OPENING DOORS

A recommendation to readers:

The kind of momentum readers will need to carry them through this densely structured argument is likely to be broken if they pause to look up the often long endnotes every time they come upon one. I would, therefore, strongly recommend that readers don't try to read the endnotes until after they have gone through the body of the text. At that point I hope they will find a number of other paths worth exploring.

OPENING DOORS

Thought From (and of) the Outside

Volume One
of
RETHINKING RELIGION

Garry Watson

The Davies Group, Publishers
Aurora, Colorado

Library of Congress Cataloging-in publication data:

Watson, Garry, 1944-
  Opening doors : thought from (and of) the outside / Garry Watson.
      p. cm.
  Includes bibliographical references and index.
  ISBN 978-1-934542-06-4 (alk. paper)
  1. Religion. I. Title.
  BL51.W33 2008
  200--dc22

                          2008019763

Cover photo © Karen Samuel | Dreamstime.com
Printed in the United States of America
0123456789

For Betsy

It is very much easier to shatter prison bars than to open undiscovered doors to life.

—D.H.Lawrence
(*The Virgin and the Gipsy*, 1925–6, 1930)

Contents

Acknowledgements

Much of the material making up three of the chapters in this book was delivered as lectures devoted to the task of "Rethinking Religion" under the auspices of the Program of Religious Studies at the University of Alberta in October and November 2005. I am especially grateful to Stephen Reimer for organizing that and for other thoughtful and kind actions. I also want to thank David Gay, Brad Bucknell, Francis Landy, Karyn Ball and Corinne Harol for their helpful and encouraging responses on this occasion.

I am very grateful to Tom Adamowski for reading and commenting helpfully on a draft of the manuscript.

Parts of the material were delivered at two International D.H.Lawrence conferences, in Paris in 1999 and in Santa Fe in 2005. Here I want to thank Ginette Roy, John Worthen, Charles Barack and especially Paul Poplawski for much-needed encouragment.

Catherine Rock and Don Fisher finished PhD theses under my supervision in 2004 and over a number of years each of these very different projects helped keep alive my interest in the subject explored in this book.

The Graduate course that I taught at the U. of A. in the Winter of 2007 on "The Return to Ethics (and Religion)" helped me to clarify a number of my ideas on the subject and I am grateful to the lively group of students who participated in it.

Without Catherine Madsen's generosity I am not sure this book would now be in print. I am indebted to her for that and for suggesting I contact The Davies Group, Publishers with whom it has been a pleasure to work.

Finally, I thank my wife, someone who started to do her own rethinking of religion decades before I got around to it.

Preface

A Different Kind of Meditation

Because our tragedy is that we diverge...further and further away from one another, like a space ship broken apart in flight which now drifts mournfully in isolated orbits, satellites to each other, planets none, communication faint.

—Norman Mailer[1]

Let us recall that Emerson depicts his immediate and constant audience as the young scholar or student (which, as he and Thoreau never tire of saying, is a capacity residing in each human being, the best part, even the essential, of the human being), and in particular depicts them, in "The American Scholar," as disgusted by the principles on which the world is managed, or ready to die of disgust, and in "Self-Reliance" as losing heart.

—Stanley Cavell[2]

This attempt to start rethinking religion will take the form of a different kind of meditation—on the one hand, different from and (as will be made clear in the opening chapter) frankly hostile to the kind offered by the currently best-selling "new atheists" (Richard Dawkins, Ed Harris, Christopher Hitchens etc.); on the other, also different from but extremely sympathetic to the kind associated with "the 'postsecular' Messianic turn of deconstruction" that is (as we will shortly see) credited with giving "the theological dimension...a new lease on life." One of the things that makes my approach differ from the former is my interest in both the latter (the "turn" brought about by one philosopher's, Jacques Derrida's, reading of another, Emmanuel Levinas) and in some of the theologically-inflected, philosophical work (Gilles Deleuze, Georgio Agamben, Alain Badiou etc.) that is sometimes seen as constituting alternatives to it. And what makes my own way of proceeding very different to those approaches adopted by the latter (by both Derrida-Levinas and those offering alternatives) is the fact that, while they have occasionally devoted essays to such writers as Hölderlin, Celan, Melville, Kafka and Joyce, what they have in common is a primarily philosophical culture, whereas my own culture is primarily grounded in literature.

Though the case is by no means identical, I can perhaps best explain what I mean by referring to an "Open Letter" that the socialist historian, E.P.Thompson (author of the classic *The Making of the English Working Class* [1963]), wrote to the Polish philosopher Leszek Kolakowski back in 1973. "If," Thompson writes, "I may borrow your own image of the Priest and the Jester, English intellectuals have played the role of jesters to the universalist priests (Catholic or anti-Catholic) of Western Europe for several hundred years."[3] And for part of the time, at least, this is the role Thompson plays in this "Open Letter":

> When you spread your wings and soar into the firmament where Kierkegaard and Husserl, Heidegger, Jaspers and Sartre and the other great eagles soar, I remain on the ground like one of the last of the great bustards, awaiting the extinction of my species on the diminishing soil of an eroding idiom, craning my neck into the air, flapping my paltry wings. All around me my younger feathered cousins are managing mutations; they are turning into little eagles, and whirr! with a rush of wind they are off to Paris, to Rome, to California. I had thought of trying to join them (I have been practising the words "essence," "syntagm," "conjuncture," "problematic," "sign") but my wings grow no bigger. (17)

Actually, considering the obvious distaste with which he viewed the "new Marxism" ("with its obligatory face-making at 'humanism,' 'moralism,' etc.—its inability to discuss the arts except by translating them into cerebration—and its lack of terms with which to handle moral or value-making process" [13]) that he saw taking over the younger generation at the time, it is impossible to believe that he could have entertained the "thought of trying to join them" for very long. But the sense he conveys of feeling painfully excluded is clearly every bit as genuine as his desire to enter into dialogue with "a familiar voice" out of an "unassimilated past" (18) (Kolakowski having recently moved to England). Unfortunately, however, this desire was doomed to be disappointed, as, judging by the following passage, Thompson seems to have half-suspected it would be:

> In the view of one of your editors, in your "post-revisionist writings," you "Show the influence, in about equal measure, of the philosophical ideas of Spinoza, Kant, Hegel, Marx, Dilthey, Mannheim, Husserl, Sartre, Heidegger, and Camus." To this pantheon...my first instinctive, but irrepressible, comment would be: "Humph!"—a term too inexact to introduce into philosophic discourse. (13–14)

This is immediately followed by the sentence I have already quoted about the Priest and the Jester, after which we get the following:

> Our best idiom has been protestant, individualist, empirical, disintegrative of universals; our best moralism has been contextual. Our poets have, on occasion, advanced philosophy further than our philosophers. If I who have been formed in this idiom think about problems of determinism and free-will, of social process and individual agency, I fall into a different kind of meditation, conditioned by a literary culture, among instances, objections, qualifications, ambiguous metaphors. (14)

Now if, in one sense, the intellectual climate in the West has, as one might expect, undergone some radical changes over the last three and a half decades, there is another sense in which it could be said that the situation we face today is oddly similar to the one Thompson found himself in in the 1970s. As for the changes, perhaps the most surprising is the one Žižek describes in the opening paragraph of his 2003 book *The Puppet and the Dwarf*:

> Today, when the historical materialist analysis is receding, practiced as it were under cover, rarely called by its proper name, while the theological dimension is given a new lease on life in the guise of the "postsecular" Messianic turn of deconstruction,

the time has come to reverse Walter Benjamin's first thesis on the philosophy of history: "The puppet called 'theology' is to win all the time. It can easily be a match for anyone if it enlists the service of historical materialism, which today, as we know, is wizened and has to keep out of sight."[4]

Of course, it has to be recognized that the number of intellectuals even aware of the deconstructive turn to which Žižek refers is very small, as is the number of intellectuals still interested in Walter Benjamin, or in the possibility of reviving historical materialism. As Jacques Derrida put it, in conversation with Maurizio Ferraris and Gianni Vattimo in 1995, the "German, Nietzschean, Heideggerian, phenomenological, hermeneutical culture" all three had in common is actually "the common capital of a very small number of people." Why, he then went on to ask, "are these few people, today, in Italy, in France, in Europe, in spite of not being widely read, still not *totally* ignored?"[5] (my italics, 86) I have italicized the word "totally" in order to emphasize the point that, as Derrida was obviously well aware, they were being largely ignored. But to recognize this is not to say that either they or the deconstructive "turn" are therefore insignificant. Intellectual significance is not to be measured in terms of popularity.

The sense in which the situation we find ourselves in today might be said to be somewhat similar to the one Thompson described in 1973 is less obvious but it has to do with the further decline that has taken place in the status of literary culture, or (in the words of Adam Phillips) of "what was once called Literature."[6] "For years now," a journalist interviewing Camille Paglia recently noted, "you've been contemptuous of the post-modern intellectual climate in the elite universities. Is it," the journalist then asked, "as bad as it was a decade ago?" Here is part of Paglia's response:

> It's improved. The prestige of the leading poststructuralists and postmodernists has vanished. But they still have genuine power and they have destroyed the next generation of scholars. There is not a single new interesting voice among the younger generation of literary critics...Wherever I go, people come up to me and tell the same story—they entered graduate school and left it or staggered through it and could not get a job because of their refusal to

spend their time on Foucault. All they wanted to do was immerse themselves in great literature and great works of art. They were treated as naïve, or as traitors, and driven out. The most lively and interesting minds have been driven out of American academe.[7]

One doesn't have to (and I don't) share Paglia's contempt for the so-called "leading poststructuralists and postmodernists" to recognize and be concerned about (indeed, to deeply deplore) the fact that for a number of decades graduate students in many university departments of English have indeed been discouraged from spending a good deal of their time immersing "themselves in great literature and great works of art." And there can be no denying but that, as an academic discipline, literary criticism has all but disappeared. All of which makes things extremely difficult for the critic who would like to be taken seriously, while also wanting his or her thought to be "conditioned by a literary culture, among instances, objections, qualifications, ambiguous metaphors."

Things might not, however, be *quite* so difficult for the critic in question if he or she *did* feel the same contempt for the discourses that have effectively replaced literary criticism that Paglia feels. (At an earlier moment, E.P.Thompson came to express a similar contempt for the Althusserian brand of Marxism that replaced for a while the kind he himself practiced.[8]) But as I started off by saying, I personally am actually sympathetic to both "the 'postsecular' Messianic turn of deconstruction" *and* to some of the proposed alternatives to it. And not only this: I am also indebted. I will spend the next three paragraphs indicating the nature of the debt.

To begin with, then, my title: *Thought from (and of) the Outside*. If the idea for this first came to me while reading the essay by Michel Foucault entitled "Maurice Blanchot: The Thought from Outside" (*La pensée du dehors*), my feeling that the "Outside" was a good idea to organize my reflections around was subsequently strengthened when I began to notice some of the ways in which a number of other French philosophers have been making use of it. Jean-Luc Nancy, for example, maintains that "there is no 'outside.' The event of existence, the 'there is,' means," according to Nancy (who has Bataille and Heidegger in mind), "that there is *nothing else*."[9] What is meant by this insistence? We can perhaps best understand it with the help of the distinction between other and extra-worldly that Peter

Hallward makes in his recent book on Gilles Deleuze entitled *Out of this World*:

> Philosophy [for Deleuze]...must lead out of the world. Does this mean a return to transcendence, a leap into an otherworldly beyond? Not at all: "out" doesn't mean "beyond." Extra-worldly doesn't mean other-worldly. To move virtually out—to *out*—involves neither actual externality nor a transcendent ideal; the *outing* that is a line of flight or deterritorialisation need not move through actual space.[10]

In terms of this distinction I take Nancy's insistence to mean that there is no "otherworldly beyond," which is to say, that the kind of otherworldly beyond in which one might hope to find God, or oneself, does not exist. Even though Foucault (unlike Nancy) *did* want to talk about the outside, this would seem to have been his concern too when he tried to distinguish the outside of negative theology from the outside he found in Blanchot. Although the experience of the former also "involves going 'outside of oneself,' this," said Foucault, is unlike the experience of the latter, in that it "is done ultimately in order to find oneself [and also, presumably, to find God]."[11] On the other hand, where Deleuze is concerned, Hallward insists that we simply can't leave God out of the discussion. As he sees it, "the logic of Deleuze's work tends to proceed broadly in line with a *theophanic* conception of things, whereby every individual process or thing is conceived as a manifestation or expression of God or a conceptual equivalent of God (pure creative potential, force, energy, life ...)" (*Out* 4). Yet at the same time, we have seen that even if Hallward wants God *in* the discussion about the Outside, he also tries to make sure that certain of the terms often associated with God (transcendence and beyond) are kept *out*.

What ought we to make of this? At one point in his contribution to a collection of essays on *Deleuze and Religion*, Philip Goodchild notes that the "danger of Deleuze's use of Spinoza and Scotus is that the concept of God may be smuggled back in." And Goodchild ends his piece by claiming that "to raise [as Deleuze does] the question of transcendence *qua* transcendence, even if encountered implicitly on a plane of immanence, is to raise a theological question. In its most rigorous purity, philosophy finds itself once more compromised with God."[12] In other words, the moral, as

I understand it, is that if we want (as I obviously do) to talk about the Outside then we had best recognize that it is futile to try to prohibit the use of certain terms just because they are (in the eyes of some) contaminated by association with theology. There will be no question, then, of my trying to *smuggle* the name of God back in; it is simply impossible to keep it out.

Finally, at the end of an essay on Deleuze and Foucault entitled "Absolute Immanence," Giorgio Agamben speaks of the need to "reconstruct a genealogy that will clearly distinguish in modern philosophy...between a line of immanence and a line of transcendence, approximately according to the following diagram"[13]:

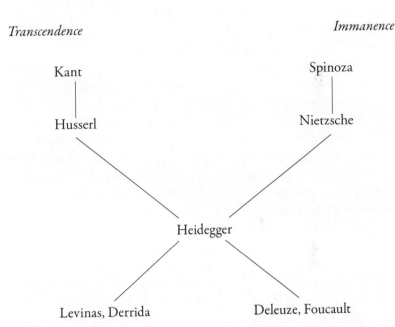

As Agamben knows better than most, it is not easy to make such a clear distinction. And not just because of Heidegger's positioning in the middle of this diagram. "I think," says Levinas, "that the truly new moment in the whole of modern philosophy is the recognition that the human is not the knowledge of God, but rather the place where God *works*, where 'God lives.' Hence, an immanent transcendence."[14]

My indebtedness to the philosophers I have been mentioning is mostly a matter of my being roused into thought by some of the questions they raise. These are the questions—concerning such things as, precisely, the Outside, but also Identity, Violence, Sacrifice, Hospitality and Otherness (and the larger question as to how these things might affect our understanding of Religion, God and Idolatry)—I am interested in pursuing. Not, however, in the way the philosophers themselves tend to pursue them. I will not, for example, be attempting to reconstruct such a genealogy as Agamben calls for. And not only, incidentally, because I am certainly not qualified to undertake such a task. Admittedly, that is a good enough reason in itself but over and beyond that is the (for me) more pressing consideration, which is that I have my own work to do, the work of raising and addressing such questions while engaging in *much more of a literary-critical than a philosophical engagement with the literary text.*

At the beginning of his essay on Herman Melville's "Bartleby," Agamben first allows that, "[a]s a scrivener, Bartleby belongs to a literary constellation," a constellation Agamben takes two sentences to sketch in with references to Gorky, Flaubert, Dostoevsky and Kafka. "But," he then claims, "Bartleby also belongs to a philosophical constellation, and it may be," he suggests, "that it alone contains the figure merely traced by the literary constellation to which Bartleby belongs."[15] Possibly. In any case, I find Agamben's essay fascinating but, in the heart of what follows, I myself will be exploring a basically literary constellation. More specifically, the particular literary constellation I will be reconstructing (mainly in chapters four and five) is one that I see arranging itself around the once famous but now largely forgotten literary critic, F.R.Leavis. The main focus will be on texts by Joseph Conrad and the now often detested D.H.Lawrence (if not perhaps as detested as much as Leavis himself is detested), with important references being made to Blake, Dickens, George Eliot and T.S. Eliot.

I am aware of the fact not only that this kind of focus on a national literature[16] is often frowned upon today but also that the prominence I am giving to Leavis and Lawrence, and the seriousness with which I propose to take them, flies directly in the face of that "set of unwritten prohibitions that [these days] define," according to Žižek, "the positions one is allowed to adopt" (*Puppet* 5). I know enough about these "unwritten prohibitions" to realize that ignoring them can indeed have serious consequences and in itself be responsible for severely reducing the size of one's readership. This is too bad but it is sometimes a risk one has to run, especially, for example, when one is convinced, as I am, that the thinkers in question are "genuine authors." I am thinking here of some of the things Stanley Cavell had to say back on the subject in the 1960s, in his essay on Kierkegaard's book *On Authority and Revelation*.

According to Cavell (who is here paraphrasing Kierkegaard), the point about a genuine-(as distinct from a premise-) author is that he or she "can give to the age what the age needs, not what it demands, whereas the fraudulent artist [or thinker] will 'make use of the sickness of our age' by satisfying its demands."[17] In terms furthermore of Kierkegaard's description of the apostle's position that Cavell again paraphrases (claiming that it "characterises in detail the position...the genuine modern artist...find[s] himself in"), I want to suggest the relevance of the following propositions (which of course—despite my retention of Cavell's masculine pronouns— I take to apply as much to my female as to my male "authors"):

(i) that "he is pulled out of the ranks by a message which he must, on pain of loss of self, communicate";

(ii) that "he knows that there are no techniques at anyone's proposal for saying what he has to say" ("artistically speaking, this is expressed by the absence of conventions within which to compose");

(iii) that "he must deny his personal or worldly authority in accomplishing what he has to do (artistically, this means that he cannot rely on his past achievements as securing the relevance of his new impulse; each work requires, spiritually speaking, a new step)";

(iv) and finally, that "the burden of being called to produce it [modern art, but also the kind of thought that concerns us here] is matched by the risk of accepting it (religiously speaking, in accepting or rejecting it, the heart is revealed)" (177).

It seems to me, incidentally, that all of the above applies to Derrida and Levinas as well as to Lawrence and Leavis (and to a number of the other writers I will be drawing on in this book).

Two further points. First, a few remarks on the kind of readers I would ideally hope to find. If, on the one hand, there is no denying but that novelists typically reach much wider audiences than philosophers (especially when the novelists are, say, Dickens, Conrad and Lawrence and the philosophers are, for example, Kant, Spinoza, Husserl and Heidegger); on the other hand, literary criticism has never reached anywhere near as many readers as the novel. Nor would one expect it to, given that literary criticism is a secondary (some would say, parasitic) discourse, that it is criticism after all (which can and does, it may be worth recalling, just as easily and frequently take the form of praise as of censure), criticism *of* some already existing literary text. So that there is always the question as to whether, or to what degree, literary criticism will make sense to the reader who has not in fact read the text being commented on. And even if the literary critic makes the effort to provide the kind of context that will make her commentary intelligible to the reader who hasn't (yet) read the text being commented on, still, this will also require some effort on the part of the reader, a different kind of effort to the kind required to read a novel, and it in itself is bound to limit the number of readers a literary critic can hope to reach. (Of course, the same consideration will apply to those works of philosophy that take the form of commentary on other philosophical texts.)

Nevertheless, during the 1950s and 1960s *some* literary criticism, at least, was addressed to the kind of reader a modernist like Virginia Woolf thought of herself as addressing: the Common Reader. This reader (educated but non-specialist) was assumed to exist at least as much outside of, as well as inside, the University and the books in which a critic like Leavis addressed him or her were usually published by non university presses (like Chatto & Windus). While realizing how very different is the situation in which we find ourselves today, and even though I am not by any means offering this as a work of *pure* literary criticism, this is still the kind of reader I would ideally hope to reach.

Finally, what I especially like about the idea of "the Outside" is that it is so unassuming, so ordinary-sounding, a term and my hope is that using it so extensively may make it possible to revivify questions and potentialities that many of us may have lost sight of—concerning, for example, "transcendence" and "immanence" (terms that I will also be using but more sparingly). I would like to think that as they work their way through the following pages at least some readers might find find some previously undiscovered doors to life beginning to open up for them. If not, what is the point? At any rate, that's my aim.

PART ONE

INTRODUCTION

We act as though we had some common sense of what "religion" means ... [W]e believe ... we preunderstand the meaning of this word, if only to be able to question and in order to interrogate ourselves on this subject ... [N]othing is less pre-assured ... and the entire question of religion comes down, perhaps, to this lack of assurance.

—Jacques Derrida (1996)[1]

Chapter One

A Polemical Clearing of the Ground

Harris, Hitchens and Dawkins' lack of scruple: the unimpressive face of atheism (and what—with the help of its other face—we can learn from it)

> *Scruple*, hesitation, indecision, reticence (hence modesty <*pudeur*>, respect, r*estraint* before that which should remain sacred, holy or safe: unscathed, immune)—this too is what is meant by *religio*.
>
> —Jacques Derrida (*FK* 31)[2]

As I will be explaining in the next chapter, what I think we urgently need to do with religion is rethink it. And if I was at first reluctant to spend any time on the four books that I have now read and wish to comment on here—Sam Harris's *The End of Faith: Religion, Terror, and the Future of Reason* (2004) and his *Letter to a Christian Nation* (2006), Richard Dawkins's *The God Delusion* (2006) and Christopher Hitchens's *God Is Not Great: How Religion Poisons Everything* (2007)—this was due to my strong suspicion that they would fall into the category of those works that seem to be written out of the conviction that *rethinking* religion is a waste of time since we already know (or ought to know) that it is an entirely Bad Thing and that any energy we feel able to devote to the subject should therefore be spent attacking it. I can now see that simply registering the fact that my suspicion has largely been confirmed is not enough: I need to say more than that about both them and the phenomenon they represent.

These four books belong to what Brian Bethune refers to (in April 2007) as "the steady stream of atheist texts that began five years ago, after 9/11 so brutally demonstrated that religious fanaticism is still a force to be reckoned with. So too," he claims, "is atheism, at least as far as book sales go." As far as book sales go, this would seem to be undeniable—with, for example, Bethune able to report that "*The God Delusion* ... has been a

fixture on bestseller lists since the fall" and *Letter to a Christian Nation*
... became a Book-of-the-Month club selection last year."[3] And as I write
this, Hitchens' book is also in the process of becoming a best-seller, having
been favourably reviewed by, among others, Anthony Gottlieb in the *New
Yorker* ("Atheists with Attitude") and Michael Kinsley in the *New York
Times Book Review* ("In God, Distrust").[4]

So while thoughtful critiques have been written of Harris's *The End of
Faith* (by Ronald Aronson)[5] and of Dawkins's *The God Delusion* (by Marilynne Robinson and Terry Eagleton),[6] there seems at the present moment
to be a widespread assumption out there that the combined efforts of such
writers as Harris, Dawkins and Hitchens have made contemporary atheism not just into a commercial success but also into an intellectual and
ethical force to be reckoned with.[7] Unfortunately, this seems to me very
far from being the case—"unfortunately" because I believe that atheism
has a major contribution to make to the urgent task of *rethinking* religion.
But nevertheless, insofar as it can challenge us to clarify what we ourselves
think about things, criticism is always, in my view, something to be thank-
ful for, and this seems to me true even of the extremely crude kind of criticism on display here.

So I want to acknowledge my gratitude to these writers. I am
prompted to do so by something the distinguished scientist and practising Christian Michael Polanyi had to say a half century ago. "Today," he
maintained, "we should be grateful for the prolonged attacks made by rationalists on religion for forcing us to renew the grounds of the Christian
faith."[8] Though I do not consider myself a Christian, I do have faith and,
somewhat to my surprise, I find that confronting this latest "rationalist"
challenge has helped strengthen it. This is the faith that Derrida claims
justice inscribes itself in, "in the act of faith or in the appeal to faith that
inhabits every act of language and every address to the other." This justice
"allows the hope, beyond all 'messianisms,' of a universalizable culture of
singularities." The faith it inscribes itself in is a "faith without dogma"
and is linked to a messianic expectation that "does not depend upon any
messianism," that "follows no determinate revelation" and that "belongs
properly to no Abrahamic religion" (*FK* 18). (I have no more to say about
this here but I will be engaging with questions concerning the messianic
in chapter five.)

From now on I will usually be referring to Harris, Dawkins and Hitchens as H.H. & D. I will be doing this for the sake of convenience but it seems to me justified by the fact that, while there are some differences between them, these are slight compared to what they share. Ideally, what H.H. & D would like to see happen is the "eradicating [of] religion" (Harris[9]); the "enemy" (Hitchens[10]), as they see it, is made up of "all religions" (*Letter* 7):

> There is no need to overstate the difficulty of understanding Islam's alleged profundities. If one comprehends the fallacies of *any* 'revealed' religion, one comprehends them all. (Hitchens, my italics 126).

Since for H.H.& D the profundities don't exist (since they are all merely "alleged"), it isn't difficult to comprehend the fallacies in question. As for the differences, unlike the other two, Harris thinks highly of Eastern mysticism; it is, according to him, an "astonishing fact" that "not a single Western thinker can be named who rivals the great philosopher-mystics of the East" [11]; he maintains "that meetings between the Dalai Lama and Christian ecclesiastics to mutually honor their religious traditions are like meetings between physicists from Cambridge and the Bushmen of the Kalahari to mutually honour their respective understandings of the physical universe" (*End* 284). In case anyone is wondering, Harris does absolutely nothing to try to substantiate these judgements but the main point I want to make here is that Hitchens is far from sharing them: he is more struck by how "absurd" the Dalai Lama's pronouncements are (200). Another difference is that, unlike Hitchens, both Harris (*End* 137) and Dawkins[12] have some positive things to say about the Sermon on the Mount. But since they are only passing comments, these count for very little (no more, really, than Harris' weightless because unsubstantiated judgements) in the steady stream of dismissive remarks directed at all three of the monotheistic religions, entirely characteristic of which is Dawkins' reference to "the ethical disaster area that is the Old Testament" (*God Delusion* 251).

Where do I stand in relation to all of this? Like Dawkins, Harris and Hitchens, I am writing from a position outside of any *community* of faith and like them (and also many believers[13]) I too find most God-talk on the public stage intolerable and wish that politicians could be prevented from indulging in it.[14] Like Hitchens, I believe that "[r]eligion is man-made" (or, as he also puts it, that "holy institutions are" [10, 240]) and I share H.H.&D's concern over the poisonous effect I agree religion often does produce. On the other hand, very much *un*like H.H.&D, I also believe that there are other sides to religion too, not the least important of which is perhaps best caught in Karl Marx's phrase "the heart of a heartless world," a phrase that Hitchens quotes (9-10) but a sentiment the implications of which he seems, judging by the evidence of his book, completely unable or unwilling either to credit or to take in (just like Dawkins and Harris in their books). My point, however, is not that H.H.&D are heartless. My main criticism of these three writers is that they are (in the four books I've read by them) both insufficiently intelligent and deeply irresponsible.

The "not-so-brights": A condescension that fails to recognize itself

I will begin by saying something about intelligence, for two reasons: (i) because of the considerable reputations for intelligence and wit that Dawkins and Hitchens seem to enjoy; and (ii) because they themselves make intelligence (or the lack of it) a key issue. I feel that I need to say no more here about the first reason since it is clear enough that all three are highly articulate and often quite clever. But I will explain what I have in mind when I say that they foreground the question of intelligence. Consider first the "cringe-making proposal" Hitchens tells us that Dawkins and Daniel Dennett apparently made: "that atheists should conceitedly nominate themselves to be called 'brights'" (*God* etc. 5). Yes, "cringe-making" seems exactly right. But though Hitchens sees this clearly enough, he appears completely and genuinely unaware of his own arrogance, which seems like second-nature to him. On the one hand, at one point, we get this: "All he [Socrates] really 'knew,' he said was the extent of his own ignorance. (This to me is still the definition of an educated person)" (256). What could be more modest? And in a similar vein, there is the moment when, after referring to "bogus arguments over the Trinity, or the Muslim *hadith*, or the arrival of a false Messiah," Hitchens pauses to remind himself that "it is better for us not to fall into relativism, or what E.P.Thompson called 'the enormous condescension of posterity'" (68).

But funnily enough, the very next sentence to this is the following: "The scholastic obsessives of the Middle Ages were doing the best they could on the basis of hopelessly limited information, ever-present fear of death and judgment, very low life expectancy, and an audience of illiterates." It would seem that Hitchens has difficulty recognizing condescension for what it is. Forget about "obsessives," notice only the sheer oddity of that last phrase: "on the basis of ... an audience of illiterates." Scholasticism for illiterates? What an idea! And as one reads through *God Is Not Great* one soon comes to see that references to illiterates (or associated terms) function in the text as a kind of nervous tic. Let's look at a few examples:

> ... the context [of the Old Testament] is oppressively confined and *local*. None of these provincials, or their deity, seems to have any idea of a world beyond the desert, the flocks and herds, and the imperatives of nomadic subsistence. This is forgivable on the part of the provincial yokels, obviously , but ... (107)
>
> Even if god is or was an Arab (an unsafe assumption), how could he expect to "reveal" himself by way of an illiterate person ... To Muslims, the annunciation of the divine to a person of extreme unlettered simplicity has something of the same value as the humble vessel of the Virgin Mary has to Christians. (124)
>
> The record of [Muhammad's] seventh-century career, like the books of the Old Testament, swiftly becomes an account of vicious quarrels between a few hundred or sometimes a few thousand unlearned villagers and townspeople ... (129)
>
> Almost all religions from Buddhism to Islam feature either a humble prophet or a prince who comes to identify with the poor, but what is this if not populism? It is hardly a surprise if religions choose to address themselves first to the majority who are poor and bewildered and uneducated. (115).

But then, when it comes to religion it seems that, from Hitchens' point of view, the lettered or the learned are almost as bad:

> Aquinas half believed in astrology ... Augustine was a self-centered fantasist and an earth-centered ignoramus ... Luther was terrified by demons ...

One must state it plainly. Religion comes from the period
of human prehistory where nobody—not even the mighty Democritus who concluded that all matter was made from atoms—
had the smallest idea what was going on. It comes from the bawling and fearful infancy of our species, and is a babyish attempt to
meet our inescapable demand for knowledge (as well as for comfort, reassurance, and other infantile needs). (64)   .

"Remember," Hitchens tells us many pages later, "we are examining the
childhood of our species" (267). As if he is afraid that we haven't been
completely persuaded by the references to bawling, infancy, babyish and
the infantile earlier. Perhaps we drifted off while pausing to wonder why
the need for comfort *has* to be infantile?

 Whatever. We will, in any case, inevitably notice other examples of
condescension as we proceed, for the simple reason that it is difficult to
find a passage produced by H.H.&D that is free of it.[15] It often seems as if
all three are personally offended by the fact that religion is not primarily
addressed to those who have (as they themselves have) a certain education.
But at the same time, what we now need to take note of is the fact that
when it *is* so addressed, it no longer counts for them *as religion*.

*Narrowing down what is allowed to count as religion: the high price we pay
for a certain kind of clarity*

> *Why not say things more simply?* ... [W]hy not reduce the Freud-
> ian "super-ego" to the "moral conscience" of classical psychology?
> *What! Is that all it is?* Yes, if one abolishes all the rest.
>   —Roland Barthes (1966)[16]

> We owe our mental existence predominantly to works of art,
> morality, religious worship, scientific theory and other articulate
> systems which we accept as our dwelling place and as the soil of
> our mental development.
>   —Michael Polanyi (286)

 We must now carefully examine the way in which Dawkins begins
his book. He does so by trying to bring his fellow scientists into line.

Unfortunately (from his point of view), it seems that a number of them call themselves religious and make approving references to God. Hence, the need Dawkins feels to explain that he is "calling only *supernatural* gods delusional" (15). "I," Einstein once said, "am a deeply religious non-believer. This," he added, "is a somewhat new kind of religion" (qtd by Dawkins 15). With reference to this, Dawkins titles his opening chapter "A Deeply Religious Non-Believer" and he chooses another of Einstein's remarks as epigraph to the chapter:

> I don't try to imagine a personal God; it suffices to stand in awe at the structure of the world, insofar as it allows our inadequate senses to appreciate it.

Dawkins then proceeds to inform us that a "quasi-mystical response to nature and the universe is common among scientists and rationalists" (11). "All [Carl] Sagan's books," for example, "touch the nerve-endings of transcendent wonder that religion monopolized in past centuries" and Dawkins maintains that his "own books have the same aspiration." As a result, Dawkins often hears himself "described as a deeply religious man ... But is 'religion' the right word?" (13) He doesn't think so. As he sees it, "[m]uch unfortunate confusion is caused by failure to distinguish what can be called Einsteinian religion from supernatural religion." While it is true that "Einstein sometimes invoked the name of God (and he is not the only atheist scientist to do so)," he (and they) did not intend the word to "be used in the way people have generally understood it: to denote a supernatural creator that is 'appropriate for us to worship.'" And "if the word God is not to become completely useless," *we should use it only in this sense.* We will then realize that a number of Dawkins' fellow scientists are labouring under a mistake:

> The dramatic (or was it mischievous?) ending of Stephen Hawking's *A Brief History of Time*, "For then we should know the mind of God," is notoriously misconstrued. It has led people to believe, mistakenly of course, that Hawking is a religious man. The cell biologist Ursula Goodenough, in *The Sacred Depths of Nature*, sounds more religious than Hawking or Einstein ... She goes so far as to call herself a "Religious Naturalist." Yet a care-

ful reading of her book shows that she is really as staunch an atheist as I am. (13)

Whether Goodenough likes it or not is clearly beside the point: she is an atheist because (if Dawkins is right) she doesn't believe in the existence of a "supernatural creator." The problem lies in "a confused and confusing willingness to label as 'religion' the pantheistic reverence which many of us share with its most distinguished exponent, Albert Einstein" (14). This doesn't mean "that Einstein contradicted himself." It simply means that "[b]y 'religion' Einstein meant something entirely different from what is conventionally meant" (15).

So what *was* Einstein? Dawkins maintains that Einstein was neither a theist (someone who "believes in a supernatural intelligence who, in addition to his main work of creating the universe in the first place, is still around to oversee and influence [by intervening in] the subsequent fate of his initial creation") nor a deist (someone who also believes "in a supernatural intelligence, but one whose activities were confined to setting up the laws that govern the universe in the first place. The deist God never intervenes thereafter ... ") but a pantheist ("Pantheists don't believe in a supernatural God at all, but use the word God as a non-supernatural synonym for Nature, or for the Universe, or for the lawfulness that governs its workings"). And as for Pantheism, it, according to Dawkins, ought not to be seen as a religious phenomenon, but rather as "sexed-up atheism" (18).

The following passage, which condenses three paragraphs into two, seems to me key to an understanding of Dawkins' polemic:

> There is every reason to think that famous Einsteinisms like "God is subtle but he is not malicious" or "He does not play dice" or "Did God have a choice in creating the universe?" are pantheistic, not deistic, and certainly not theistic. "God does not play dice" should be translated as "Randomness does not lie at the heart of all things." "Did God have a choice in creating the Universe?" means "Could the universe have begun in any other way?" Einstein was using "God" in a purely metaphorical, poetic sense. So is Stephen Hawking, and so are most of those physicists who occasionally slip into the language of religious metaphor. Paul

Davies's *The Mind of God* seems to hover somewhere between Einsteinian pantheism and an obscure form of deism—for which he was rewarded with the Templeton Prize (a very large sum of money given annually by the Templeton Foundation, usually to a scientist who is prepared to say something nice about religion).

Let me sum up Einsteinian religion in one more quotation from Einstein himself: "To sense that behind anything that can be experienced there is a something that our mind cannot grasp and whose beauty and sublimity reaches us only indirectly and as a feeble reflection, this is religiousness. In this sense I am religious." In this sense I too am religious, with the reservation that "cannot grasp" does not have to mean "forever ungraspable." But I prefer not to call myself religious because it is misleading. It is destructively misleading because, for the vast majority of people, "religion" implies "supernatural" ... I wish that physicists would refrain from using the word God in their special metaphorical sense. The metaphorical or pantheistic God of the physicists is light years away from the interventionist, miracle-wreaking, thought-reading, sin-punishing, prayer-answering God of the Bible, of priests, mullahs and rabbis, and of ordinary language. Deliberately to confuse the two is, in my opinion, an act of intellectual high treason. (18–19)

The God of the Bible is obviously and inevitably at least as metaphorical and poetic as the God of the physicists but leaving this aside and foregoing the temptation to comment on Dawkins' confession that he is more grasping than Einstein, what this passage reveals is the nature of Dawkins' irresponsibility. As seems usual in such cases, the irresponsibility may well be attributable to a kind of innocence (or ignorance). The idea that intellectuals might have a responsibility to *question* "what is conventionally meant" (15) by a term—or what "the vast majority of people" mean by it (19)—doesn't seem to have occurred to him. It would seem that for him if a term has more than one meaning then it is misleading and we need to redefine it in such a way as to eliminate alternative meanings. Otherwise we are left with confusion and, in the case of the god of the physicists and the god of the Bible, "*deliberately* to confuse the two is ... an act of intellectual high treason." But what ought we to call the act of producing clarity by the means we have seen Dawkins employ? I'm thinking here not so much of the totally confident way he translates those "famous Einsteinisms" as of his refusal to tolerate alternative understandings of religion and God. Or to put it another way, of his inability or unwillingness to consider the possibility that a more nuanced position than his own, one that "seems to *hover* somewhere between Einsteinian pantheism and an obscure form of deism," might be an expression not so much (as he rather nastily insinuates) of willingness to betray principle (by saying "something nice about religion" in order to make some money) as of intellectual honesty, that it might be more intellectually honest than the kind of black and white certainty he himself demands.

Like Dawkins (and Hitchens), Harris also has no patience with ambiguity. Take, for example, the for him completely unproblematical "original import of a term" like "faith." "Throughout this book," he tells us, "I am criticizing faith in its ordinary, scriptural sense—as belief in, and life orientation toward, certain historical and metaphysical propositions. *The meaning of the term, both in the Bible and upon the lips of the faithful, seems to be entirely unambiguous*" (*End*, my italics 65). As for those ("certain theologians and contemplatives") who "have attempted to recast faith as a spiritual principle that transcends mere motivated credulity," Harris accuses them of sophistry (to use his word: of being "rarefied") and of deceit (hiding serpents):

> Paul Tillich, in his *Dynamics of Faith* (1957), rarefied the original import of the term out of existence, casting away what he called "idolatrous faith" and, indeed, all equations between faith and belief. Surely other theologians have done likewise. Of course, anyone is free to redefine the term "faith" however he sees fit and thereby bring it into conformity with some rational or mystical ideal. But this is not the "faith" that has animated the faithful for millenia. The faith that I am calling into question is precisely the gesture that Tillich himself decried as "an act of knowledge that has a low degree of evidence." My argument, after all, is aimed at the majority of the faithful in every religious tradition, not at Tillich's blameless parish of one.
>
> Despite the considerable extertions of men like Tillich who have attempted to hide the serpent lurking at the foot of every

altar, the truth is that religious faith is simply *unjustified* belief in matters of ultimate concern ... (*End* 65)

If only things were that simple. But the truth in question is considerably more complex than Harris either allows or realizes, as we can see by turning (again) to Michael Polanyi's *Personal Knowledge*.

What Polanyi has to say both about faith and other related matters is very suggestive in this context. As he sees it, "[s]cientists—that is, creative scientists—spend their lives in trying to guess right. They are sustained and guided therein by their heuristic passion" (143). But the point about an "heuristic impulse" is that it "can live only in the pursuit of its proper enquiry" and, as Polanyi understands it, the "Christian enquiry is worship" (281): the "Christian religious service" is "a framework of clues which are apt to induce a passionate search for God" (282). Like "a theory, or a mathematical discovery, or a symphony," religious worship takes the form of a "valid articulate framework" that we make use of if and when we dwell in it. "Astronomic observations," for example, "are made by dwelling in astronomic theory" (195). Here is Polanyi's explanation of what the "indwelling of the Christian worshipper" is like:

> It resembles not the dwelling within a great theory of which we enjoy the complete understanding, nor an immersion in the pattern of a musical masterpiece, but the heuristic upsurge which strives to break through the accepted framework of thought, guided by the intimations of discoveries still beyond our horizon. Christian worship sustains, as it were, an eternal, never to be consummated hunch: a heuristic vision which is accepted for the sake of its unresolvable tension. It is like an obsession with a problem known to be insoluble, which yet follows, against reason, unswervingly, the heuristic command: "Look at the unknown!" (199)

The idea of an "unresolvable tension" is obviously central to this and we get a sharper sense of just *how* tense Polanyi sees it as being when he explains that if an "heuristic impulse is never without a sense of its possible inadequacy, and [if] what it lacks in absolute assurance may be described as its inherent doubt," then "the sense of inadequacy inherent in the Christian faith goes beyond this, for it is part of the Christian faith that its striving can never reach an endpoint ... 'Faith embraces itself and the doubt about itself,' writes Tillich":

> Yet according to the Christian faith this inherent dubiety of the true faith is sinful and this sin is an ineradicable source of anguish. Take away doubt, sin and anguish [*or, in other words, take away the tension*], *and Christian faith turns into a caricature of itself. It becomes a set of inaccurate, often false and largely meaningless statements, accompanied by conventional gestures and complacent moralizing.* (my italics 280)

Why it is sometimes necessary to criticize caricatures (so long as we realize that that is what we are doing)

From Polanyi's (Christian) point of view, it would seem that at any given time much of what passes for Christianity is likely to be a caricature of it. And by now no reader of this piece is likely to be too surprised if I say that H.H.&D concentrate their attack on caricatures of religion. What Terry Eagleton says about "[c]ard-carrying rationalists like Dawkins" in his review of *The God Delusion*—that they "are in one sense the least well-equipped to understand what they castigate, since they don't believe there is anything to be understood, or at least anything worth understanding. This is why they invariably come up with vulgar caricatures of religious faith that would make a first-year theology student wince"—this seems to me true and to apply at least as much to Harris and Hitchens as well. All three write as if (in Eagleton's words), "[w]hen it comes to theology, ... any old travesty will pass muster."[17] On the other hand, as Gottlieb sees it (in his "Atheists With Attitude"), "[t]hat is unfair, because millions of the faithful around the world believe things that would make a first-year theology student wince"(1).[18] And though I do not myself believe Eagleton is being unfair, I think that what Gottlieb says in the rest of his sentence is also probably true and worth pausing to consider.

Noting in her review of *The God Delusion* that for Dawkins (as for H.&H.) the positive alternative to religion is science, Marilynne Robinson suggests that if we are to compare religion with science then we ought to compare the best of one with the best of the other. "To set the declared hopes of one against the real-world record of the other is clearly not useful, no matter which of them is flattered by the comparison." And "if religion is to be blamed for the fraud done in its name, then what of science?" (84) Robinson is surely right about this and also, incidentally, in her contention that, no matter how greatly religion may have contributed, and be contributing, to violence around the world, science is *much* more responsible for the *largest* threats we face (nuclear catastrophe, ecological disaster etc.). But even so, it is of course still possible and legitimate to be concerned about the damage done in the name of religion, regardless as to whether or not it is actually a product of a fraudulent or caricatured version of the latter.

In the "Note to the Reader" with which he begins his *Letter to a Christian Nation* Harris tells us that "[f]orty-four percent of the American population is convinced that Jesus will return to judge the living and the dead *sometime in the next fifty years*" (*Letter* xi). This is indeed strange but I'm not sure that it should, as Harris maintains, "be considered a moral and intellectual emergency" (xii). (As Gottlieb points out with reference to this statistic, in "some religious research, it is not necessarily the respondents who are credulous" (2). After all, "in 1998, a fifth of non-Christians in America told a poll for *Newsweek* that they, too, expected Jesus to return. What does Harris make of that? Any excuse for a party, perhaps" [3]). But even if Harris were right to think that the "fact" that so alarms him—"that nearly half of the American population apparently believes" (*Letter* xii) Jesus will soon return—constitutes a real emergency ("The book," he tells his readers, "you are about to read is my response to this emergency" [Ibid]), this would still not justify a determination to disregard (or to ride rough-shod over) fine distinctions; it would still be necessary to preserve a sense of scruple and to respect the need to make careful qualifications.

Consider, for example, the simple but important distinction Francis Fitzgerald makes after noting (in her recent "The Evangelical Surprise") that Evangelicals "make up a quarter of the [US] population—around 75 million people":

According to polls, some 60 percent [of them] are biblical literalists, who believe, for example, that God created the universe in exactly six days and a few thousand years ago, and who insist that their interpretation of the Bible is the eternal and only true reading of it.

The others believe, as most mainline Protestants do, that the Bible should be read in the light of the rest of human knowledge and that its interpretation is not a simple matter.[19]

I take it that from the point of view of the latter 40%, the beliefs of the former 60% would seem (as they seem to me and to Eagleton) to be "vulgar caricatures of religious faith." But while one might well want to express some concern about the beliefs held by the former 60%, I find it odd (at best) to ignore those of the latter 40% and odder still (*much* odder) to effectively *imitate* those biblical literalists in one's own readings of the Bible. Yet that's exactly what H.H.&D do.

The morality of good conscience: H.H.&D. as (literalist) readers of Christianity and its (immoral) Bible

> ... error, recklessness, the unthought, and irresponsibility are given the so very presentable face of good conscience.
>   —Derrida (1993)[20]

> All major confrontations over the right to free thought, free speech, and free inquiry have taken the same form—of a religious attempt to assert the literal and limited mind over the ironic and inquiring one.
>   —Hitchens (*God* 258).

I imagine that Dawkins would agree in principle both with the second of these two epigraphs and also with Hitchens' further claim that "the literal mind does not understand the ironic mind, and sees it always as a source of danger" (*God* 29). But in practice he (like H&H) reads literally. The first example he provides in the section entitled "The Old Testament" is that of "the well-loved story of Noah," the "moral" of which he finds "appalling" and summarizes in one sentence: "God took a dim view of humans, so he (with the exception of one family) drowned the lot of them including children and also, for good measure, the rest of the (presumably blameless) animals as well." "Of course," says Dawkins by way of anticipating the obvious objection, "irritated theologians will protest that we don't take the book of Genesis literally any more." Perhaps not, but Dawkins' point is that "a frighteningly large number of people still do take their scriptures, including the story of Noah, literally. According to Gallup, they include approximately 50 per cent of the US electorate" (237–8).

Here is Hitchens commenting on the beatitudes in a passage that seems to me *so* asinine I have become rather fond of it:

> Many of the sayings and deeds of Jesus are innocuous, most espe-
> cially the "beatitudes" which express such fanciful wish-thinking
> about the meek and peacemakers. But many are unintelligible and
> show a belief in magic, several are absurd and show a primitive at-
> titude to agriculture (this extends to all mentions of plowing and
> sowing, and all allusions to mustard or fig trees), and many are on
> the face of it flat-out immoral. The analogy of humans to lilies,
> for instance, suggests—along with many other injunctions—that
> things like thrift, innovation, family life, and so forth are a sheer
> waste of time. ("Take no thought for the morrow.") This is why
> some of the Gospels, synoptic and apocryphal, report people (in-
> cluding his family members) saying at the time that they thought
> Jesus must be mad. (*God* 118) [21]

In some ways, none more so than in his idea of morality, Hitchens seems such an innocent! (I prefer this word to the ones he tends to favour: simple-ton, boob etc.) Obviously, by the standards of worldly morality, now just as much as then, obviously Jesus must have appeared (must still appear) mad; and equally obviously, by the same token, his comparison of humans to lil-ies must make him appear immoral, at least in the eyes of those adhering to the Protestant Work Ethic. Just imagine!—implying "that things like thrift, innovation, family life, and so forth" might be, no "*are* a sheer waste of time." [22] How irresponsible of him! And how splendid of Hitchens to point all this out. He ought to be given a medal for good citizenship.

Another example is that of "the infamous tale," as Dawkins calls it, of Abraham's "sacrificing of his son Isaac":

> By the standards of modern morality, this disgraceful story
> is an example simultaneously of child abuse, bullying in two

asymmetrical power relationships, and the first recorded use of
the Nuremberg defense: "I was only obeying orders." Yet the leg-
end is one of the great foundational myths of all three monotheistic religions.

Once again, modern theologians will protest that the story
of Abraham sacrificing Isaac should not be taken as a literal fact.
And, once again, the appropriate response is twofold. First, many
many people, even to this day, do take the whole of their scripture
to be literal fact ... Second, if not as literal fact, how should we
take the story? As an allegory? Then an allegory for what? Surely
nothing praiseworthy. As a moral lesson? But what kind of morals could one derive from this appalling story? (242–3)

It would seem that Dawkins has simply not heard of either *Fear and Trembling* (Kierkegaard's meditation on the story of Abraham and Isaac) or
Derrida's reflection on the Kierkegaardian and Biblical texts in his *The
Gift of Death*. Both Kierkegaard and Derrida are of course fully aware of
just how shocking the story is. But unlike Dawkins, they also find it challenging, in deeply troubling ways, to their own sense of morality. However, this is something I go into in considerable detail in my fifth chapter and
my immediate concern here is to draw attention to the fact that, where
morality is concerned, H.H.& D. exhibit a remarkably untroubled and
complacent form of good conscience.

They give the distinct impression that they are largely writing about,
and to some extent also writing *to*, a large group of know-nothings whom
they are determined to free of their dearest illusion: the illusion that their
bible (whichever one they are using) is the source of our morality; or even
the illusion that, where morality is concerned, their bible might have *anything* of value to teach us. Hitchens, for example, follows his chapter on
"The Nightmare of the 'Old' Testament" with a chapter entitled "The
'New' Testament Exceeds the Evil of the 'Old' One." Harris maintains
that the "pervasive idea that religion is somehow the *source* of our deepest
ethical intuitions is absurd" (*End* 171). And Dawkins has this to say:

There are two ways in which scripture might be a source of morals or rules for living. One is by direct instruction, for example,
through the Ten Commandments ... The other is by example:

God, or some other biblical character, might serve as ... a role model. Both scriptural routes, if followed through religiously (the adverb is used in its metaphoric sense but with an eye to its origin), encourage a system of morals which any civilized modern person, whether religious or not, would find—I can put it no more gently—obnoxious.

To be fair, much of the Bible is not systematically evil but just plain weird, as you would expect of a chaotically cobbled-together anthology ... (237)

Whatever Dawkins *himself* thinks he means by following scriptural routes religiously, in practice it invariably comes down to an amazingly reductive and literalist reading of the Bible. But this aside, we can quickly note (in passing) that H.H.&D seem to find nothing remotely problematical about the idea of setting up "any civilized modern person" as a judge of these matters (since for them "the standards of modern morality" (242) are the best available to us) and we can then ask the naïve question as to whether or not it mightn't be possible to point to some modern example of a Christian whose life might be thought to provide a model worth emulating.

It is very revealing to see how H.H.&D have anticipated this question in the way all three deal with Martin Luther King. But first, a clarification. If, as Hitchens (who seems to think Dawkins has made a point worth repeating when he calls the Bible "cobbled-together"), if, as he would have it, "the cobbled-together ancient Jewish books had an ill-tempered and implacable and bloody and provincial god ... [w]hereas the cobbled-together books of the last two thousand years contained handholds for the hopeful, and references to meekness," Hitchens claims that "[[t]his distinction is more apparent than real, since it is only in the reported observations of Jesus that we find any mention of hell and eternal punishment." This is meant to prepare us for the following hilarious example (it deserves to be enshrined as a classic of its kind) of Hitchens making what he clearly considers to be a rational argument:

The god of Moses would brusquely call for other tribes, including his favorite one, to suffer massacre and plague and even extirpation, but when the grave closed over his victims he was essentially finished with them unless he remembered to curse their

succeeding progeny. Not until the advent of the Prince of Peace
do we hear of the ghastly idea of further punishing and torturing
the dead ... At no point did Dr. King ... even hint that those who
injured and reviled him were to be threatened with any revenge
or punishment, in this world or the next ... [And "the examples
King gave from the books of Moses were, fortunately for all of
us, metaphors and allegories ... In his version of the story, there
are no savage punishments and genocidal bloodlettings" (174–5)]
[*Therefore*, in] no real as opposed to nominal sense ... was he a
Christian. (175–6)

Having made in the pages preceding this a big point of saying how much
he admires Dr King, we might have known that he would end up by denying that King was a Christian. Harris doesn't seem to share Hitchens'
admiration but since "many Christians believe that a harmless person like
Martin King, Jr., is the best exemplar of their religion," he also feels the
need to deny that King was a Christian:

> ... the doctrine of Jainism is an objectively better guide for
> becoming like Martin Luther King, Jr., than the doctrine of
> Christianity is. While King undoubtedly considered himself a
> devout Christian, he acquired his commitment to nonviolence
> primarily from the writings of Mohandas K. Gandhi. In 1959,
> he even traveled to India to learn the principles of nonviolent
> social protest directly from Gandhi's disciples. Where did Gan-
> dhi, a Hindu, get his doctrine of nonviolence? He got it from
> the Jains. (*Letter* 12)

But didn't Gandhi derive *some*, at least, of his inspiration from Tolstoy,
who clearly—surely—got most of *his* from Christianity? Possibly, but
don't expect Harris to acknowledge that. Astonishingly, Dawkins does
offer the thought that the "Sermon on the Mount is way ahead of its time"
and that Jesus's "'turn the other cheek' anticipated Gandhi and Martin
Luther King by two thousand years" (250). More characteristically, however, we later find him chiming in to tell us that, "[a]lthough Martin Luther King was a Christian, he derived his philosophy of non-violent civil
disobedience directly from Gandhi, who was not" (*God Delusion* 271).

So nakedly and relentlessly do H.H.&D display their animus towards religion in general and the three monotheisms in particular that
it fairly takes the breath away. It so heedlessly flies in the face of the most
elementary of the lessons we try to teach our students when they are com-
posing an argument. "If you hope to persuade anyone then you must," we
tell our students, "try to recognize and do justice to the strong points of
the opposition. Whatever you do, don't try to defend or explain away the
indefensible but concede what needs to be conceded." But if, on the one
hand, H.H.&D. refuse to give Christianity any of the credit for somone
like Martin Luther King, on the other hand, consider for a moment how
they deal with atheistic dictators.

"Christians like yourself," Harris lectures his reader (in a section of
his *Letter* entitled "Are Atheists Evil?"), "invariably declare that monsters
like Adolf Hitler, Joseph Stalin, Mao Zedong, Pol Pot, and Kim Il Sung
spring from the womb of atheism. While it is true," he then concedes,
"that such men are sometimes enemies of religion, they are never especially rational" (*Letter* 39-40). His point? That because such men are not
"especially rational," they are not good atheists. In a similar vein, in a
chapter devoted to what he calls "The Last-Ditch 'Case' Against Secularism" Hitchens maintains that "Totalitarian systems, whatever outward
form they may take, are fundamentalist and, as we would now say, 'faith-
based'" (*God* 250). And as for Dawkins, in a section entitled "What
About Hitler and Stalin? Weren't they Atheists?" he claims that "the evils
of Hitler's regime can hardly be held up as flowing from atheism" (277).
In itself, each one of these three assertions seems to me reasonable: my
point is simply that a double-standard is in operation here, flagrantly so,
to such an extent that one feels slightly embarrassed for H.H.&D—they
too much resemble little boys shamefacedly caught in the act of trying
to pull a fast one but actually perpetrating something so blatant that not
even the most dull-witted among us can fail to notice.

According to Harris (who is objecting here to Edward Said's critique
of Samuel Huntingdon's description of the conflict between Islam and
the West as a "clash of civilizations"), "One need only read the Koran *to
know, with something approaching mathematical certainty*, that all truly
devout Muslims will be 'convinced of the superiority of their culture, and
obsessed with the inferiority of their power,' just as Huntingdon alleges"

(*End*, my italics 130). A year later, in his *Letter to a Christian Nation*, two other things about Islam were certain to Harris: (i) "The idea that Islam is a 'peaceful religion hijacked by extremists' is a fantasy" and (ii) "most Muslims are *utterly deranged by their religious faith*" (85).[23] But why should I have any more confidence in these judgements than I have when Hitchens claims that "Shakespeare has much more moral salience than the Talmud or the Koran or any account of the fearful squabbles of Iron Age tribes" (*God* 151)? I do know that Shakespeare is one of the greatest writers but since I also know how badly H.H.&D read the Bible, why should I believe they will be any better at reading the Koran or the Talmud?

If H.H.&D don't know the Bible then of course it can't come as a surprise that they also don't know any theology—if they did, they wouldn't be insisting that the question as to whether or not God exists is "a scientific question" (Dawkins 48). But then, the question naturally arises, What *do* these three know? Here is Hitchens on what almost seems like his favourite subject, fools:

> Whoever the psalmist turns out to have been, he was obviously pleased enough with the polish and address of psalm 14 to repeat it virtually word for word as psalm 53. Both versions begin with the identical statement that "The fool has said in his heart, there is no God." For some reason, this null remark is considered significant enough to be recycled throughout all religious apologetics. All that we can tell for sure from the otherwise meaningless assertion is that unbelief—not just heresy and backsliding but unbelief—must have been known to exist even in that remote epoch. Given the then absolute rule of unchallenged and brutally punitive faith, it would perhaps have been a fool who did *not* keep this conclusion buried deep inside himself, in which case it would be interesting to know how the psalmist knew it was there. (254)

Hitchens obviously protests too much ("this null remark," this "otherwise meaningless assertion" which, if neither null nor meaningless, would of course make Hitchens the fool), but what seems to me most interesting and revealing here is his obviously genuine puzzlement over the fact that "unbelief ... must have been known to exist even in that remote epoch." But *how was that possible if there was indeed an "absolute rule of unchallenged and brutally punitive faith" in place back then?* Actually, much of Hitchens' commentary on the last two thousand years leave us with the clear impression he thinks such a rule was in place during practically the entire period.[24] As for Harris, here is his view of the same period:

> The only reason anyone is "moderate" in matters of faith these days is that he has assimilated some of the fruits of the last two thousand years of human thought (democratic politics, scientific advancement on every front, concern for human rights, an end to cultural and geographic isolation, etc.) (*End* 18)
>
> ...
>
> The Bible, it seems certain, was the work of sand-strewn men and women who thought the earth was flat and for whom a wheelbarrow would have been a breathtaking example of emerging technology. To rely on such a document as the basis for our worldview—however heroic the efforts of redactors—is to repudiate two thousand years of civilizing insights that the human mind has only just begun to inscribe upon itself through secular politics and scientific culture. (45)

What were all those "insights" doing before the mind (the human mind) suddenly began to "inscribe" them "upon itself"? This seems to me unclear but I take Harris to be *implying*, at least, that "two thousand years of civilizing insights," "the fruits of the last two thousand years of human thought," were produced with very little, if any, help from the Bible. Or as Hitchens would have it, "when we read of the glories of 'Christian' devotional painting and architecture, or 'Islamic' astronomy and medicine, we are talking about advances of civilization and culture—some of them anticipated by Aztecs and Chinese—that have as much to do with 'faith' as their predecessors had to do with human sacrifice and imperialism" (*God* 254). *It seems that H.H.&D will say almost anything, however improbable it may sound, in order to avoid giving even the slightest appearance of moral credit to Judaism or Islam or Christianity.*

Some atheists who can (and do) do much better

It will be salutary to recall, in striking contrast to this meanness of spirit, the generosity of Nietzsche, who is also of course an incomparably more perceptive critic of religion than H.H.&D. In his *Letter to a Christian Nation*, Harris reminds his readers that the "core of science is not controlled experiment or mathematical modeling; it is intellectual honesty ... Religion," he then claims, "is the one area of our lives where people imagine that some other standard of intellectual integrity applies" (64-5). Really? Here is the (once, and still, in some quarters) famous passage that comes near the end of Nietzsche's *The Genealogy of Morals*:

What is it, in truth, that has triumphed over the Christian god? The answer may be found in my *Gay Science*: "The Christian ethics with its key notion, ever more strictly applied, of truthfulness; the casuistic finesse of the Christian conscience, translated and sublimated into the scholarly conscience, into intellectual integrity to be maintained at all costs; the interpretation of nature as a proof of God's beneficent care; the interpretation of history to the glory of divine providence, as perpetual testimony of a moral order and moral ends; the interpretation of individual experience as preordained, purposely arranged for the salvation of the soul— all these are now things of the past: they revolt our consciences as being indecent, dishonest, cowardly, effeminate. It is this rigor, if anything, that makes us good Europeans and the heirs of Europe's longest, most courageous self-conquest." All great things perish of their own accord, by an act of self-cancellation: so the law of life decrees ... Thus Christianity as dogma perished of its own ethics, and in the same way Christianity as ethics must perish; we are standing on the threshold of this event. After drawing a whole series of conclusions, Christian truthfulness must now draw its strongest conclusion, the one by which it shall do away with itself. This will be accomplished by Christianity's asking itself, "What does all will to truth signify?"[25]

My point, in quoting this, is not that I think it is obviously and (to use Hitchens' term) unanswerably right—either in its account of Christian ethics (as producing "scholarly conscience" and "intellectual integrity at all costs") or in its conclusion (that "Christianity as ethics must perish"). It can of course be argued and disagreed with (and, as always with Nietzsche, there is enough provocation to irritate just about everyone—that "effeminate" jab, for example). But my point is that the passage oughtn't to be ignored, especially not by anyone planning to think about the subject themselves. If only H.H.&D had shown themselves able to engage with it but, so far as I can see, there are only two references to Nietzsche in the four books I have been commenting on and they are sadly predictable. For Harris Nietzsche can be quoted approvingly when he says what Harris wants to hear: he tells us that "Nietzsche had it right when he wrote, 'The most pitiful example: the corruption of Pascal, who believed in the corruption of his reason through original sin when it had in fact been corrupted only by his Christianity'" (*End* 247, n.35). And Hitchens writes this: "The decay and collapse and discredit of god-worship does not begin at any dramatic moment, such as Nietzsche's histrionic and self-contradictory pronouncement that god was dead. Nietzsche could no more have known this, or made the assumption that god had ever been alive, than a priest or witch doctor could ever declare that he knew god's will" (67). Even by Hitchens's standards this is a bit much. He reads and condescends to genius in the literalist, flat-footed way he reads and condescends to the Bible; his crass assumption that Nietzsche must understand a "dramatic moment" as happening instantaneously when in fact the contexts in *Thus Spoke Zarathrustra* make it plain that he sees it stretching out like the "event" he says (in the passage I've just quoted) we are "on the threshold of," an event that will be made up of a "great spectacle of a hundred acts that will occupy Europe for the next two centuries, the most terrible and problematical but also the most hopeful of spectacles ... " (*Genealogy* 297–8).[26]

When I said earlier on that atheists can do much, much better than the performance staged by H.H.&D, Nietzsche was one of the figures I had in mind[27] but I was also thinking of such recent books as Alain Badiou's *Saint Paul: The Foundation of Universalism* (1997), Eric Santner's *On the Psychotheology of Everyday Life: Refections on Freud and Rosenzweig* (2001), Slavoj Žižek's *The Puppet and the Dwarf: The Perverse Core of Christianity* (2003), Slavoj Žižek, Eric Santner and Kenneth Reinhard's *The Neighbor:*

Three Inquiries in Political Theology (2005), all of which—like the late work of Derrida—are in a different league to the one H.H.&D play in. What *these* atheistic authors have in common is that, like Nietzsche (and of course unlike H.H.&D), they are able to recognize Christianity and Judaism (and in Derrida's case, Islam too) as "great things," things from which we can still learn what may well turn out to be indispensable lessons. As a result, they are all engaged in trying (in Žižek's words[28]) to find "new way[s] to reactualize the Judaeo-Christian legacy." (Which helps us to see that what H.H.&D seem to be trying to do is liquidate it.[29]) Thus, Badiou (who confesses to being "irreligious by heredity, and even encouraged in the desire to crush the clerical infamy by my four grandparents, all of whom were teachers") is undeterred by the fact that (from his point of view) Christ's resurrection is "a fable" and sees Paul as "a poet-thinker of the event" and "one of the very first theoreticians of the universal."[30] At the same time, if (like H.H.&D) these authors are all describable as atheists, there are substantial differences between the kinds of atheism they represent (as opposed to the minor differences between H.H.&D), with for example, Žižek explaining that "one of the trends to which [he is] very much opposed is the recent post-secular theological turn of deconstruction,"[31] which is associated with Derrida and Levinas and which I find particularly attractive and persuasive.

I will now bring these preliminary reflections to a close by saying something about my own position on some of the issues surrounding belief and the supernatural.

Faith, Belief, Evidence, the Supernatural and the Cross

> Ever since the attacks of philosophers like Bayle and Hume on the credibility of miracles, rationalists have urged that the acknowledgement of miracles must rest on the strength of factual evidence. But actually, the contrary is true: if the conversion of water into wine or the resuscitation of the dead could be experimentally verified, this would strictly disprove their miraculous nature. Indeed, to the extent to which any event can be established in the terms of natural science, it belongs to the natural order of things ... It is illogical to attempt the proof of the supernatural by natural tests ... Observation may supply us with rich

clues for our belief in God; but any scientifically convincing observation of God would turn religious worship into an idolatrous
adoration of a mere object, or natural person.
                                    —Polanyi (*Personal Knowledge* 284)

On the inside of its dust jacket we learn that "A preeminent scientist—and
the world's most prominent atheist—asserts the irrationality of belief in
God"; inside the book itself Dawkins tells us "religious faith" is captured
"perfectly" by the definition of "delusion as 'a persistent false belief held
in the face of strong contradictory evidence'" (*God Delusion* 5); and we
have already noted his saying that he is "calling only *supernatural* gods
delusional" (15). Hitchens doesn't have much to say about belief and what
he does say—asserting of himself and his "co-thinkers" that "[o]ur belief is
not a belief. Our principles are not a faith" (*God* 5)—suggests to me that
he hasn't given it much thought. Harris has a good deal to say about belief,
which he invariably links to the need for evidence. Over and over again,
he insists that "religious beliefs, to be beliefs about the way the world *is*,
must be as evidentiary in spirit as any other" (*End* 63). "The corrective
to the worldview of Osama bin Laden is not," in his view, "to point out
the single line in the Koran that condemns suicide because this ambiguous statement is set in a thicket of other passages that can be read only
as direct summons to war against the 'friends of Satan.' The appropriate
response to the bin Ladens of the world is to correct everyone's reading of
these texts by making the same evidentiary demands in religious matters
that we make in all others" (35). Finally, Harris insists that "[w]e must
find our way to a time when faith, without evidence, disgraces anyone who
would claim it" (48).
    Given the way in which Dawkins and Harris talk about belief, it may
be a good idea to turn next to something Slavoj Žižek has had to say on
the subject:

    In our politically correct times, it is always advisable to start with
    the set of unwritten prohibitions that define the positions one is
    allowed to adopt. The first thing to note with regard to religious
    matters is that reference to "deep spirituality" is in again: direct
    materialism is out; one is, rather, enjoined to harbor openness
    toward a radical Otherness beyond the ontotheological God.

Consequently, when, today, one directly asks an intellectual: "OK, let's cut the crap and get down to basics: do you believe in some form of the divine or not?," the first answer is an embarrassed withdrawal, as if the question is too intimate, too probing; this withdrawal is then usually explained in more "theoretical" terms: "That is the wrong question to ask! It is not simply a matter of believing or not … " Against this attitude, one should insist even more emphatically that the "vulgar" question "Do you really believe or not?" matters—more than ever, perhaps. (*Puppet* 5–6)

Though they are all academics, Dawkins, Harris and Hitchens belong to a different universe than this, one that knows nothing of the specific "unwritten prohibitions" Žižek mentions (which is not to say that their writing is unaffected by other prohibitions but that's another story). But when it comes to the question of belief, all three momentarily seem to be on the same wavelength as Žižek, which is odd because, as he goes on to explain two sentences further on, he actually knows better. Claiming that "the direct belief in a truth that is subjectively fully assumed ('Here I stand!') is a modern phenomenon," Žižek contrasts it "to traditional beliefs-through-distance, like politeness or rituals." He thinks the fact that "[p]remodern societies did not believe directly but through distance" explains "why Enlightenment critics misread 'primitive' myths—they first took the notion that a tribe originated from a fish or a bird as a literal direct belief, then rejected it as stupid, 'fetishist,' naïve. They thereby imposed their own notion of belief on the 'primitivized' Other" (*Puppet* 6). My point is simply that H.H.&D do to the "faithful" (all of whom they lump into one bag) pretty much what Žižek describes these Enlightenment critics doing to "the 'primitivized' Other."

While I agree that there is sometimes a need to ask "vulgar" questions, I am much more impressed by the attitude towards belief we see the philosopher Jacques Derrida displaying in his response to John Caputo's asking him what he means when he says, not that he *is* an atheist but that he "rightly pass[es] for [one]":

If I believe in what is beyond being, then I believe as an atheist, in a certain way … [A]lthough I confirm that it is right to say that I am an atheist, I can't say, myself, "I am an atheist." It's not a *position*. I cannot say, "I *know* what I am: I am this and nothing else." I wouldn't say, "I am an atheist" and "I wouldn't say, "I am a believer" either. I find the statement absolutely ridiculous. Who can say, "I am a believer?" Who *knows* that?[32]

Playful? Yes. Another hoverer? Yes, certainly. Somewhat slippery even? No doubt. But irresponsible? I might have once thought so but I don't any longer, not in the light of how we've seen H.H.&D discuss such things.

So here's what I want to do in the rest of this Preface. Without either believing in the supernatural or considering myself a Christian, I want to explain why *I* think Christianity deserves to be taken seriously and with respect and also why I think it is not necessarily irrational to believe in the supernatural. This means of course that I will be giving reasons and explaining what I think counts as evidence in these matters. (If I focus on Christianity here this is simply because it is the form of religion I know best.)

Let's start by noting the sentences in which Dawkins gets warm before he immediately wanders off and gets lost again:

> New Testament theology adds a new injustice, topped off by a new sado-masochism whose viciousness even the Old Testament barely exceeds. It is, when you think about it, remarkable that a religion should adopt an instrument of torture and execution as its sacred symbol, often worn around the neck. (*God Delusion* 251)

Why sado-masochism? In part this is no doubt due to the fact that, as Eagleton points out, "Dawkins sees Christianity in terms of a narrowly legalistic notion of atonement—of a brutally vindictive God sacrificing his own child in recompense for being offended—and describes the belief as vicious and obnoxious. It's a safe bet that the Archbishop of Canterbury couldn't agree more. It was the imperial Roman state, not God, that murdered Jesus" (33).[33] But of course it is also the case that the crucifixion is a grotesquely violent form of execution, so much so that when Mel Gibson did his best to film it in all its horror he ran the risk that there would inevitably be someone like Hitchens who would see it as "an exercise in sadomasochistic homoeroticism" (*God* 111). Yet, as René Girard says in his piece "On Mel Gibson's *The Passion of the Christ*," to reproach the film for "going too far," for "gratuitously exaggerating Christ's sufferings," is absurd. "How can one exaggerate the sufferings of a man who must suffer, one after the other, the two most excruciating tortures devised by Roman cruelty?"[34]

In any case, the idea that God would descend to the earth and then, in human form, be willing to allow himself to go through such unspeakable agony is astounding and it seems beyond the power of the human imagination to conceive of; it's almost enough to make me, at least, believe in the existence of a supernatural realm. I would be happy to agree, therefore, when Dawkins says it is "remarkable that a religion should adopt an instrument of torture and execution as its sacred symbol," if not for the fact that *he* seems to means only "remarkably perverse," whereas, what seems to *me* truly remarkable and profound is the fact that what we have here implicitly claims to be (in Eagleton's words) "the traumatic truth of human history" as "a tortured body" (33). So that, in the circumstances, the fact that the symbol often seems to be worn as a kind of pretty decoration, while in a way obscene, nevertheless, seems to me perfectly understandable. Because a religion that asks its faithful to look steadily at the crucifixion and accept "this dreadful image of a mutilated innocent as the truth of history" (ibid) is asking too much.

I am *not*, however, saying that it *oughtn't* to be asking too much, not even if this means, as it surely does, that what is being asked of us is the impossible. Here we can return to Hitchens who, after pointing out that "regulations that are often immoral and impossible at the same time" are characteristic of totalitarianism, gives some "examples of rules that must, yet cannot, be followed":

> The commandment at Sinai which forbade people even to *think* about coveting goods is the first clue. It is echoed in the New Testament by the injunction which says that a man who looks upon a woman in the wrong way has actually committed adultery already ... [These] attempt to place impossible restraints on human initiative ...
>
> This objection applies even to some of the noblest and some of the basest rules. The order to "love thy neighbor" is mild and yet stern: a reminder of one's duty to others. The order to "love thy neighbor *as thyself*" is too extreme and too strenuous to be

obeyed, as is the hard-to-interpret instruction to love others "as
I have loved you" ... The so-called Golden Rule ... simply enjoins
us to treat others as one would wish to be treated by them. This
sober and rational precept, which one can teach to any child with
its innate sense of fairness (and which predates all Jesus's "beatitudes" and parables), is well within the compass of any atheist
and does not require masochism and hysteria, or sadism and hysteria, when it is breached. (*God* 213)

There is no doubt but that the Golden Rule sounds simpler and it is certainly easier to carry out than, for example, the injunction ("But when
thou doest alms, let not thy left hand know what thy right hand doeth"
[*Matthew* 6:3]) that Hitchens cites elsewhere and that seems every bit as
impossible as the ones mentioned above. But is this the "piece of pseudo-
profundity" (*God* 133) Hitchens takes it to be? I don't think so. Citing
near the beginning of *The Gift of Death*, Jan Patočka's claim to the effect
that "Christianity understands the good in a different way from Plato, as
goodness that is forgetful of itself and as love (in no way orgiastic) that
denies itself,"[35] Derrida goes on to meditate on the significance of the fact
that goodness can only "exist beyond all calculation" on "the condition
that goodness forget itself, that the movement be a movement of the gift
that renounces itself, hence a movement of infinite love ... I have", he then
adds, "never been and never will be up to the level of this infinite goodness
nor up to the immensity of the gift" (50-1). And in *Given Time*, he defines
the "gift" as the "figure of the impossible" and tends to follow references to
it (the gift) with the words "*if there is any.*"[36]

   I am not claiming that the fact we are being asked something impossible in these cases *proves* the existence of a supernatural realm and *proves*
that the request comes from it. Of course not. All I am saying is that it
makes some sense to me, it doesn't strike me as being deeply irrational,
that some might take it as the kind of sign or clue—or even as the sort of
possible, debatable, "evidence"—that strengthens their faith. And I can
certainly see why, among others, Simone Weil and René Girard feel this
way about the extraordinary moment during the crucifixion when we are
told that "Jesus cried with a loud voice, saying, *Eli, Eli, lama sabachthani?*
That is to say, My God, my God, why hast thou forsaken me?" (*Matthew*
27: 46). "There," says Weil, "we have the real proof that Christianity is

something divine."[37] Noting how, in *"La Chute*, Albert Camus makes his
central character observe that 'Eli, Eli, lama sabachtani' has been 'cen-
sored' by two Gospels out of four," Girard makes the following claims:

> Simone Weil shows herself to be incomparably more profound
> when she takes the presence of this particular sentence in the
> other two Gospels as a striking sign of their supernatural ori-
> gin. To take upon itself so radically the naturalistic character of
> the death, the gospel text must be founded upon the unshakable
> certainty of a form of transcendence that leaves this death com-
> pletely behind.[38]

If the crucifixion sequence and especially this, its perhaps most shocking moment are the most dramatic of the signs that the God of Christianity came among us humans in the least prepossessing, the most vulnerable,
of forms imaginable, an important part of the explanation is to be found
in Christ's reflections on the Kingdom of Heaven in *Matthew* 25: 34-46:

> 34. Then shall the King say unto them on his right hand, Come,
> ye blessed of my Father, inherit the kingdom prepared for you
> from the foundation of the world:
> 35. For I was ahungered, and ye gave me meat: I was thirsty, and
> ye gave me drink: I was a stranger, and ye took me in:
> 36. Naked, and ye clothed me: I was sick, and ye visited me: I was
> in prison, and ye came unto me.
> 37. Then shall the righteous answer him, saying, Lord, when
> saw we thee ahungered, and fed thee? or thirsty, and gave thee
> drink?
> 38. When saw we thee a stranger, and took thee in? or naked, and
> clothed thee?
> 39. Or when saw we thee sick, or in prison, and came unto thee?
> 40. And the King shall answer and say unto them, Verily I say
> unto you, Inasmuch as ye have done it unto one of the least of
> these my brethren, ye have done it unto me.
> 41. Then shall he say also unto them on the left hand, Depart
> from me, ye cursed, into everlasting fire, prepared for the devil
> and his angels:

42. For I was ahungered, and ye gave me no meat: I was thirsty, and ye gave me no drink:

43. I was a stranger, and ye took me not in: naked, and ye clothed me not: sick, and in prison, and ye visited me not.

44. Then shall they also answer him, saying, Lord, when saw we thee ahungered, or athirst, or a stranger, or naked, or sick, or in prison, and did not minister unto thee?

45. Then shall he answer them, saying, Verily I say unto you, Inasmuch as ye did it not to one of the least of these, ye did it not to me.

46. And these shall go away into everlasting punishment: but the righteous into life eternal.

Here, in my view, we have the heart, I'm tempted to say the compromised heart, of Christianity. For me, the heart of it is in the idea that God manifests himself in the one who either comes to us in need (the hungry, the thirsty, the stranger) or whom we visit in his or her need (the prisoner); it's in the idea that God manifests himself in "one of the least of these." As for the temptation to see it as "compromised," I'm referring to the framework that neatly separates the saved from the damned, with the latter condemned to "everlasting fire," "everlasting punishment." Here I agree with Hitchens: this strikes me too as being a "ghastly idea." And insofar as the passage encourages us to see the damned as being made up of *others*, who are getting their just deserts, then it seems to me to belong to the psychology that Nietzsche and Kierkegaard famously diagnosed (of *ressentiment* or revenge). But is this an accurate reading? Mightn't it be more to the point to recognize that if this is the way God manifests himself then most of *us* are more likely than not to miss him? And if this is the case, then the point of the threat of eternal punishment might be to frighten us into realizing that doing the right thing on behalf of "the least among us" is a never-ending task.[39]

   If there is a God and if he (or she) indeed comes among us in this terribly afflicted way, then it seems to me more likely than not that we *would* miss him (or her). For two reasons, one provided by Weil, the other by Girard. I'm thinking first of two of Weil's reflections on affliction: that "it is as easy to direct one's thought voluntarily towards affliction as it would be to persuade an untrained dog to walk into a fire and let itself be burnt";

and that "thought flees from affliction as promptly and irresistibly as an animal flies from death."[40] And secondly, I'm thinking of Girard's reflections on the almost irresistible force of mimetic desire and on the frequency and significance of scapegoating.[41] As for the force of mimetic desire, there may be no more dramatic example than Peter's denials of Christ, his inability (in Girard's words) "to resist the new form of violent mimetic contagion that ... arise[s] when public opinion turns completely against Jesus" (*Things Hidden* 419). When mimetic desire reaches the point of greatest intensity Girard argues that it results in scapegoating and he further argues that the "biblical text alone carries [scapegoat demythologization] to its extreme conclusion."[42] Among other things, this would explain why Hitchens finds that "religion is scapegoating writ large" (*God* 211).[43]

Chapter Two

Why We Need to Rethink Religion

Fate doesn't work things out. Man is a thought-adventurer, and only his adventuring in thought rediscovers a way...The adventure is gone out of Christianity. We must start on a new venture towards God.

—D.H.Lawrence (1924)[1]

It seems we are unable to eliminate or suppress the phenomenon of religion. It reemerges in different forms, some of them perverse: sectarianism, theoretical or political dogmatism, religiosity...Therefore, it is crucial that we rethink religion...

—Luce Irigaray (1984)[2]

Ultimately it can be argued that the term *God* is something of a placeholder, the name for responsibility within the interhuman. That God is a preeminently empty notion, that to subject God to thematization entails a destruction of transcendence, Levinas had established in the 1975 essay "God and Philosophy"...

—Jill Robbins (2001)[3]

Whether we consider ourselves to be believers or unbelievers—whether we are enthusiastically *for*, angrily *against*, or indifferent to it—religion is one subject many (I suspect most) of us feel we already know about. Not of course everything about it but enough, quite enough, thank you: enough, in short, to know that we either love or hate it, or that the merest reference to it bores us silly.

My choice of epigraphs is designed to encourage the beginning of the process of putting this assumption (or conviction) into question. I will shortly explain exactly *why* I think we need to start rethinking religion but, since I feel that those who propose to address this subject had better be ready for a question concerning their hidden agenda, I want to *begin* by speaking more personally than I plan to do throughout most of this book, by first explaining both where (as we say these days) I am "coming from" and, if not exactly my "agenda," at least the kind of agenda I *don't* have.

(i) A personal note

As it happens, this will be my second attempt at trying seriously to think about religion; I mean at trying to think it (or some aspects of it) *through*, to give it the kind of sustained and open-ended thought that might possibly result in my having to re-assess where I stand on the subject.

I'm strongly *tempted* to say that I first began to think seriously about religion when—living on the South coast of England, in my late teens, in the early 1960s—I started to read writers like Jean-Paul Sartre and Albert Camus and began to think of myself as an existentialist (in philosophy), as an anarchist (in politics), and (where religion was concerned) as an atheist. But, as for the latter, it would be more accurate to say that what I got from Sartre, Camus and others was the assurance that the religious question was effectively settled (there is no God, God is no longer an issue)—so that it was OK *not* to think about it.

As a result, I personally didn't *actually* start to give some serious thought to religious matters until 1978 when I read René Girard's *Deceit, Desire and the Novel*. What initially fascinated me about this book was my realization that the kind of mimetic desire Girard convincingly shows to be at work in a number of major European novels could also be found at the centre of some of the English and American novels I had by that time been teaching (in Canada) for years. So that in the first instance Girard's work led me to rethink some of the literary texts I knew best and cared most about. And gradually, as this process of rethinking deepened and was fed by my reading of Girard's subsequent work—first *Violence and the Sacred*, then the essays collected in *"To Double-Business Bound,"* and finally the more overtly Christian-inspired *Things Hidden From the Foundation of the World*—I found myself rethinking not just literary texts but also the religious questions they were often raising but that I had previously felt in good conscience able to overlook. In short, one thing led to another and I found myself in the process of being—and remaining for three or four years—converted.

Though I did not stay converted, the experience—both of moving into a community of faith and then of returning to the outside—inevitably changed me in some ways, mainly (I think) by leaving me with a greater feeling of respect for some *aspects* at least of religion than I had had before it. Since an essential part of what happened during that period (that extended from 1978 to 1982) took the form of my reading and pondering such writers as Kierkegaard, Simone Weil, Pascal and Augustine, this will not (to anyone familiar with them) seem surprising. I particularly remember being impressed by something I read at that time that made me realise how attractive Christianity can sometimes be. It was something two Christian thinkers (Pascal and Eric Voegelin) had to say about a state of uncertainty (regarding the question as to whether or not God exists) that they see as being inescapable but also (in Voegelin's words, in 1968) "so hard to bear that it may be acknowledged sufficient motive for the creation of fantasy assurances."[4] If, as Voegelin implied, the desire for "a stronger certainty" (Ibid) concerning God's existence is a perfectly understandable one, Voegelin clearly felt that Pascal was right to maintain that on the question "as to whether man was created by a good God, an evil demon, or just by chance," there *can* be "no certainty"—not, at any rate, "apart from faith."[5] And as Voegelin pointed out, this "thread of faith, on which hangs all certainty regarding divine, transcendent being, is indeed very thin. Man is given nothing tangible" (*Science*, 108). It is quite natural, therefore, even for the faithful, to wish, as (back in the 17th century) Pascal says he wished, "a hundred times over that, if there is a God supporting nature, she should unequivocally proclaim him, and that, if the signs in nature are deceptive, they should be completely erased" (*Pensées* 162). Such wishing will not help, however: the uncertainty remains.

Of course, this is the reverse of the impression one gets from today's Evangelical right-wingers, who appear to have no doubts at all.[6] But then, to be honest, there are atheists too who seem (in the words of James Wood) to be "drunk on certainty"[7] and in Voegelin's view, at any rate (as expressed in 1952), "[u]ncertainty is the very essence of Christianity."[8] And not only of Christianity: "the absence of a secure hold on reality and the demanding spiritual strain are generally characteristic of border experiences in which man's knowledge of transcendent being, and thereby of the origin and meaning of mundane being, is constituted" (*New Science*

109–10). One of his examples of "a high demand in spiritual tension" (that seems especially pertinent today) is that of "the Islamic prayer exercises that have developed since the ninth century":

> When I want to pray, says the rule, I go to the place where I wish to say my prayer. I sit still until I am composed. Then I stand up: the Kaaba is in front of me, paradise to my right, hell to my left, and the angel of death stands behind me. Then I say my prayer as if it were my last. And thus I stand, between hope and fear, not knowing whether God has received my prayer favourably or not. (*New Science* 113–14)

But though I still find this moving, I have to admit that, on the rare occasions when (usually as a tourist) I enter churches today, I usually find their atmosphere to be as oppressive now as I experienced it when I was forced to attend as a child—up to the age of thirteen, when I told my parents that I could stand it no longer and was allowed to absent myself. As for the agenda I *don't* have, there will be no question then of my wanting to persuade anyone to go to church. Nor, perhaps I should add, of my being so foolish as to try to persuade anyone who already goes to stop going.

(ii) Three (of the four) reasons why we need to rethink Religion

By "we" I mean first of all, of course, those of us who haven't already begun doing so but, beyond that, when I speak of "we" I am also thinking of the (by no means necessarily academic) student and scholar in each of us. Why, then, do we students, we scholars and (I would add) we believers in criticism, why (supposing we haven't already started) do *we* need to rethink religion?

As I see it, there are four main reasons, the last of which I will leave to the end of the next section. *The first and most obvious* of these reasons is the fact that, in the last couple of decades, religion—most strikingly manifested in the growing strength of two opposed forms of (what, with some reluctance but for want of a better word, I will call) fundamentalism, Islamic and Christian—has made a dramatic return to the world stage. Recall just three examples: (i) the *fatwa* issued on February 14, 1989 against the novelist Salman Rushdie by the then leader of the Islamic Republic of Iran, the Ayatolla Khomeini; (ii) the attack on the World Trade Centre on September 11, 2001; and (iii), more generally, the increasing influence of right-wing Evangelicalism on the politics of the world's dominant power. In the face of these and other such events, it would seem that the French philosopher/psychoanalyst Luce Irigaray got it right in 1984. Leaving aside for the moment the question as to whether we should *want* "to eliminate or suppress the phenomenon of religion," it seems more likely now than it did a few decades ago that it simply can't *be* eliminated. Suppressed, yes, for a time but, in one way or another, religion will always reemerge, sometimes (as in the three instances just mentioned) with a vengeance. And, as Irigaray said, this is what makes it "crucial that we *rethink* religion."

Or so some of us might conclude. But by no means everyone would agree with this. Indeed, I assume that quite a few of the readers I would like to reach would agree with two critics who, back in the 1980s (only yesterday, as it were), took the trouble to speak out *against* religion, two critics who give the impression that *they* believe it would be a waste of time to rethink it—since we already know (or ought to know) that it is an entirely Bad Thing—and that, if we are forced to give it any thought at all, our energies ought to be devoted either to opposing it or at least to ensuring that our critical practice is uncontaminated by it. In fact, this seems to me the most influential of the ways in which Criticism (and not only but especially the kinds of criticism deriving from some combination of Marx, Nietzsche, Freud and/or some of their Enlightenment predecessors) has viewed (and continues to view) Religion.

So, *the second reason we now need to rethink religion* is that this way of regarding Religion will no longer do. It won't do because its confidence and morale-boosting clarity actually generates serious confusion. But if the view in question is indeed as influential as I am maintaining, then before starting to explain why it won't do I had first better make sure that I have presented it clearly and carefully. And I think I can best do this (and best hope to avoid charges of having set up a straw man) by turning to and drawing on the two critics (Jonathan Culler and Edward Said) I just mentioned.

I will take Edward Said first and will note (for what it says about influence) that Giles Gunn was no doubt speaking for many others when he began his recent tribute by saying that the now deceased "Said, as virtually no one else in literary and cultural studies in America during the last two decades, became the conscience of our profession." [9] What concerns us here, however, is the significance of the way in which his 1983 book *The World, the Text, and the Critic* is framed by its advocacy of "Secular Criticism" (the title of its Introduction) and its opposition to "Religious Criticism" (the title of the book's Conclusion). In the ending of this book, then, Said makes it emphatically clear that, as he understands it, "religious discourse...serves as an agent of closure, shutting off human investigation, criticism and effort in deference to the authority of the more-than-human, the supernatural, the other-worldly." Its "regular effect is either to compel subservience or to gain adherents" and it necessarily threatens secular criticism since "what a secular attitude enables...is [inevitably] diminished, if not eliminated, by appeals to what cannot be thought through and explained, except by consensus and appeals to authority."[10] Here are the last two sentences of Said's book:

> Once an intellectual, the modern critic has become a cleric in the worst sense of the word. How their discourse can once again collectively become a truly secular enterprise is, it seems to me, the most serious question critics can be asking one another. (292)

There is no doubt, therefore, but that, as William D. Hart (the author of *Edward Said and the Religious Effects of Culture* [2000]) maintains, "Said thinks of secularism as religion-abolished or as religion-strictly-quarantined." [11] As Hart says, where religion is concerned, Said's stance is one of "strict rejection" (8); he "describes those things that he does not like as sacred, religious, or theological, and what he does like as secular" (12).

As for Jonathan Culler, I'm thinking specifically of his 1984 *TLS* review ("A Critic against the Christians") of William Empson's posthumously published *Using Biography* and his 1986 piece ("Comparative Literature and the Pieties") that was addressed to his academic colleagues and written to further develop the anti-religion argument Culler had first presented to a wider audience in the review two years earlier. I want to make it quite clear that I am (to put it mildly) no more enthusiastic than Culler is about the fact that "religious discourse" (or, as I would prefer to say, a certain kind of religious discourse) is, as Culler noticed it was already back in 1986, "playing an increasingly greater role in our political and cultural life."[12] If only, as he says, there was "a vigorous tradition of antireligious satire to keep the sanctimonious in check" (31).[13] And like Culler, I too think it vitally important that every effort be made to keep alive and to strengthen the possibility of *criticism*, one highly significant expression of which takes the form of critical theory. Which means that I too believe "we should work to keep alive the critical, demythologizing force of contemporary theory" (32).

Taking it for granted (as I do myself) that any self-respecting literary academic is bound to be a critic, Culler argued, then, that, as far as religion is concerned, there is only one position that a critic can responsibly adopt, that of being *against* it. Here is an excerpt from his 1984 piece:

> It could be argued that despite its beneficent effects in certain times and places, religion is historically one of the greatest sources of evil in the world, but we pass over this in silence. We have no evidence for the existence of God, but we do not speak out against idolatry. Religion is the most potent repressive force in America today, but teachers of literature do not raise their voices against it—thinking it irrelevant...Religion provides the ideological legitimation for anti-feminist politics and other movements of political reaction, yet feminist critics do not attack religion itself, only its patriarchy. In America politicians of all stripes now appeal to God without fear of ridicule. Arguments about prayer in the schools never attack religion itself, and priests call, without fear of reprisal, for laws to conform to their religion.[14]

I would suggest that, *on the one hand*, when we read this today, just after the middle of the second term of George Bush's presidency, *parts* of it seem even more relevant and forceful than they must have done twenty years ago. At least for those of us who also find it hard to stomach the fact that American "politicians of all stripes now appeal to God without fear of ridicule"and who share Culler's concern over the kinds of ideological legitimation that religion continues to provide. It seems increasingly possible that certain usages of Christianity *may* indeed be making it into "the most potent repressive force in America today" and there is much to be worried about. But, *on the other hand*, Culler's failure or refusal to make distinctions is also worrying. The impression he conveys is that he thinks we should be (not just criticizing but) attacking (not this or that manifestation of religion but) "religion *itself*." Thus, immediately after claiming that we should honour Empson for his "attack on superstition," Culler maintains that the "best way to honour him would be to continue the critique of religious values" ("A critic" 1328).[15] Not the critique of *certain* "religious values" but of religious values *as such*, which from this point of view, can never be anything *but* "superstition."[16]

In other words, as Culler invited us to see the issue, criticism (or critique) is to religion as light (that of the Enlightenment) is to the dark (the darkness of superstition). Or, at least, this is how it *ought to be*. But in the mid 1980s Culler's own academic discipline of Comparative Literature in particular, and academic literary study in general, seemed to him to be in "complicity" with religion. Ironically, religion formed the "one area" in which his own discipline had "conspicuously failed to live up to its Enlightenment heritage" ("Comparative" 30). Ironically because he thought of "the critique of religion" as forming "the proudest [part of this] heritage and perhaps the one region in which the comparative perspective and literary criticism demonstrably had a major effect on the thought and discourse of Western culture." Culler summarized this effect as follows:

> At the beginning of the eighteenth century, one might say without greatly oversimplifying, Protestants took the Bible to be the word of God; by the beginning of the twentieth century this belief was untenable in intellectual circles...Radical scepticism, it has been suggested, is a characteristic result of the literary criticism of the Gospels. (31)

Now even if (as we shall see in the next paragraph) it immediately gives rise to a further question, one way of explaining what is wrong with the attitude towards Religion that is shared by Said and Culler is to say that it rests on the naïve or mistaken belief that the French deconstructionist philosopher Jacques Derrida was to identify in his 1994 essay on "Faith and Knowledge: the Two Sources of 'Religion' at the Limits of Reason Alone":

> Why [Derrida asked]does [the return of religions, or of the religious] particularly astonish those who believed naively that an alternative opposed Religion, on the one side, and on the other, Reason, Enlightenment, Science, Criticism (Marxist Criticism, Nietzschean Genealogy, Freudian Psychoanalysis and their heritage), as though one could not but put an end to the other? (*FK* 5)

In light of what we've just been looking at, it might almost seem as if Derrida, whose earlier work Culler had played a big role in introducing to the English-speaking world, had Culler specifically in mind when he asked the question that obviously answers itself. But more significant than the possibility that Derrida might have had Culler (or Said for that matter) specifically in mind when he asked it is the fact that, as its parenthetical reference makes clear, he could equally well have been thinking of virtually *any* of the *numerous* admirers of Marx, Nietzsche and Freud—the three masters of (what Paul Ricoeur had called in 1970) "the school of suspicion," united only in "their common opposition to a phenomenology of the sacred."[17] I would submit, therefore, that this in itself testifies to the fact that what we have here is a major break with an (among intellectuals) widely and long-held consensus on these matters. But in any event, both his essay on "Faith and Knowledge" and other related texts by Derrida form an important part of what I have in mind when I say that *the third reason we need to rethink religion* is that, for some time now, forms of radical rethinking have in fact already got underway and, in my view, the thinking in question constitutes a challenge that we can't afford to ignore.

Why, for example, is it naively mistaken (if it is) to believe "that an alternative oppose[s] Religion, on the one side, and on the other, Reason, Enlightenment, Science, Criticism (Marxist Criticism, Nietzschean Genealogy, Freudian Psychoanalysis and their heritage), as though one could not but put an end to the other?" After all, this can't either be or not be the case just because Derrida said so. We need to give it some thought, which is what I now propose to do. Except that I intend to approach the matter somewhat indirectly, by addressing another closely related question instead. In some quarters, any hint of a turn to religion is likely to be greeted by the kind of suspicion implicit in the question What might this mean for Politics? So the question I want to address now is this: Why is it naïvely mistaken to believe (as so many still do) that it is possible to set up *Politics* and Religion in easy opposition to one another? In the next section I will set out the answer that I think we most need to consider here, the one Régis Debray provided in his 1981 *Critique of Political Reason.*

(iii) Group Identity, Belief, the question of Belonging and the fourth reason we need to rethink Religion: Régis Debray on Politics as Religion

God does not exist, but politically we are condemned to an essentially theological collective existence. If we want to understand anything about our immediate political life, we have to become theologians.[18]

—Debray (1981)

On September 11 it was nineteen men with box cutters. The Pentagon was preparing for cyberterrorism and got pocket knives... The United States, a nation of engineers, is in thrall to a technological illusion and thinks of arms rather than men, visible devices rather than interior dispositions (belief in the afterlife is undetectable via infrared). The alliance of the two is certainly volatile, but *the detonator is belief.*[19] ("Indispensable" 16-17, my italics)

—Debray (2004)

If, as Levinas affirms, religion is etymologically that which binds, that which holds together ...[20]

—Maurice Blanchot (1980)

Debray first became famous when (having associated himself with the Cuban revolution, and Che Guevara in particular) he got arrested in Bolivia in 1967. Though sentenced to thirty years in prison, he was released in 1970 and returned to France in 1971, where he has written a number of books and made a name for himself as a critic and theorist of the media; as someone who tries to combine leftist politics and patriotism (in this respect, at least, like Richard Rorty in the US); for having served as an advisor on Third World Affairs in the government of François Mitterand from 1981 to 1985, and from 1987 to 1988; and most recently for having taken the side of those in France who supported the passing of a law prohibiting "Muslim headscarves and other overt religious insignia (such as Jewish skullcaps and large Christian crosses) in state schools."[21]

According to Debray, then, "the *political as such* is ultimately religious in nature" (*Critique* 48, my italics). How so? To put it very simply, this is because of the nature of group organization and of the fact—obvious enough when one thinks about it—that there can be no politics without groups. Debray reminds us, then, that the political realm centres on "the formation and disintegration of large (and non-natural) human groups" (30). And he makes it plain that when he uses the term "group" he wants us to understand it as "a fundamental concept or category of pure politics," which means that "its field of application immediately excludes non-structured physical aggregates (a crowd in a department store, a queue at a bus stop, etc.) and non-practical logical aggregates (a socio-occupational category, an age group, a sex-structure, etc)" (185–86).

So what is it about the nature of group organization that makes politics religious? The point to grasp here is that groups, systems and societies can never be either entirely open or entirely closed. Thus, on the one hand, there can be no entirely "open society, no society whose essence or identity (or both) is not to some extent threatened by a neighbouring or more distant society. Enclosure is the basic category of the political world, since the opposition between inside and outside establishes both its identity and its necessity" (277). But on the other hand, it is also simultaneously true that there can be no entirely closed society (which means that "enclosure" turns out to be a somewhat ambiguous term) because "*no system can be closed by elements internal to that system alone.* Contradictory as it may seem, a field can therefore only be closed by being opened up to an element external to it" (170, Debray's italics).

Another way of putting this is to say that any "collective body" is "born by being separated from itself (that is, subordinated to a point of extrinsic coherence) and it has to live in separation from itself" (179). But to say that a group is separated from itself is to say that by its very definition "its *disposition* [is] towards the '*sacred*'" (191, my italics), at least when the latter is understood as "'something external and superior to individuals,'" which Debray calls "a minimal but universally accepted definition of the sacred" (192). This becomes a bit clearer perhaps once we realize that the external element (or "point of extrinsic coherence") to which the group is subordinated is necessarily either invisible—"no one has actually seen God, the Republic or the Working Class"—or at least absent. Debray calls it, therefore, "the founding absence" (179) and he claims that the group that it founds has to find some way of making it visible, or present. This, as he sees it, is where "religion" comes in, "religion" understood as "a way of managing the sacred element in society" (192):

> Being completed by an invisible Yahweh, Israel requires a Moses it can have, see and believe. The problematic Covenant requires a tangible Ark to bridge the gap between the Other and us and it makes no difference if the Other is the world Proletariat, the Nation, the Grand Master, the Sovereign People or God the Father.

Here, however, I need to register a partial disagreement. It seems to me that the identity of this particular Other can actually make a *major* difference. If, as Melissa Orlie has recently put it, "each human association must have its god," and if this means that "we must determine which deities we revere," then a lot will depend on their identity.[22] Here, for example, is part of Charles Dickens's description of the reverence accorded one such deity in his novel *Little Dorrit*:

> Merdle! O ye sun, moon, and stars, the great man! The rich man, who had in a manner revised the New Testament, and already entered into the kingdom of Heaven. The man who could have any one he chose to dine with him, and who had made the money! As he went up the [hotel] stairs, people were already posted on the lower stairs, that his shadow might fall upon them when he came down. So were the sick brought out and laid in the track of the Apostle—who had *not* got into the good society, and had *not* made the money.[23]

A reminder, among other things, that, even if it needs to be handled with care, the concept of idolatry may still be as indispensable today as it used to seem yesterday.

But, at the same time, I take Debray's point to be that the identity of the Other in question here makes no difference in terms of the group's own structure and with this I agree. In each of the cases he mentions, the "group's inability to appear transparently to itself as a founded totality" ensures that this Other—"the figure of Mediation"—turns out to be "the kingpin of the whole" (180).[24] It is this Other that constitutes the "'secret' of human behaviour," the "inhuman and therefore theological" secret (176), insofar as we all belong to one or another of its various avatars.

Because, if the group is separated from itself, so are its members. One of the effects "of the group's eccentricity with regard to itself" is that *no* "element within a social set has its necessity within itself" (179). Not even the individual, the "social decentring" of whom—which is to say, "the recognition that an individual's centre of gravity does not lie within himself—is an important link in a chain of truths that is humiliating for reason" (176).[25] As Debray invites us to see it, to the extent that the "group both exists beyond the individual and is immanent to him," the "status of 'group member' is not added to a substantial subject as one property among others: it relates to the very constitution of the subject." We can therefore say that in this sense the subject "does not belong to himself and...his innermost personality is not a personal but a patrimonial possession" (141). No matter how "free-thinking" the community to which they belong, members "cannot establish immediately transparent relations with one another, since these are necessarily mediated by the organization that relates them to one another." Debray offers the following explanation:

> [T]he believer has his supreme reality in his church, the militant in his party, the patriot in his community, the Afghan tribesman in his tribe, the footballer in his team, and so on ad infinitum. Between abstractions like the individual and his generic essence, *belonging intervenes* both to give and to take away humanity. Ever slipping between man and man as a third and more powerful party, an institution or an individual brings them into one another's presence as members of the same group. No group can achieve self-recognition without making a detour through the untouchable first principle which acts as its touchstone. (227, my italics)

All of which means that a *crisis* within the group—church, party, community, tribe, team etc.—leaves its members in an extremely vulnerable
situation. Necessarily separated from themselves, essentially belonging to
the group (the status of "group member" relating to "the very constitution
of the subject"), what else are they to do if not answer when "the group
summons"? The alternative would be to enter a kind of chaos. In a crisis,
"Fatherland, Church, Party and Family call upon us to remember that
they have made us what we are. Our ideologies are our marching orders"
(141). *So long, at any rate, as we continue to believe in them* (admittedly a
crucial qualification to which I'll return).

Though Debray too is a kind of sceptic ("God does not exist" [176]),
we can now note that he is nowhere near as impressed by radical scepticism as Jonathan Culler seems to be. "Non-believers," he maintains, "are
solitary men":

> They lay down the law in their rooms at home, but as soon as
> they go out into the streets, one of two things happens. Either
> they become believers (against their will) or they give way to the
> believers. Sceptics have the ability to respect the law without re-
> ally believing in it, but not to pass laws in the City or to convince
> others that they should abandon their beliefs. (122)

From this point of view, radical scepticism is all very well in the study but
of no use whatsoever in the world of politics: what moves and to a large
extent constitutes the latter is *belief.*

This follows from the fact that politics is an "organizational," more
than a "representative or symbolic" practice (37) because the *"work of
organization is by its very nature 'religious,' simultaneously producing an
opening and a closure, saturating the 'below' with an absence 'on high'"* (my
italics, 175). Politics is an organizational practice because it is a specific
field of reality delineated not only by the formation of large and (non-
natural) human groups but also by their disintegration. In other words,
the fact that groups can never be entirely open or entirely closed means
that their existence is constantly being threatened both from within and
from without. It means that a group is always in danger of disintegrating
back into the "atomized swarm" of unrelated beings that it was before it

was organized (175). In short, it means that the work of organization is never done. And as Debray says, there "are many types of group, but there are not many ways for a stable, organized group to go on existing" (47). Hence, the need for representation, for ceremonies, for the things "that can bind—alliances, charters, oaths, pacts, friendship, memory, doctrines, principles" (268). Hence, too, the significance of the distinction Debray finds himself having to make between two kinds of socialism: "theoretical" and "actually existing," the one "iconoclastic," the other "iconomaniac"—in other words, the "doctrine is naked, but the state is dressed in flags" (310). Except that in once actually existing socialism—no longer today, of course, but still actually existing when Debray's book first appeared in France in 1981—it wasn't just a matter of flags:

> In the heartlands of "real socialism," collective life expresses and exhausts itself in the repetitive enthusiasm of endless popular processions, military parades, corteges, anniversaries, inaugurations, closures, festivals, congresses, tributes, funerals, visits, meetings, galas, exhibitions of medals, flags, trophies, diplomas, pennants, and so on. The organization of ceremonies is the prime function of the authorities...(9)

In other words, actually existing socialism "has at all times, though in varying degrees, renewed religious forms of social existence, which were thought to have been excluded by the new relations of production" (36). Like it or not, the point about all of this iconomania is that actually existing socialism was religious through and through.

At least, this would seem to be the inescapable conclusion if we go by (or at least emphasize) what I take to be one of the principal meanings of the word "religion." As Debray sees it, "there is no need to take sides in the old quarrel between those who, like Cicero, connect *religio* with *legere* (to collect, to assemble) and those who, like Tertullian, opt for *ligare* (to bind)" (265). I think the reason he feels this is that he sees no conflict between them: what are *collecting* and *assembling* if not ways of *binding*? And as Mark Taylor says, while introducing his recent edition of *Critical Terms for Religious Studies*, though "its etymology is uncertain, 'religion' appears to be derived from the Latin stem *leig*, which means 'to bind.'"[26]

In summary, according to Debray, it isn't just "the political as such [that] is ultimately religious in nature" (48), "social man qua social must naturally be religious" too (187). And if, like Levinas (and others), we understand "religion" as "that which binds, that which holds [us, men and women,] together," then this would indeed seem (quite inescapably) to be the case. Indeed, it's worth noting the way in which George Grant, a Christian thinker and arguably Canada's most important political philosopher, reached a similar conclusion back in 1963:

> The central controversy about the use of the word [religion] has been whether it should be confined to those systems of belief which include reference to a "higher" divine power or whether it should be extended to include those beliefs which exclude any reference to such a power. I intend to use it in the latter and broader sense. The origin of the word is, of course, shrouded in uncertainty, but the most likely account is that it arises from the Latin "to bind together." It is in this sense that I intend to use it. That is, as that system of belief (whether true or false) which binds together the life of individuals and gives to those lives whatever consistency of purpose they have. Such use implies that I would describe liberal humanists or Marxists as religious people; indeed that I would say that all persons (in so far as they are rational beings) are religious. [27]

Like Debray, Grant too thinks that we are all religious but for him this is true insofar as we are rational beings, whereas for Debray it is true insofar as we are social beings. But at the same time, since in this passage Grant understands a rational being *as* a social one (as someone who gives her allegiance to one of those "system[s] of belief (whether true or false) which bind[...] together the life of individuals and give[...] to those lives whatever consistency of purpose they have") he and Debray would seem to be in basic agreement here.

So here we have an answer to the question as to why it is naïvely mistaken to believe (as many still do) that it is possible to set up Politics and Religion in easy opposition to one another.

Still, it is ironic that Debray should have mounted his argument—about the impossibility of our having either politics or society without religion—just at a moment in history (a "moment" stretching back over at least the last few decades) when many people were beginning to think it might now be quite possible to get by *without* these things, without politics and even without society. It is clear that liberal humanism and Marxism, the two systems of belief to which Grant referred in 1963, are nowhere near as strong now as they were then. Debray may be right to say that "[n]on-believers are solitary men" but, in that case, whether we (men and women) like it or not, don't many of us, these days, feel fairly "solitary"? As if, for us, belonging (*pace* Debray) had not yet intervened? Indeed, isn't this the point the philosopher Alasdair MacIntyre is making in the following sentences from his book *After Virtue* (1981)?:

> E.M.Forster once remarked that if it came to a choice between betraying his country and betraying his friend, he hoped he would have the courage to betray his country. In an Aristotelian perspective anyone who can formulate such a contrast has no country, has no *polis*; he is a citizen of nowhere, an internal exile wherever he lives. Indeed from an Aristotelian point of view a modern liberal political society can appear only as a collection of citizens of nowhere who have banded together for their common protection.[28]

My own sense is that—even if "internal exile" is likely to seem a somewhat exaggerated description of the way many of us now feel—the experience of feeling much of the time like an outsider is growing more common. And given the options more or less available, wouldn't many of us prefer, on balance, to remain *un*bound? This state of affairs seems to me of such significance that I think of it as *the fourth major reason we need to rethink religion*. Among other things, we need to arrive at a better (less mystified) understanding of where exactly we stand on a number of the most important issues, in the face of some of the most fundamental questions. With this in mind I now want to try to deepen the thrust of Debray's argument.

(iv) Questions concerning Sacrificial Logic, Individual Identity, and Religion

> We must exclude someone from our gathering, or we shall be left with nothing.
>
> —E.M.Forster (1924)[29]

We now need to note something that a number of other thinkers have made more of than Debray himself does: namely, the significance in these contexts of scapegoating (Girard), exclusion (Kristeva) or sacrifice (Derrida). This, in effect, is what is necessarily entailed by the fact of what Debray calls "[e]nclosure" ("the basic category of the political world") and in fact Debray admits as much in the following sentences:

> To each his own scapegoat. In the nineteenth century, political guilt was transferred to the fetish of "religion"; in the twentieth it is transferred to the fetish of "ideology." Every epoch projects its lack on to a "bad object," believing that the lack will end when the bad object is expelled. (*Critique* 224–25).

Notice how this neatly anticipates what we saw earlier of Jonathan Culler's diatribe against religion, which we can *now* see constitutes further evidence in support of Debray's thesis concerning its inescapability. What we now need to grasp is that this scapegoating—this exclusion, or expulsion, of a bad object—is one of the two *essentially religious* (or binding) strategies (the *other* one involving Culler's appropriation of an Enlightenment heritage, the "absence 'on high'" that is brought down "below" through the mediation first of Empson and then of Culler himself) by means of which he constructs the group to which he makes his appeal. Judging, furthermore, by the confident manner in which Culler declares that "we do not speak out against idolatry," there would seem to be no doubt but that in *his* mind at least "idolatry" can *only* belong to the world of the completely Other, which for him is the world of "religion," of "priests," of "piety" and of "superstition."[30] How could he not have realized that he was repeating the self-contradictory gesture identified by René Girard in an interview given to *diacritics* in 1978, that of re-arranging things "in a manner more compatible with the self-esteem of an intelligentsia whose sole common ground and binding theme—*religio*—has become the systematic expulsion of everything biblical, our last sacrificial operation in the grand manner."[31]

The point is that treating religion solely as a Bad Object for which Others are responsible and in the construction of which we ourselves are in no way implicated leads to confusion.[32] (And the first advantage of working with the admittedly thin definition of religion as that which binds us together is that it results in greater clarity. If we are all religious insofar as we are social beings, then it has to be recognized that some of us are in this sense much less religious than others. But even so, even if we never go to church or don't belong to any political parties, even if we are not very "social" at all, even if our social being is much reduced, to the degree that it exists at all, to that degree we too are religious. The second advantage of the thin definition is that it encourages us to think more seriously than we might otherwise be inclined to do about questions relating, on the one hand, to the outside [and possible forms of transcendence] and, on the other, to belonging—questions we might previously have thought the exclusive concern of thicker conceptions of religion, and therefore ones we could safely ignore.)

I would say, for example, that Wendy Steiner is doing essentially the same thing as Culler when she claims—in her 1995 book on *The Scandal of Pleasure: Art in an Age of Fundamentalism*—that, "[I]f liberalism welcomes diversity and disjunction, fundamentalism casts these out in the name of purity, creating a system of inside and outside—the pure within, the barbarian without."[33] Who or what is doing the casting out here, if not "liberalism" itself? Indeed, in this very formulation (its construction of a Bad Object) "liberalism" repeats the gesture it accuses "fundamentalism" of using. "Liberalism," Steiner tells us, "wants everyone inside, allied by a premise of solidarity overarching unlimited, non-violent disagreement" (Ibid). But it is all very well for liberalism to *want* "everyone inside." The question is: Is it *possible*?

Or to rephrase the question: Is it possible to move from a sacrificial logic of identity to a nonsacrificial logic of inclusion? Among other things, I'm thinking here of Allison Weir's 1996 account of the ways in which a number of feminist thinkers have been engaging in a critique of the logic of identity, which they understand as a "sacrificial logic of opposition and exclusion."[34] As Weir understands it, for example, "[Judith] Butler's central argument...is that *any* identity is always a product of a logic of exclusion or of sacrifice" (my italics, Weir 6). And of course my point here is that this logic is an essentially religious logic, at least in *one* of the ways in which religion has to be understood. But if this is true, then it would also seem that, even if we were to somehow escape the group life of politics and society, we would still not have escaped religion—not, at any rate, unless we had somehow managed to do without an identity and the kind of sacrificial logic that constitutes it.

But *is* it true that (in at least one of its guises) religion can be understood in terms of a sacrificial logic of opposition and exclusion? By way of demonstrating that it *is*, at least as far as the three Abrahamic religions are concerned, I will now cite two examples (the first from the "Old," the second from the "New Testament") and then ask not only whether we can escape a sacrificial logic but also whether we should *want* to escape it.

First, then, Julia Kristeva's argument in her book *Powers of Horror* that *Leviticus* is a text that constitutes a "tremendous project of separation."[35] In the light of such passages as, for example, "I am the Lord your God, which have separated you from other people ... that ye may put difference between holy and unholy, and between unclean and clean" (*Leviticus* 20:24; 10:10;[36] qtd. in *Powers* 97), who could disagree?

Second, an equally striking example of sacrificial logic in the Bible is (in the words of Kierkegaard's book *Fear and Trembling*) the "remarkable teaching on the absolute duty to God" in *Luke* 14:26:

> If any man come to me, and hate not his father, and mother, and wife, and children, and brethren, and sisters, yea, and his own life also, he cannot be my disciple.[37]

As Kierkegaard says, "[t]his is a hard saying, who can bear to hear it?" (Ibid) But of course, over the years a number of people *have* been able to hear it. On the one hand, for example, we can surely hear a somewhat muted echo of it in the excerpt from the Doukhobor psalm sung at the 1895 Burning of Arms Resistance:

> For the sake of Thee, Lord, I loved the narrow gate; I left the material life; I left father and mother; I left brother and sister; I left my whole race and tribe; I bear hardness and persecution; I bear scorn and slander; I am hungry and thirsty; I am walking naked; For the sake of Thee, Lord.[38]

And there is an unmistakable, direct, and even more forceful allusion to Luke's hard saying in a passage from Ralph Waldo Emerson's "Self-

Reliance" that Stanley Cavell calls a favourite of his and quotes and comments on in his essay "An Emerson Mood":

> The doctrine of hatred must be preached, as the counteraction of the doctrine of love, when that pules and whines. I shun father and mother and wife and brother when my genius calls me. I would write on the lintels of the door-post, *Whim*. I hope it is somewhat better than whim at last, but we cannot spend the day in explanation. Expect me not to show cause why I seek or why I exclude company. Then again, do not tell me, as a good man did today, of my obligation to put all poor men in good situations. Are they *my* poor? I tell thee, thou foolish philanthropist, that I grudge the dollar, the dime, the cent I give to such men as do not belong to me and to whom I do not belong.[39]

As Cavell notes, the "general background of substitution could hardly be clearer":

> What Jesus required of one who would follow him Emerson requires of himself in following his genius—to hate his father, and mother, and wife, and children, and brethren, and sisters, yea, and his own life (*Luke* 14:26); to recognize that the promise of the kingdom of heaven is not an unconditional promise of peace but a fair warning that the time for decision and division will come. (*Senses of Walden* 153)

"But why," Cavell asks a bit later, does Emerson "mark whim on the lintels of his door-post? Why mark anything?" Here is part of his answer:

> We may understand this marking to invoke the passover blood, and accordingly again see writing as creating a division—between people we may call Egyptians and those we may call Jews—which is a matter of life and death, of the life and death of one's first-born. (*Senses* 155)[40]

My point is that we could hardly hope to find more striking testimony to the presence of sacrificial logic than these references to "division," especially Cavell's insistence that *"the promise of the kingdom of heaven is not an unconditional promise of peace but a fair warning that the time for decision and division will come"* (my italics).

But even if, in the light of this, we accept the idea that a sacrificial logic of opposition and exclusion is indeed a religious logic, there are still two questions that need to be raised here (even though this is not the place to try to answer them); the question as to whether or not we might be *able* to escape this logic, and the question as to whether we should *want* to escape it. It would seem, for example, that the English Marxist critic, Terry Eagleton is in no doubt on the subject:

> [S]ome postmodern radicals detest the idea of closure so cordially that they would wish to exclude nobody whatsoever from their desired social order, which sounds touchingly generous-hearted but is clearly absurd. Closure and exclusion, for radical thought, are by no means to be unequivocally censured in some sentimental liberal spirit.[41]

And I take it that the following 1982 declaration made by the English historian (and committed socialist) E.P.Thompson shows that he too would question not only the possibility but also the desirability of our moving beyond a sacrificial logic:

> The fear or threat of the Other is grounded upon a profound and universal need. It is intrinsic to human bonding. We cannot define whom "we" are without also defining "them"—those who are not "us"...
> This bonding-by-exclusion is intrinsic to human socialization. "Love and hate," William Blake wrote, "are necessary to Human existence." This will not go away because we do not think it nice. It is present in every human association: the family, the church or political party, in class formation and class consciousness. Moreover, this bonding-by-exclusion establishes not only the identity of a group, but some part of the self-identity of the individuals within it.[42]

On the other hand, more recently (in 1997), we find Hent De Vries and Samuel Weber coming at the question from a slightly different angle, one that foregrounds the violence involved:

Since the breakup of the former Soviet Union, the disintegration of the former Yugoslavia, and the spread of civil strife throughout much of Eastern Europe, the ideal of self-determination and the value system of which it has long been the cornerstone can no longer be accepted as self-evident...Values based upon the ontological and deontological priority of identity over difference, of sameness over alterity—and such priorities are perhaps inseparable from the notion of value itself—are demonstrating in practice what thinkers from Nietzsche through Adorno to Levinas and Derrida have long suspected: that violence is not necessarily the exclusive characteristic of the other but rather, and perhaps even above all, a means through which the self, whether individual or collective, is constituted and maintained.[43]

Though this does not obviously contradict the positions staked out by Eagleton and Thompson, it seems to me that it does give us a significantly different emphasis. To say that "the ideal of self-determination and the value system of which it has long been the cornerstone *can* no longer be accepted as self-evident" is surely to imply that it *should* no longer be so accepted. And this leaves us with an open question as to whether or not it might be possible to constitute and maintain "the self, whether individual or collective," differently. It is by no means obvious that this is a real possibility but, if it is, De Vries and Weber are clearly aware of the fact that it would have to be done in full awareness of the difficulties Derrida had in mind when he admitted, on the one hand, that, while he is "constantly against," and "trying to deconstruct[,] the logic of sacrifice," while he tries "not to be simply sacrificialistic," he "cannot deny that sacrifice is unavoidable"[44]; and, on the other hand (with reference to Carl Schmitt's argument that politics depends on the distinction between friend and enemy[45]), that "*losing* the enemy would not [from a Nietzschean or Schmittian point of view] *necessarily* be progress, reconciliation, or the opening of an era of peace and human fraternity."[46]

As I have already been trying to show, a significant change has begun to occur in the intellectual climate over the last couple of decades. I now want to take more explicit note of this change, which forms, as I noted earlier, *the third reason I believe we need to rethink Religion*. Though I am certainly not proposing to offer anything like a survey, I do want to now glance, in slightly (only slightly) more detail, at some of the radical re-thinking that is already out there.

(v) The recent philosophical turn to religion

Of course, religion has been crucial to Western traditions of radical egalitarianism, from the movement to abolish slavery, to the US civil rights movement, to liberation theology in Latin America; Marxist atheism was often more apparent than real.[47]
—Susan Buck-Morss (2003)

Today...the theological dimension is given a new lease on life in the guise of the "postsecular" Messianic turn of deconstruction.
—Slavoj Žižek (2003; *Puppet* 3)

If Derrida's late reflections on religion must surely have left some, at least, of his early admirers feeling disappointed, others—not surprisingly—were clearly delighted. Consider, for example, the openly triumphant tone adopted (in 1997) by John Caputo, at the time a Professor in Philosophy at Villanova (a Catholic University), as he announced (and one can practically hear him chortling) that the "news [coming from Derrida's late work] could not be worse for Derrida's secularizing, Nietzscheanizing admirers."[48] Caputo made this announcement in a book-length Commentary he wrote in response to a round-table discussion with Derrida that took place (in October 1994) as part of the inauguration of the new doctoral program in philosophy at Villanova.[49] Here is Caputo on "Derrida's secularizing, Nietzscheaning admirers":

They thought they found in deconstruction the consummating conclusion of the Death-of-God, the final stake in the still-twitching heart of the old God. If the first version of the Death-of-God, in Feuerbach and the young Hegelians, turned into the Birth of Man, then according to this atheistic metanarrative, deconstruction has been sent into the world to proclaim the End of Man, to deconstruct the subject and all metaphysical humanisms, and hence finally to scatter the ashes of the old deity to the four winds of *différance*. However much that line on Derrida may conform to the requisite academic dogmas about religion—if there is one "other" that is just too other, too, too *tout autre* for academics to swallow, it is religion!—it has nothing to do with deconstruction. (*Nutshell* 158)

At the same time, Caputo maintained that the "messianic turn in deconstruction, if it is a turn...also gives the lie to Derrida's critics...who take deconstruction to be the enemy...of religion." The truth, according to Caputo, is that deconstruction turns out to be "a blessing for religion." It is not, in his view, "the destruction of religion but its reinvention" (*Nutshell* 158, 159).

Although the relish with which Caputo recounts this development seems to me understandable and easy to forgive, I want to make it clear here (what will be obvious in chapters four or five) that Nietzsche nevertheless remains one of those thinkers whom I, at least, continue to find indispensable in my own attempt at rethinking religion.

That said, whatever one makes of Caputo's claim about deconstruction constituting the reinvention of religion, it is important to note that Derrida is by no means the only major intellectual figure involved in the climactic change to which I am trying to draw attention. Consider first, for example, Eduardo Mendieta's reminder that "an atheistic Jewish Messianism" was an important ingredient in "the critical theory tradition inaugurated by the Frankfurt School" as the latter attempted "to rescue the Enlightenment, and with it reason, by means of a refusal to grant immanence the last word."[50] To be sure, this is in one obvious sense not new at all. But it effectively becomes new when we find it in the Introduction to a recent collection of essays significant devoted (another sign of the times) to *The Frankfurt School on Religion* (2005). It is as if, finally, in the last few years, there are readers who may now be readier than they used to be to listen to what Adorno and his colleagues had to say on this subject too. And the fact that one of the essays in this collection is by the influential German philosopher Jürgen Habermas is also worth mentioning here.

It is not, as Edmund Arens assures us at the end of *The Frankfurt School on Religion*, that Habermas has "gone through a clandestine conversion" (384). But his attitude to religion *has* changed, some would say softened, and they would say it angrily. I am thinking here of the obvious disapproval with which Perry Anderson, the Marxist editor of the *New Left Review*, has reacted to Habermas's decision to endorse John Rawls's "claim that human rights are validated by all world religions." According to Anderson, "the slightest acquaintance with the Pentateuch, Revelations, the Koran or the Bhagavadgita—replete with every kind of injunction to persecution and massacre—is enough to show how absurd such an anachronistic notion must be." It would seem that for Anderson all that needs to be said about "transcendent faiths" is that they "continue to represent contradictory ethical imperatives" and to wage "ideological or literal war with each other."[51]

Still, however much Anderson may regret it, when a collection of Derrida's own essays appears under the title *Acts of Religion* (2002) and of essays *on* him is called *Derrida and Religion: Other Testaments* (2005), when a collection of Habermas's essays appears under the title *Religion and Rationality: Essays on Reason, God, and Modernity* (2002), and when books with titles like *Religion and Culture: Michel Foucault* (1999), *Deleuze and Religion* (2001) and *The Frankfurt School on Religion* (2005) start coming out, it seems safe to say that a change has occurred in the intellectual climate—the kind of change that is summed up in the title *Philosophy and the Turn to Religion* (1999), one of the three big, difficult and intellectually ambitious books by Hent De Vries (the other two being *Religion and Violence* [2001] and *Minimal Theologies: Critiques of Secular Reason in Adorno and Levinas* [2005]) that— heavily and openly under the influence of Derrida/Levinas—have done a good deal to define it.

And, however we determine the *size* of the change that has been taking place, what makes it *significant* is the challenging nature of the thought it has produced.[52]

Take, for example, Derrida's comments on the word "religion" in the epigraph to Part One. In the light of this epigraph perhaps we oughtn't to be *too* surprised to find Derrida elsewhere referring, on the one hand, to "my religion about which nobody understands anything" while confessing, on the other, that he "rightly pass[es] for an atheist."[53] All of which invites us to consider the possibility that the meaning of the word "religion" may only seem simple and clear when one is not thinking about it, when one is either an unreflective believer in, or an unreflective dismisser of, religion.[54] And if that is so, then perhaps the same thing applies to some of those other words that are also easy to take for granted, to use automatically, without thought, such words as "believer" or "atheist" or "Christian."

As T.S.Eliot once put it (in "Burnt Norton"):

> Words strain
> Crack and sometimes break, under the burden,
> Under the tension, slip, slide, perish,
> Decay with imprecision, will not stay in place,
> Will not stay still.[55]

But surely, some will protest, Eliot wasn't thinking here of words like "believer," "atheist" and "Christian"? Surely these are among the words whose stable—simple and unequivocal—meanings we ought to be able to count on?

Let's look at a few more examples—nuggets, food for thought—in the form of usages that can make us wonder if our confidence that we know the meaning of some of these words is as well-founded as we have been assuming it is. First, from Mendietta's Introduction to *The Frankfurt School on Religion*:

> The motto that hangs over the Frankfurt School's negative theology, is one that Ernst Bloch articulated thus: "Only an atheist can be a good Christian; only a Christian can be a good atheist." (11)

Second, from an exchange in 1998 between Catherine Clément and Julia Kristeva in their book *Feminine and the Sacred*:

> [CC] You are a Christian atheist and I a Jewish atheist ...
> [JK] If atheism did exist—which is not certain—it would belong to no religion, but rather to the depletion of all religions, in full knowledge of the facts, as old Hegel wanted it, without forgetting the Universal, the Christian. Yet the tendency to forget Christianity, which sometimes puts on the airs of a liberating blasphemy, characterizes a number of modern "atheists."[56]

Third, an excerpt from one of a number of recent studies of Georges Bataille, Peter Tracey Connor's *George Bataille and the Mysticism of Sin*
(2000):

> It was ... a matter, in Bataille's blunt phrase, of "doing justice to
> Christianity in all hostility" (V1, 316). The violence of such a "rig-
> orous hostility" finds expression in the contradictory utterances
> that Bataille makes regarding himself; both "ferociously religious"
> and "profoundly atheist," Bataille sidesteps every attempt to label
> him. One might well say of Bataille's attitude to Christianity what
> Jaspers, in a book highly praised by Bataille, wrote of Nietzsche:
> "His *opposition* to Christianity as a reality is inseparable from his
> *tie* to Christianity as a postulate."[57]

Fourth, from De Vries's *Minimal Theologies*:

> Reiterating his radicalization of the ban on graven images, [Ador-
> no] writes, in *Negative Dialectics*: "one who believes in God there-
> fore cannot believe in Him. The possibility for which the divine
> name stands is maintained by whoever does not believe ..."[58]

Fifth, from one of Levinas's interviews:

> Everyone is a little bit Jewish...Moreover, Jews are people who
> doubt themselves, who in a certain sense, belong to a religion of
> unbelievers.[59]

Sixth, from John Caputo:

> In a certain way, the most important feature of this postmodern
> desire for God is...that it throws the very distinction between the-
> ism and atheism into undecidability. Take Derrida's work on hos-
> pitality...by the standards of religious orthodoxy—and this is what
> Derrida says about himself—he "rightly passes as an atheist." But
> given what he says about hospitality and the passion for justice,
> which for him is the passion for God, the desire for God, I under-
> stand less and less each day what such atheism would mean.[60]

Seventh, from Eric Santner:

> When ... one has lost the capacity to pray, "God," in essence, as-
> sumes the status of a designated signifier, a stand-in for an other-
> wise nameless loss; the word signifies, *but not for us* even though we
> continue, in some sense, to be addressed by it, to live, as [Gershom]
> Scholem so powerfully phrased it, within the space of its validity
> beyond and in excess of its meaning. (*Psychotheology* 44)[61]

What, I can imagine someone (whose sense of frustration has been mount-
ing) now bursting out with, What is the point of all of this? If, as T.S.Eliot
observed back in 1920, "it becomes increasingly difficult for anyone to
know whether he knows what he is talking about or not,"[62] why go out
of one's way to increase the difficulty? That would seem to me an understandable response. But I also think it would be a mistake. Sometimes
things turn out to be not as clear-cut as we imagine them to have been
and this is now true, it seems to me, of some of those things (God, belief,
atheism, Christianity, the sacred etc.) we associate with religion, as well as
with religion itself.

Hence (again, then), the need for some rethinking.

One thing of which I am quite sure, however, is that there are many
very different ways in which this could usefully be done and so it may be
appropriate here to issue one last warning before we plunge in. The next
three chapters will *not* take the form of a general *Introduction* to the kinds
of radical rethinking of Religion I have been mentioning. What they *do*
offer is something much more restricted in scope. To put it very simply,
my contribution is organized around reference to two specific aspects of
the recent attempts at rethinking the subject: my aim is to zero in on (i)
the so-called "'postsecular' Messianic turn of deconstruction" and (ii) to
examine it under the rubric of the Outside. And to remind the reader of
what I said in the Preface, my approach is somewhat idiosyncratic in that
I will be using the still controversial English writer D.H.Lawrence (along
with Nietzsche, Kierkegaard, Žižek, F.R.Leavis and two other English
novelists, Joseph Conrad and George Eliot) to help me make sense both
of the Levinasian-inspired postsecular, Messianic turn taken by Derrida's
late work and also of the Outside. I should also make it clear here that
while Levinas and Derrida will have major roles to play in the following

discussion, I will have very little to say about the text (Michel Foucault's essay on "Maurice Blanchot: The Thought from Outside") that initially aroused my interest in the Outside. This is not because I share the view of a common reader with whom on other occasions I find myself agreeing but according to whom Foucault's essay is no better than pretentious rubbish.[63] Like its subject, the essay *is* an exceptionally difficult one to make anything of but that, in itself, is not why I will be referring so little to it. I *will* be referring briefly to both Blanchot's notion of the Outside and to the way in which it has been taken up by Foucault and (more recently) by John Paul Ricco but the fact is that I find other versions of, and ways of talking about, the Outside—including Levinas's and Derrida's but especially Lawrence's—more congenial and more rewarding than the version that spurred me to thought in the first place

I should also explain that what follows in the next three chapters mostly focusses on the individual's experience of Religion and I plan to focus more on the collective or group experience in a subsequent work. In his 2002 book *Varieties of Religion Today: William James Revisited*, Charles Taylor associates the two most influential ways of discussing Religion in the last century with William James and Emile Durkheim. In terms of this distinction, this book is closer in spirit to James (even though I hardly mention him) while the other book will be closer in spirit to Durkheim (who in fact I will be discussing, along with Bataille, Kristeva, Girard, Shakespeare, Melville, Hawthorne, Conrad and Peckinpah).

PART TWO

THE OUTSIDE

In its acuter stages every religion must be a homeless Arab of the desert.

...

The religious experience which we are studying is that which lives itself out within the private breast. First-hand experience of this kind has always appeared as a heretical sort of innovation to those who witnessed its birth. Naked comes it into the word and lonely; and it has always, for a time at least, driven him who had it into the wilderness, often into the literal wilderness out of doors, where the Buddha, Jesus, Mohammed, St. Francis, George Fox, and so many others had to go.

—William James (1902)[1]

And that I have not got a thousand friends, and a place in England among the esteemed, is entirely my own fault. The door to "success" has been held open to me. The social ladder has been put ready for me to climb. I have known all kinds of people, and been treated quite well by everyone, practically, whom I have known personally.

Yet here I am, nowhere, as it were, and infinitely an outsider. And of my own choice.

—D.H.Lawrence (1927)[2]

Someone asked me the other day if, as a Jew, I didn't feel like an outsider in France. I replied to him that wherever I am, I feel like I'm in the way, and I quoted a Psalm: "I am a stranger upon the earth" (Ps. 119:19).

—Levinas (*Righteous?* 92)[3]

I am a Jew from Algeria, from a certain type of community, in which belonging to Judaism was problematic, belonging to Algeria was problematic, belonging to France was problematic, etc. So all this predisposed me to not-belonging ...

—Derrida (1997)[4]

[W]e indulge a somber fear ... of the outsiders among us ...

...

"[E]gregious" means at root "outside the flock" ... a minor and insidious fear is the prod that coaxes us toward conforming our lives, and even our thoughts, to norms that are effective markers of group identity precisely because they are shibboleths, a contemporary equivalent of using the correct fork. These signals of inclusion and exclusion, minor as they seem, have huge consequences ...

—Marilynne Robinson[5]

Chapter Three

Shifting focus from the "outsider" to the outside

He [the Nawab Bahadur] had spoken in the little room near the Courts where the pleaders waited for clients; clients, waiting for pleaders, sat in the dust outside. These had not received a card from Mr. Turton. And there were circles even beyond these— people who wore nothing but a loincloth, people who wore not even that, and spent their lives in knocking two sticks together before a scarlet doll—humanity grading and drifting beyond the educated vision, until no earthly invitation can embrace it.
—E.M.Forster (1924)[6]

Famine, like genocide, destroys the capillary system of social relations that sustains each individual's system of entitlements. In so doing, genocide and famine create a new human subject—the pure victim stripped of social identity, and thus bereft of the specific moral audience that would in normal times be there to hear his cry. The family, the tribe, the faith, the nation no longer exist as a moral audience for these people. If they are to be saved at all, they must put their faith in that most fearful of dependency relations: the charity of strangers.
—Michael Ignatieff (1997)[7]

As we noted in the last chapter, Régis Debray thinks that "[n]on-believers are solitary men." And as I reflected then, if that is the case, then whether we like it or not, many of us, these days, must be feeling fairly "solitary." As if, for us, belonging (*pace* Debray) has not yet intervened. As if we are outsiders.

By way of starting to try to get some kind of historical perspective on this, it may be useful to take William James and Emile Durkheim as representing two basic alternatives. If, as James put it in *The Varieties of Religious Experience* (1901-02), there is "one great partition which divides the religious field," with "institutional" religion on the one side and "personal religion" on the other, then he chose to confine himself as far as he could "to personal religion pure and simple" (34), whereas (in *The Elementary Forms of the Religious Life* [1915]) Durkheim chose to focus on the institutional or collective side of religious life. So that one way of understanding the situation in which we find ourselves today is in terms of the three "ideal types" ("Paleo-, neo-, post-Durkheimian") that Charles Taylor proposes in his recent *Varieties of Religion Today: William James Revisited* (2002).[8] Taylor explains the first two types as follows:

> Under the Paleo-Durkheimian dispensation, my connection to the sacred entailed my belonging to a church, in principle coextensive with society ... The neo-Durkheimian dispensation saw me enter the denomination of my choice, but that in turn connected me to a broader, more elusive "church," and, more important, to a political entity with a providential role to play. In both these cases, there was a link between adhering to God and belonging to the state—hence my epithet "Durkheimian." (93–4)

As Taylor sees it, these are the dispensations our history has moved through, with the result that it is the *post*-Dukheimian dispensation (of "expressive individualism") that "has come more and more to color our age" (97, 96). So that over the last few decades in France, for example, not only has the church seen "a sharp drop in adherence, but young people [have begun] to drop out of the rival Jacobin and/or Communist worldviews as well" (95). Taylor concludes, therefore, by claiming that in some ways "our post-Durkheimian world" seems to be "a paradigmatically Jamesian one," while at the same time warning us against taking away "a too-simple notion of James's undoubted prescience" (111). If we were to do that we would be overlooking "the continuing importance of the neo-Durkheimian identities," which in some societies are "in a quasi-agonistic relation to the post-Durkheimian climate (111, 114).

After all, as Taylor has noted early on in his book, if, on the one hand, there are moments in the Psalms (see, for example, Psalm 51) that already put us "on the road to our contemporary notion of personal religion," on the other hand, "there were many stages on the way, and not every culture has pressed as singlemindedly toward this ultimate point as the Latin

Christendom to which we are heirs in the West" (12). If it is in "the North Atlantic regions" that "the movement toward committed inwardness has gone the farthest" (if it is there that "James's stress on personal religion, even his insistence that this is what religion *really* is, as against collective practice, can seem entirely understandable, even axiomatic, to lots of people" [12–13]), there are two striking and fairly dramatic exceptions to this trend. If Taylor only notices one of these, it has to be admitted that the other one is far easier to spot now than it was (history having speeded up to such an extent) even five years ago, when his book came out. I'm referring of course to some of the ways in which Muslim communities have begun to make their presence felt in Western societies, ways that would now it seems to me force Taylor to seriously consider revising the sentence in which he claims that "James is very close to the spirit of contemporary society" (111).

As for the other exception, Taylor explains that, in "a sense, part of what drove the Moral Majority and motivates the Christian right in the United States is an aspiration to reestablish something of the fractured neo-Durkheimian understanding that [they believe] used to define the nation, where being American would once more have a connection with theism, with being 'one people under God,' or at least with the ethic which was interwoven with this" (97-8). But my own view is that, in the case of the U.S., the neo-Durkheimian identity is so strong there that it might be more accurate to speak of the post-Durkheimian minority being in "a quasi-agonistic relation to" *it*.

Indeed, where the U.S. is concerned, outside the sphere of higher education,[9] in American society-at-large, the influence of institutionalized religion is now so great that Harold Bloom doesn't seem to have been exaggerating when he claimed in 1992 that the "United States of America is a religion-mad country" and that the "central fact about American life, as we enter the final decade of the twentieth century, is that our religiosity is everywhere"— "the flag and the fetus, our Cross and our Divine Child," forming the "linked emblems" of the US's "national religion."[10]

It's interesting to note that, in relation to this, Bloom identifies himself as both an outsider and an insider. Or in his own words, he confesses to being, on the one hand, "an unbelieving Jew of strong gnostic tendencies" (*American* 30), while claiming, on the other, that "[i]f we are

Americans, then to some degree we share in the American Religion, however unknowingly or unwillingly" (28). Possibly, but I am sure there are many Americans who are less happily resigned to that fate than Bloom himself seems to be.

Still, it is certainly possible to be, from a certain point of view, technically or objectively an insider, while nevertheless *feeling* like an outsider. Like countless others, I know this from my own experience, as I will now briefly explain.

Even though I don't think of any one of them as having been necessarily determining, I will begin by noting three things, starting with the fact that I am one of those who has moved around a bit—first from Wales to the South of England, when I was thirteen, then from England to North America, as a young adult. By the time I came to make that second move in 1968 my cultural and political interests were just about equally divided between France (Sartre, Camus, Godard etc.) and the US (Mailer, Baldwin, jazz, the antiwar movement) and the move took me and my French wife and son first to the States and two years later to Canada, where I have been living and working ever since. More recently, my second marriage to an American citizen has meant (among other things) that I have begun to spend more of my time than I used to south of the border.

These moves would not, I think, necessarily be enough to explain why I have always felt more like an outsider than an insider—not, at least, in and of themselves. Nor, in and of itself, would my age. But the fact is that I am also one of those for whom a formative influence was the discovery—as we entered our late teens at the beginning of the 1960s—of existentialism and one could hardly think of oneself as an existentialist (as many of us learned to do at that time) without also thinking of oneself as something of a rebel (Camus's *L'Homme Révolté*) and an outsider (the title both of a popular, non-academic, introduction to existentialism by Colin Wilson and also of the English edition of the translation of Camus's *L'Étranger*). Indeed, as I explained in the last chapter, it was during this period that (besides becoming an existentialist in philosophy) I also began to think of myself as an anarchist or libertarian socialist in politics and (where religion was concerned) as an atheist. But in practical terms, these were just two more ways of considering oneself something of a rebel and an outsider.

All of which meant that, by the time I moved to North American, my sense of politics and attitude towards religion made it more likely than not that for much of the time I would continue to feel like an outsider, whose loyalties are sometimes divided and whose feelings sometimes come as a surprise even to myself. If, for example, one of the reasons I had for admiring Sartre in the 1960s was his refusal to accept the Nobel Prize,[11] I was recently startled to discover—in the aftermath of Mick Jagger's acceptance of a knighthood in the UK—that I still cared about such things, something that was brought home to me by the keen pleasure I experienced on reading that, over the years, a significant number of writers and actors have declined such honours as the one Jagger accepted (with, for example, Michael Frayn, Albert Finney, Alan Bennett, Aldous Huxley, Paul Schofied and the painter David Hockney all having declined knighthoods).[12] Good for them, I thought. Of course, these figures are all known for being highly successful *inside* of their chosen professions but all the more reason—or so it seems to me—to applaud their determination to stand *outside* that particular system of awards.

In any case, I am among those who—even though we are capable of rejoicing and feeling less alone when others do the sort of things we admire—do not think of ourselves as "believers," at least not in Debray's strong sense of the term, which is to say as people whose very individuality (or subjecthood) is constituted by our status as members of a particular group. And among other things this means that, in relation to politics, even though I have always considered it a major part of life, I have spent most of my adult years unhappily feeling like a disillusioned spectator.

So I will confess that I now have mixed feelings when I discover, on the one hand, someone of my own generation and profession proclaiming that "the outside is the only place to be" and, on the other, a young film actress talking about the "attraction of outsider status, the attraction of the power there." I'm thinking first of a moment in his book *Secular Vocations* when Bruce Robbins notes Donald Davie's remark that his fellow literary critic Stanley Fish "has a respectful tenderness" for "professionalism in literary studies" that Davie, who prefers "the less easily institutionalized concept of 'vocation' or 'calling,'" can't share. Maintaining (what I have to admit I myself don't believe[13]) that "no distinction between vocation and profession can be sustained," Robbins responds to Davie's telling us that he was "educated by men and women who in their own time and place were 'mavericks'" by claiming that what used to be thought "rare and transcendent"—such things as culture or the "maverick"—have now been institutionalized.[14] He draws the following conclusion:

> It is because culture and the 'maverick' have been institutional-
> ized and generalized that, as our intellectual instincts tell us, the
> outside is the only place to be. Thanks to culture, the disciplinary
> object which provided the ground or rationale for criticism's ac-
> tivities, every literary critic could be a permanent outsider. Criti-
> cism itself as an institution became a *bande à part*. (Ibid)

One of the things this overlooks, however, is the existence of certain obvious differences within the university system itself. For our purposes here,
it is Frank Lentricchia who makes this point most effectively in his 1980
book *After the New Criticism*. Drawing on Michel Foucault's realization
that, if they want to be taken seriously, "medical statements cannot come
from anybody," "that it is not enough to speak the truth—one must be
'within the truth' (*dans le vrai*),"[15] Lentricchia applies what Foucault says
about medical doctors to the situation of the literary critic. And even if
some of the details (concerning, for example, "Saussurean linguistics") no
longer fit, the overall message seems as relevant today as it did then:

> To probe the source of a speaker's authority is very quickly, as
> Foucault shows, to discover impregnable interlocking institutions
> which force expression into certain thoroughly architected places
> of confinement ... [T]he literary critic ... will, at a minimum, have
> a Ph.D. in literature, and preferably from one of a small group of
> celebrated universities. He will need a university appointment or
> a position at a small "respected" college: a letterhead announcing
> his name, an M.A. degree, and his home address as Commerce,
> Oklahoma, will constitute a distinct disadvantage. An ambitious
> literary critic who desires to lodge his statements within our cur-
> rent sense of critical truth would seek "co-existence," as Foucault
> puts it, with certain other disciplines—Saussurean linguistics,
> anthropology in the structuralist mode, deconstructionist phi-
> losophies, and so on. And his books and articles will speak from

institutionally sanctioned sites: a university press, a scholarly journal, but again this is only minimal, for to be critically *dans le vrai* in 1980 is to speak under the imprimatur of certain preferred presses and journals. Above all, certain doctrines will be paid reverence. (*After* 198-99)

Either that or else, Foucault maintains, one will end up "speak[ing] the truth in a void" (qtd. by Lentricchia 197), which means that one simply won't be *heard*.[16] My point, then, is that while many academic literary critics might like to *think* of themselves as "outsiders," some of them are obviously much closer to certain "insides" than others, who in turn can therefore more legitimately be said to be on the "outside" of things. At the same time, these latter (in so far as they do after all have jobs as university teachers of literature) may be objectively describable as insiders, especially in relation to those who don't have (but would like, and are qualified, to have) such jobs.

Here is the actress Tilda Swinton commenting in a recent interview on her appearance in David Mackenzie's 2003 film *Young Adam* (an adaptation of Alexander Trocchi's novel of that name[17]):

... the story of a middle-class artist who is alienated and determined not to align himself with a disenfranchised and discredited society is absolutely modern, and in that sense, I would call this a New Beat society. The attraction of outsider status, the attraction of the power there—it's very real now. For many people, for most kids, it's the most powerful place to be.

...

The question that remains relevant at the heart of this story is the question of loneliness. As well as the question of godlessness, and the question of "society-lessness" ... What existentialism does is it presses your nose right up against the window, rubs it at loneliness. It says, "this is the deal, and that's not either a bad or a good thing." It's just the deal, and you have to work it out. And of course my belief is that once you've worked it out, you find the best company you can imagine, that of other lonely people! [Laughter][18]

It would appear that for Tilda Swinton, then, just as much as for Bruce Robbins, "the outside is the only place to be." But while it would be easy enough to make fun of the fact that a successful academic and a young film actress can feel like outsiders, I am not interested in being ironical at their expense. Partly, as I'll explain later, because there is a sense in which I think they are quite right: as I will try to show in the next chapter, when it is understood in a certain way, "the outside" can indeed stand for something highly desirable. Yet at the risk of stating the obvious, I *do* want to draw attention to what may be in some danger of getting overlooked.

When we say that "the outside is the only place to be" or that there is "power" in "outsider status," we are obviously not thinking of those who are *doomed* to be on various kinds of outsides either because they are disabled (the blind, the deaf etc.) or the victims of national or man-made disasters (famine or genocide), or because they are single when they would prefer to be in a relationship, or because they have been forcibly ejected and then shut or locked out (King Lear, for example, locked outside of Gloucester's castle in the storm; the homeless in our city streets etc.). We are not thinking either of those who have—for whatever reason, sexual disposition, race etc.—been stigmatized, ostracized or scapegoated. A moment in an episode in the popular TV series *NYPD* Blue comes to mind here. Having noticed that a murder suspect (an AWOL Marine named Russell Stokes) seems to be going through something similar to what he himself went through fifteen years earlier (the difficulty of admitting to oneself and then to the world that one is gay), the Police Administrative Aide John Irvin tells Andy Sipowicz that he believes Stokes may find it easier to confess to a crime he didn't commit than to admit to being gay. After realising that Stokes is indeed innocent, Andy then allows John to visit Stokes's cell to have a few words with him. John's way of trying to reassure Stokes that after he has accepted his gayness he'll still have a life to look forward to, is to point to the life he has made for himself working with the 15th squad. "I fit in," the now openly gay John tells him, adding that he sometimes babysits for his colleagues.[19] And there is no doubt at all but that the words *fitting in* say it all: in this particular context, they powerfully describe the desirable state to attain.

But when fitting in seems the last thing we want to do, and when our identities seem closer to suffocating rather than protecting us, the model many of my generation are more likely to have in mind is that of the alienated modernist artist (or Kierkegaardian "apostle," or "genuine author")—Baudelaire, perhaps, or Melville, or Van Gogh. Or the writers Ian Watt draws to our attention when he reminds us, in his book on *Conrad in the Nineteenth Century*, that Conrad's peers tended "to equate individuality with alienation":

> [T]he poetry of Eliot and Pound, for instance, typically leads us away in critical revulsion from all contemporary actuality, *while the novels of Lawrence and Joyce present the breaking of ties with family, home, class, country, and traditional beliefs as necessary stages in the achievement of spiritual and intellectual freedom*: both the novelists and the poets incite us to a sharper sense of separateness.[20]

It is worth noting, incidentally, that Edward Said sees this—the rejection of "filial relationship[s] ... held together by natural bonds and natural forms of authority" (*World* 20)—as forming the first part of a "strong three-part pattern" that he finds originating in a number of "late nineteenth- and early twentieth-century writers" (16). He thinks that it resulted in "the pressure to produce new and different ways of conceiving human relationships"; in the search for "some other way by which men and women can create social bonds between each other that would substitute for those ties that connect members of the same family across generations." With T.S.Eliot in mind—and more specifically, the failure of the latter's first marriage, a failure to which Said claims "Eliot's mind gave a far wider application"—Said maintains that for him (Eliot) the "only other alternatives seemed to be provided by institutions, associations, and communities whose social existence was not in fact guaranteed by biology, but by affiliation" (17). So the first two parts of the pattern are made up of a "turn from filiation to affiliation" (18) with, on the one hand, Conrad taking on "in his own life (as did Eliot and Henry James) the adopted identity of an émigré-turned-English gentleman," while on "the other side of the spectrum we find Lukács suggesting that only class consciousness, itself an insurrectionary form of an attempt at affiliation, could possibly break through the antinomies and atomizations of reified existence in the modern capitalist world-order" (19).

What seems to make Said a little uneasy about this is the fact, as he understands it, that this "transition from a failed idea or possibility of fili-ation" to a new affiliative form of relation that is provided by "a party, an institution, a culture, a set of beliefs, or even a world-vision" is a move "to a kind of compensatory order":

> [W]hether we look at this new affiliative mode of relationship as it is to be found among conservative writers like Eliot or among progressive writers like Lukacs and, in his own special way, Freud, we will find the deliberately explicit goal of using that new order to reinstate vestiges of the kind of authority associated in the past with filiative order. This, finally, is the third part of the pattern. Freud's psychoanalytic guild and Lukács' notion of the vanguard party are no less providers of what we might call a restored au-thority. (19)

The problem (from Said's point of view) is that this latter is basically "the quasi-religious authority of being comfortably at home among one's peo-ple, supported by known powers and acceptable values, protected against the outside world" (16). And while Said is willing to concede—after maintaining that the persistence of such "religious-cultural effects" as en-forced "subservience" and "organized collective passions" testify to such apparently "necessary features of human life" as "the need for certainty, group solidarity, and a sense of communal belonging"—that "*[s]ometimes* of course these things are beneficial" (290, my italics), he seems primarily concerned with the stifling effect they can have on criticism:

> The history of thought, to say nothing of political movements, is extravagantly illustrative of how the dictum "solidarity before criticism" means the end of criticism. I take criticism so seriously as to believe that, even in the very midst of a battle in which one is unmistakably on one side against another, there should be criti-cism, because there must be critical consciousness if there are to be issues, problems, values, even lives to be fought for. (28)

For Said, then, what seems most importantly at stake in all of this is the survival of criticism, criticism as a secular enterprise that is untainted by religion, the critical spirit that keeps enquiry free and open-ended. And even though he thinks (sadly) that criticism has largely become "an academic thing, located for the most part far away from the questions that trouble the reader of a daily newspaper" (25), the critic, as Said *imagines* him or her, would seem, *ideally* at least, to be an outsider, and "criticism ... most itself" when it is *"oppositional"* (29).

If Said defines the ideal critic as an outsider, he does so because, as he sees it, that is the only way criticism can be a secular enterprise. As we noted William D. Hart saying earlier, where religion is concerned, Said's stance is one of "strict rejection" (*Edward Said* 8); he "describes those things that he does not like as sacred, religious, or theological, and what he does like as secular" (12). What Said likes is criticism, even if (as, for example, with Erich Auerbach) it derives "from a profoundly conservative outlook"; even so, "at its best" Auerbach's work "teaches us how to be critical, rather than how to be good members of a school" (*World* 29). And from the point of view that Said shares with Durkheim and Debray, one can't be a member of a "school" without being religious. I hope it is obvious by now that I agree with this. Where I disagree is first of all with Said's assumption that a "school" can't be properly critical: think, for example, of Adorno and Horkheimer's Frankfurt School, or of the kinds of unofficial "schools" that existed around Jean-Paul Sartre's *Les Temps Modernes* and F.R.Leavis's *Scrutiny*. (Since these days it is much less well-known than the other two, it may perhaps be worth recalling Terry Eagleton's claim on *Scrutiny's* behalf, that "no more militant, courageous and consistent project is to be found in the history of English criticism"[21]).

Also worth pondering in this connection is Leavis's insistence (in 1960) that "[c]riticism, with all it stands for, is collaborative and creative," and that "[m]ere lonely intransigence is barren."[22] Yet, at the same time, Adorno, Horkheimer, Sartre and Leavis would surely all have agreed with Said when the latter maintains that criticism "is most itself" in "its suspicion of totalizing concepts, in its discontent with reified objects, in its impatience with guilds, special interests, imperialised fiefdoms, and orthodox habits of mind" and "most *un*like itself at the moment it starts turning into organized dogma" (my italics, *World* 292). It is true that schools of criticism can of course degenerate into the kinds of dogma-producing "communities of opinion" we find Emerson inveighing against in (the tenth paragraph of) his great essay on "Self-Reliance":

> A man must consider what a blind-man's-buff is this game of conformity. If I know your sect I anticipate your argument ... Well, most men have bound their eyes with one or another handkerchief, and attached themselves to some of these communities of opinion. This conformity makes them not false in a few particulars, authors of a few lies, but false in all particulars.

This, it might be said, gives us one version of "merging" (one version of being on the inside), which together with "absolute isolation" or "absolute loss" (one version of being on the outside) Adam Phillips calls "the two fundamental terrors construed by psychoanalysis."[23] And if it the former that threatens, then, if one is interested in the continuing life of criticism, it is the latter (the isolation of the outside) that has to be risked. At such times the survival of criticism will be dependent on such nonconformist outsiders as Emerson, yes, but also as Adorno, Sartre, Leavis and Said all (at different stages in their careers) managed to be.

Where I also disagree, however, is with Said's apparent assumption that the critic on the outside of institutions is the one to whom we should look for secular criticism, as opposed to religious dogma. It is after all St. Paul who advises the "brethren" to "be not conformed to this world" (*Romans* 12, 2). And as Darko Suvin has recently noted, in Said's advocacy of "the migrant and suffering intellectual as liberator" there are surely "christological echoes" [24]—or echoes, at least, of prophets crying in the wilderness.[25]

With these considerations in mind, it seems to me worth noting that, for her part, though Tilda Swinton does refer to the figure of the alienated artist, *her* emphasis, like Bruce Robbins's, falls not, as one might expect, on the individual loner but rather on the group: for Robbins, a Godardian "*bande à part*," for Swinton "the best company you can imagine, that of other lonely people!"

It must be easier to be an outsider when you are not alone but rather part of a group. I recall, for example, the paradoxical but euphoric sense that so many of us had in the 1960s that we (a sizeable part of an entire generation) were *all* outsiders, but outsiders *together*. But I am mainly thinking here of such clearly defined groups as, for example, religious cults or those made up of political radicals. However isolated such groups may be, at least their members can draw on one another for support. Even then, however, the experience must be extremely painful at times. Consider an example we glanced at in the last chapter, that of the Doukhobor psalm sung in 1895 at the Burning of Arms Resistance (when the Doukhobors burned all their weapons in public bonfires):

> For the sake of Thee, Lord, I loved the narrow gate; I left the material life; I left father and mother; I left brother and sister; I left my whole race and tribe; I bear hardness and persecution; I bear scorn and slander; I am hungry and thirsty; I am walking naked; For the sake of Thee, Lord.[26]

Notice how, even though this was sung by the group, each member sings as the "I" who "bear[s] scorn and slander" and is "walking naked" etc. But still, however painful, and comfortless, the experience of being in such a group must sometimes be, it is probably not *as* painful, one imagines, as when one is completed isolated, which is to say, when one is cut off not just from all other human beings but also without any compensating belief in God.

We might usefully think here of what happens to Martin Decoud, a character who finds himself in such a situation in Joseph Conrad's novel *Nostromo*. Decoud is a sophisticated young man who we are told "had pushed the habit of universal raillery to a point where it blinded him to the genuine impulses of his own nature."[27] Though he is "no patriot" ("the word had no sense for cultured minds, to whom the narrowness of every belief is odious" [*Nostromo* 162]), he has allowed himself to be persuaded by Don José Avellanos "to take the direction of a newspaper that would 'voice the aspirations of the province'" (139) because he is in love with Don José's daughter, Antonia. In his "Author's Note," Conrad explains that Antonia was modelled on his "first love" and that she was "the only being capable of inspiring a sincere passion in the heart of a trifler" (13). He adds that "it was [he] who had to hear oftenest her scathing criticism of [his] levities—very much like poor Decoud" (14). So Conrad would seem to have a lot invested in Decoud, who becomes involved in politics not because he believes, as Antonia does, in a "great cause" (162) but because of his love for a woman. At the end of the novel's second Part, he finds himself left by Nostromo alone on an island and responsible for the safekeeping of the silver that will be used to finance the patriotic cause. Nostromo promises Decoud that he will "try to come out to [him] in a night or two" (252). But, as we learn much later in the novel, Nostromo did not keep his promise and Decoud "died from solitude and want of faith in himself and others" (408):

> Solitude from mere outward condition of existence becomes very swiftly a state of soul in which the affectations of irony and scepticism have no place. It takes possession of the mind, and drives forth the thought into the exile of utter unbelief. After three days of waiting for the sight of some human face, Decoud caught himself entertaining a doubt of his own individuality. It had merged into the world of cloud and water, of natural forces and forms of nature. In our activity alone do we find the sustaining illusion of an independent existence as against the whole scheme of things of which we form a helpless part ... Both his intelligence and his passion were swallowed up easily in this great unbroken solitude of waiting without faith ... On the tenth day, after a night spent without even dozing off once ... , the solitude appeared like a great void, and the silence of the gulf like a tense, thin cord to which he hung suspended by both hands ... Only towards the evening, ... he began to wish that this cord would snap. (408-10)

In the event, he takes out a dinghy, four silver ingots to weigh himself down, and shoots himself, rolling "overboard without having heard the cord of silence snap in the solitude of the Placid Gulf" (411):

> A victim of the disillusioned weariness which is the retribution meted out to intellectual audacity, the brilliant Don Martin Decoud, weighted by the bars of the San Tomé silver, disappeared without a trace, swallowed up by the immense indifference of things. (412)

One way of describing what happened to Decoud is to say that he lacked conviction. "It is certain," wrote Novalis (in words Conrad used as the epigraph to *Lord Jim*), "any conviction gains infinitely the moment another soul will believe in it." And of course Marlow's conviction—Marlow who tells us he "believes in the solidarity of our lives"—is that Jim is "one of us" (171),[28] which gives to the outsider Jim some of the strength he needs to behave as if he is indeed "one of us." But as he at one point makes clear to Antonia, Martin Decoud takes a cynical view of conviction:

> What is a conviction? A particular view of our personal advantage either practical or emotional. No one is a patriot for nothing. The word serves us well. But I am clear-sighted, and I shall not use that word to you, Antonia! I have no patriotic illusions. I have only the supreme illusion of a lover. (*Nostromo* 164)

When it comes down to it, this "supreme illusion" is not enough. It's worth noting that Nostromo has no convictions either, which means that when he and Decoud find themselves facing a "common danger," the fact that there is "no bond of conviction" between them means that they are "merely two adventurers, pursuing each his own adventure," and they have "nothing to say to each other" (247).

But, as Conrad surely knew, it is one thing to be able to clearly diagnose the problem and quite another to solve it. No doubt it is better, for example, for the critic (as well as for the criticism he or she produces) to be able to participate in what Leavis (following T.S.Eliot) called the common pursuit. But the fact is that such collaboration (to use another of Leavis's key terms) is not always available. And with reference to Said's definition of the political critic as "outsider," Suvin wonders what such a critic could realistically hope to achieve "unless accompanied by a careful alliance with some mass movement, into which [Said] practically entered but which he never theorized" (121, 122).[29] In any case, when someone says that he has spent a large part of life feeling like a disillusioned spectator, it doesn't help to say that he should become a participant, join in, get involved. What if he does have convictions but can't find others who share them? Here, for example, is the poignant testimony of D.H.Lawrence in 1927:

> Myself, I suffer badly from being so cut-off. But what is one to do?... At times one is *forced* to be essentially a hermit. I don't want

to be. But anything else is either a personal tussle, or a money
tussle: sickening: except, of course, for ordinary acquaintance,
which remains acquaintance. One has no real human relations—
that is so devastating.[30]

Or what if one is unable to find others who are willing to have one join in?
And of course the problem is compounded if, like Decoud (and, if Yeats
was right, like many others too—"The best lack[ing] all conviction, while ·
the worst/Are full of passionate intensity"[31]), one doesn't have any convictions to share anyway. It isn't, after all, as if a conviction or belief is something one can simply *decide* to have.

Another way of describing what happened to Decoud—"On the
tenth day, after a night spent without even dozing off once ... , the solitude appeared like a great void, and the silence of the gulf like a tense,
thin cord to which he hung suspended by both hands"—might be to say
that he was briefly exposed to the experience (or, rather, non-experience)
of the condition that the French philosopher Emmanuel Levinas calls the
il y a (or the *there is*), and that Decoud couldn't stand it. In his 1946 essay
"There is: existence without existents," Levinas asks us to "imagine all beings, things and persons, reverting to nothingness." He says that he uses
"the term *there is*" to designate the "impersonal, anonymous, yet inextin-
guishable 'consummation' of being, which murmurs in the depth of nothingness itself." He explains that '[w]e could say that the night is the very
experience of the *there is*, if the term experience were not inapplicable" and
the following passage shows us the difficulty:

> When the forms of things are dissolved in the night, the dark-
> ness of the night, which is neither an object nor the quality of an
> object, invades like a presence. In the night, where we are riven to
> it, we are not dealing with anything. But this nothing is not that
> of pure nothingness. There is no longer *this* or *that*; there is not
> "something." But this universal absence is in its turn a presence,
> an absolutely unavoidable presence ... *There is*, in general, without
> it mattering what there is ... Its anonymity is essential ... What
> we call the I is itself submerged by the night, invaded, depersonal-
> ized, stifled by it.[32]

Levinas also invites us in this connection to think of "the monotonous presence that bears down on us in insomnia" and he maintains that the "rustling of the *there is* ... is horror" ("There" 32, his ellipse). As he says, he is trying "to draw attention to the existential density of the void itself, devoid of all being ... " (35).

For our purposes here, the point to grasp is that this gives us one version of the Outside. And since, as Jill Robbins points out in her book on Levinas, from the 1940s onwards, both Maurice Blanchot (Levinas's friend) and Georges Bataille (Blanchot's friend) "developed independently [both of Levinas and of one another] the thought of the *il y a*,"[33] there are two other versions of the Outside to compare it with. As Gerald L. Bruns puts it, "The *il y a*: there is. Blanchot will later call it: the Outside, the Neutral."[34] And as for Bataille, Robbins tells us that he associates the *il y a* not with Levinasian "horror and suffocation" but rather "with ecstasy, joy, and celebration" (*Altered* 97). So far as I can see, one of the things all three of these thinkers have in common is that they all seem to value a willingness to expose oneself to, or to go through, an experience (or non-experience) of the *il y a*, which they all in different ways find in literature. Thus, as Bruns notes in his book on Blanchot, the latter understands writing as an activity that "preserves the anonymity of words and things, which is to say their density or thickness within the *il y a*" (*Maurice Blanchot* 61). Bruns explains, furthermore, that "the loss of subjectivity in writing" (66) makes it for Blanchot "an act of dying, but not like suicide is an act, since suicide is still a subjective act of self-expression." With Conrad's Decoud in mind, we can now note that Bruns (who is not thinking of Conrad) elaborates on this as follows:

> Death comes of waiting. In waiting we are already outside the world, in death's space. The suicide tries to take command of death's space as if it were part of the world, a territory like any other. (67)

So from this (extremely harsh) point of view, Decoud cheats or evades death because of his inability to wait or, in Conrad's words, because of his "waiting without faith" (*Nostromo* 409).

But as his critics mostly seem to agree (at least Robbins, Bruns and De Vries), Levinas himself attempts (in Bruns's words) "to escape the anonymity or non-sense (or poetry) of the *il y a* ... by 'a passage from *being* to a *something*' (or, alternatively and better: to a someone), while Blanchot remains behind, on the hither side of being" (*Maurice Blanchot* 61). As Levinas sees it, it is "society with the Other, which marks the end of the absurd rumbling of the *there is*."[35] It is the "relation with the Other alone [that] introduces a dimension of transcendence, and leads us to a relation totally different from experience in the sensible sense of the term, relative and egoist" (*TI* 193). In other words, when we enter into the kind of relationship with the Other or Stranger that Levinas calls the face-to-face relationship we move from one kind of Outside (the *il y a*) into another kind. As Levinas understands it, totality breaks up with "the gleam of exteriority or of transcendence in the face of the Other" (*TI* 24); the "origin of exteriority" is to be found in "the epiphany of the face" (*TI* 261).

Now we have already noted (in the Preface) the claim made by Jean-Luc Nancy that "there is no 'outside'" and "that there is *nothing else*." But of course we all know that there are obviously any number of actual outsides in relation to any number of actual insides. So it all depends; mainly, for our purposes here, on what we mean (whether or not we are making sense) when we refer—as I do in the title of this book—to Thought from (and of) *the* Outside.

In the circumstances, then, before going any further, it might be a good idea for me to try to forestall certain misunderstandings by attempting a few clarifications. Somewhat arbitrarily, I will limit myself to five (no less than three of which are indebted to George Eliot, who won't be reappearing after this until chapter five).

(i) *"Ekstasis or outside standing-ground"*

> In writing the history of unfashionable families, one is apt to fall into a tone of emphasis which is very far from being the tone of good society ... But good society, floated on gossamer wings of light irony, is of very expensive production; requiring nothing less than a wide and arduous national life condensed in unfragrant deafening factories, cramping itself in mines, sweating at furnaces, grinding, hammering, weaving ... This wide national life is entirely based on emphasis—the emphasis of want, which urges it into all the activities necessary for

the maintenance of good society and light irony ... Under such circumstances there are many among its myriads of souls who have absolutely needed an emphatic belief ... Some have an emphatic belief in alcohol, and seek their *ekstasis* or outside standing-ground in gin, but the rest require something that good society calls enthusiasm ...

—George Eliot[36]

As I noted early on in this chapter, when we say that "the outside is the only place to be" or that there is "power" in "outsider status," we are obviously not thinking of those who are for different reasons *doomed* to be on various kinds of outsides; we are not thinking of those who have no say in the matter. It might reasonably be claimed, therefore, that when we articulate such sentiments we are speaking from a (more or less) privileged position. This is why I now cite the above passage from Eliot's novel *The Mill on the Floss*, to remind us that when it is understood in a certain way (as *ekstasis* or standing-ground) the Outside can also seem highly desirable to many who are wholly lacking in privilege; indeed, to many of those who, in relation to privilege, find themselves occupying an obviously quite undesirable form of the Outside.

(ii) *"Promiscuous erotic perversity"*[37]

The "out" of *being-with-out* (a non-relational relation), is what Blanchot and Foucault refer to as the *Outside*. With every inside-outside opposition there comes something, something that is outside the closure that is this coupling, something that is not a thing at all (at least not necessarily). This is the Outside that not only remains outside of every inside, but outside of every outside.

—John Paul Ricco (*Logic* 4)

Though I intend to save (until near the end of the next chapter) the comments I promised (at the end of the last chapter) to make on the way in which Maurice Blanchot's notion of the Outside has been taken up by Michel Foucault and (more recently) by John Paul Ricco, I will note here that what draws Ricco to it is the prospect it offers of anonymous sex.

(iii) *"On the other side of silence"*

> If we had a keen vision and feeling of all ordinary human life,
> it would be like hearing the grass grow and the squirrel's heart
> beat, and we should die of that roar which lies on the other side
> of silence. As it is, the quickest of us walk about well wadded with
> stupidity.
>
> —George Eliot[38]

I will have something to say about this version of the Outside ("the other
side of silence") at the end of chapter six. For now I will just note the claim
made by a recent work of "postsecular" political theory (Melissa Orlie's
Living Ethically, Acting Politically) to the effect that "thinking's enact-
ment of what is invisible, silent, and outside constitutes a political spiritu-
ality" (208, n.1).

(iv) *Emerging from (getting Outside of) "moral stupidity"*

> We are all of us born in moral stupidity, taking the world as an
> udder to feed our supreme selves: Dorothea had early begun to
> emerge from that stupidity, but yet it had been easier for her to
> imagine how she would devote herself to Mr Casaubon, and be-
> come wise and strong in his strength and wisdom, than to con-
> ceive with that distinctness which is no longer reflection but
> feeling—an idea wrought back to the directness of sense, like
> the solidity of objects—that he had an equivalent centre of self,
> whence the lights and shadows must always fall with a certain
> difference.
>
> —George Eliot (*Middlemarch* ch. 21, 225)

> "For me—how should there be any outside-myself? There is no
> outside. But all sounds make us forget this; how lovely it is that
> we forget."
>
> —Nietzsche[39]

The reason I cite these two passages here is because, while I do myself believe in (and propose to talk about) the possibility of our engaging with

forms of otherness Outside of (also inside) the self, I also believe that our ability to do this (to get outside of ourselves) is by no means something we ought to be taking for granted. We can get some sense of the difficulty involved by noting Henry Staten's observation (made with Nietzsche and Freud in mind) that "it is not clear that there is anything besides what we call narcissism, which therefore ceases to mean what it would mean if it had any antithesis."[40] Does Eliot's Dorothea (in *some* ways, of course, almost the least narcissistic person one could think of) ever *completely* emerge from "moral stupidity"? Does anyone?

(v) *Outside of the "iron cage"?*

> [T]he modern economic order ... is now bound to the technical and economic conditions of machine production which to-day determine the lives of all the individuals who are born into this mechanism ... with irresistible force ... In [Richard] Baxter's view the care for external goods should only lie on the shoulders of the "saint like a light cloak, which can be thrown aside at any moment." But fate decreed that the cloak should become an iron cage ... [O]f the last stage of this cultural development, it might well be truly said: "Specialists without spirit, sensualists without heart; this nullity imagines that it has attained a level of civilization never before achieved."
>
> —Max Weber (1904–5)[41]

Finally, there is the question as to whether or not there is a sense in which it is possible to get outside, escape the confines, of Weber's "iron cage," whether or not it is possible to somehow elude the grasp of what Weber also referred to as the increasing "rationalization of life" (*Protestant Ethic* 136), which one commentator has usefully summarized (with Theodor Adorno, Max Horkheimer and Jürgen Habermas in mind) as "the project of scientific enlightenment and the reduction of the lifeworld to the norms of representational-calculative reason and instrumental control" (Bruns, *Maurice* xiv).

Since we are now ready to examine in the next two chapters some manifestations of what William James called simply "personal religion"— personal as opposed to institutional or group religion (*Varieties* 34)—it

might be useful for us to have in mind his claim that "a religious life, exclusively pursued, ... tend[s] to make the person exceptional and eccen-
tric" (15). Indeed, James believes that "many religious phenomena" have a
"psychopathic origin" (30) and so he not surprisingly maintains that, like
other kinds of geniuses, "religious geniuses have often shown symptoms of
nervous instability" (15). One of his examples is the founder of the Quaker
religion, which James thinks "it is impossible to overpraise":

> No one can pretend for a moment that in point of spiritual sagac-
> ity and capacity, Fox's mind was unsound. Every one who con-
> fronted him personally, from Oliver Cromwell down to county
> magistrates and jailers, seems to have acknowledged his superior
> power. Yet from the point of view of his nervous constitution,
> Fox was a psychopath or *détraqué* of the deepest dye. (15,16)

But in calling Fox and others (like Bunyan, for example, whom he calls "a
typical case of the psychopathic temperament, sensitive of conscience to
a diseased degree" [147]) psychopathic, James is definitely not intending
criticism. On the contrary, in fact, as we can see from the following:

> Few of us are not in some way infirm, or even diseased; and our
> very infirmities help us unexpectedly. In the psychopathic tem-
> perament we have the emotionality which is the *sine quâ non* of
> moral perception; we have the intensity and tendency to empha-
> sis which are the essence of practical moral vigor; and we have
> the love of metaphysics and mysticism which carry one's interests
> beyond the surface of the sensible world. (30)

It might be a good idea to have these words in mind as we prepare to move
in the next chapter into the company of, among others, D.H.Lawrence,
Jacques Derrida, Emmanuel Levinas, George Eliot, Joseph Conrad,
F.R.Leavis and Slavoj Žižek, all of whom have some of "the intensity and
tendency to emphasis" that James mentions.

Chapter Four

Thought from (and of) the outside

Part One: Lawrence, Levinas and Derrida: at the firing line and into the unknown

> ...outside the pale of all that is accepted, and nothing known applies.
> —D.H.Lawrence (1920)[1]

(i) Why Lawrence?

In the minds of some, at least, my decision to return to D.H.Lawrence probably requires some justification or explanation. So I will offer four main reasons for starting off with, and thus giving such prominence to, Lawrence.

(i) Lawrence and Critical Theory

> ...we have to unlearn, at the price of survival, the inherent domi-native mode.
> —Raymond Williams (1958)[2]

> So, we know the first great purpose of Democracy: that each man shall be spontaneously himself—each man himself, each woman herself, without any question of equality or inequality entering in at all; and that no man shall try to determine the being of any other man, or of any other woman.
> —D.H.Lawrence ("Democracy,"[3] qtd. by Williams 224)

The first reason has to do with how I understand Critical Theory. To put it simply, I do not associate Critical Theory exclusively with the Frankfurt School. I see Critical Theory as including the latter but also going way beyond it. I see Critical Theory in terms of the common project that

Raymond Williams invited the readers of his book *Culture and Society* to commit themselves to back in 1958.[4] I think we can begin to get some idea of just how common this project was to become if we now look first at the last two sentences of Said's Introduction to his book *Orientalism*:

> But what I should like also to have contributed here is a better understanding of the way cultural domination has operated. If this stimulates a new kind of dealing with the "Orient" and "Occident" altogether, then we shall have advanced a little in the process of what Raymond Williams has called "the unlearning" of the "inherent dominative mode."[5]

On the one hand, then, this project can be seen to have provided the effective rationale for the subsequent development of the field of postcolonial studies. But this is by no means all. As becomes immediately apparent when we consider that one good definition of many, perhaps most, versions of feminism might be exactly the effort "to unlearn...the inherent dominative mode." Isn't this, for example, Jane Tompkins's point when she claims, at the end of her book *West of Everything*, that "if you don't first, or also, come to recognize *the violence in yourself* and your own anger and your own destructiveness, whatever else you do [to combat these things] won't work...Genocide...starts at home."[6] Or consider something Michel Foucault had to say in an interview he gave near the end of his life:

> On the critical side—I mean critical in a very broad sense—philosophy is precisely the challenging of all phenomena of domination at whatever level or under whatever form they present themselves—political, economic, sexual, institutional, and so on.[7]

My point is *not* that Foucault was a feminist: it is that in much of his work he too was committed to the project of unlearning the inherent dominative mode, a project that (as he usefully reminds us here) should also be understood as entailing an element of *challenge* as well.[8]

As I understand it, this commitment—to both unlearning and challenging "all phenomena of domination"—describes one of the main functions of criticism in our time.

But what does this have to do with Lawrence? A careful reading of the penultimate paragraph of *Culture and Society*, in the light of some of the emphases in the earlier Lawrence section of that book,[9] reveals that when Williams formulated the phrase that Said was later to use to describe his own aims ("we have to unlearn, as the price of survival, the inherent domi-native mode") one of the most important influences Williams was writing under, one that arguably constituted (at least at that precise moment) his major inspiration, was clearly D.H.Lawrence. And this being so, my thinking that it might be possible to advance one of the key goals of Critical Theory (in the broad sense I have given it) with Lawrence's help may not sound quite so unrealistic.

(ii) *Lawrence and Religion*

The second reason it seems to me appropriate to begin with Lawrence is that he too felt the need to rethink religion. And not in any detached way either: for Lawrence, rethinking religion meant wrestling with it. In using that particular word, I'm thinking of something Lawrence had to say in the 1919 "Foreword" he wrote to his novel *Women in Love*, that it "pretends only to be a record of the writer's own desire, aspirations, struggles: in a word, a record of the profoundest experiences in the self...We are now," Lawrence then added, "in a period of crisis. Every man who is acutely alive is acutely wrestling with his own soul."[10] I suspect that Lawrence is drawing here (perhaps unconsciously) on a sentence near the beginning of *The Varieties of Religious Experience* in which William James defends what he thinks remains of the "revelation-value" of the Bible after it has been submitted to "the higher criticism" by claiming that "a book may well be a revelation in spite of errors and passions and deliberate human composition, if only it be the true record of the inner experiences of great-souled persons wrestling with the crises of their fate ..." (*Varieties* 13, 14) But whether or not Lawrence had this in mind, his preoccupation with questions concerning religion is undeniable.[11] Thus, for example, in the midst of an extraordinary letter he wrote as a twenty-two year old to Reverend Robert Reid, we find this:

Then, it appears to me, a man gradually formulates his religion, be it what it may. A man has no religion who has not slowly and

painfully gathered one together, adding to it, shaping it; and one's
religion is never complete and final, it seems, but must always be
undergoing modification.[12]

Lawrence wrote this in 1907 but he was to continue to rethink religion
until, just over two decades later, the last years of his life, during which he
wrote *Apocalypse*, his last major book, a study of the Book of *Revelation*.
(On this, see the essay by Gilles Deleuze.[13])

(iii) *Lawrence and Otherness*

The third reason for starting with Lawrence has to do with another
of the areas in which he strikingly anticipated our current concerns. "We
have thought and spoken till now," he declared in 1918, "in terms of like-
ness and oneness. Now we must learn to think in terms of difference and
otherness."[14] In fact, that is something Lawrence had already started to do
himself and I would argue that this was one of the most important of the
ways in which he undertook to rethink religion.

(iv) *At the Firing Line: Lawrence and the Unknown Outside (the French
connection)*

I wish we were all like kindled bonfires on the edge of space,
marking out the advance-posts. What is the aim of self-preservation, but to carry us right out to the firing line, where what *is* is in
contact with what is not.
                                                —D.H.Lawrence[15]

The fourth and (for our immediate purposes here) easily the most
important reason is that Lawrence has so much to teach us about the
Outside. I will begin explaining what I mean by this by pointing to the
wish Lawrence expresses in the opening of his *Study of Thomas Hardy*,
the one I have just quoted. If we were to do what Lawrence here wishes
we would do (allow ourselves to be carried "right out to the firing line,
where what *is* is in contact with what is not") then we would be behaving
like the poppy which he beautifully describes in the following words:

[H]is fire breaks out of him, and he lifts his head, slowly, subtly, tense in an ecstasy of fear overwhelmed by joy, submits to the issuing of his flame and his fire, and there it hangs at the brink of the void, scarlet and radiant for a little while, imminent on the unknown, a signal, an out-post, an advance-guard, a forlorn, splendid flag, quivering from the brink of the unfathomed void, into which it flutters silently, satisfied, whilst a little ash, a little dusty seed remains behind on the solid ledge of the earth. (*STH* 18)

This poppy is not "afraid of giving himself forth," of moving "on to expose his new nakedness[;] up there to confront the horrific space of the void, he is [not] afraid of giving himself away to the unknown" (18). In fact, this poppy has "traversed his known and come" precisely "to meet the unknown" (19). This is what Lawrence would like us humans to have the courage to be doing too. If we judge by Birkin's invitation to Ursula in the "Mino" chapter of *Women in Love*, men and women should be trying to do this together:

And it is there I would want to meet you—not in the emotional, loving plane—but there beyond, where there is no speech and no terms of agreement. There we are two stark, unknown beings, two utterly strange creatures, I would want to approach you, and you me.—And there could be no obligation, because there is no standard for action there, because no understanding has been reaped from that plane. It is quite inhuman,—so there can be no calling to book, in any form whatsover—because one is outside the pale of all that is accepted, and nothing known applies. (*WL* 146)

This isn't selfish, Birkin assures Ursula, "[b]ecause I don't *know* what I want of you. I deliver *myself* over to the unknown, in coming to you, I am without reserves or defenses, stripped entirely into the unknown" (147). (Perhaps I should explain that I read *Women in Love* as containing a succession of philosophical dialogues.[16])

I want to propose three complementary ways of understanding what is happening here, which is to say, what is happening when we meet the unknown—or give ourselves away, or expose ourselves (nakedly, stripped

entirely), to it: (i) we are opening ourselves to Otherness (understood here
as being by definition the unknown); (ii) we are encountering non-being
(since "what *is* is in contact with what is not"); and (iii) we are therefore
making contact with the Outside. I say "therefore" because I think that
when we encounter otherness or the unknown or non-being we are also
encountering, in one form or another, the Outside. Lawrence, I want to
claim here, is one of our major thinkers of the Outside and this may be
what this Englishman most importantly has in common with such later
thought-adventurers as Georges Bataille, Emmanuel Levinas, Maurice
Blanchot, Michel Foucault and Jacques Derrida.

"And I am English," Lawrence once declared, "and my Englishness
is my very vision."[17] I have no wish to deny that Lawrence was of course
English and I will admit that there are moments in his writing when he
himself produces the kind of "Britishism" that one reviewer finds Geoff
Dyer's entertaining book on him (*Out of Sheer Rage: Wrestling with
D.H.Lawrence*) occasionally collapsing into:

> When Rilke's "you must change your life" appears on page 90,
> the quote is immediately followed by Philip Larkin's put-down
> translation: "Yes, find another Princess to live off." This is accu-
> rate but petty, and seems to have been designed to protect the
> sniggering Larkin from all that unseemly continental vaporing.
> No enthusiasm please, we're British.[18]

My point, however, is not only that "enthusiasm" is much more characteristic of Lawrence than this kind of pettiness; it is also that this enthusiasm often gets expressed in passages that might well seem to those who
dislike them to be like nothing so much as "unseemly continental vaporing." "Continental vaporing" or, as the transplanted Australian writer
Clive James might put it, "rhetorical gas." Here I'm drawing on another
book review, this time by Richard Locke of Clive James's *Cultural Am-
nesia: Necessary Memories from History and the Arts*. Locke tells us that
James sees Jean-Paul Sartre (in whom he thinks "German metaphysics met
French sophistry...producing nothing but rhetorical gas") as being "the
vile progenitor of the 'pseudo-scientific casuistry' and 'exalted balderdash'
of 'Jacques Lacan, Julia Kristeva, Jean Baudrillard and the other artistes in
the flouncing kick-line of the post-modern intellectual cabaret'":

Again and again throughout the book, James denounces what he thinks of as willful obscurantism—in dozens of writers including Paul Celan and Walter Benjamin, whose "eloquent opacity" is "an intellectual multivitamin pill, the more guaranteed in its efficacy by being so hard to swallow."[19]

Interestingly, Locke notes that "there is one moment when James does acknowledge a more complicated possibility":

James grants "there is such a thing as an obscure language that contains meaning, and there is also such a thing as a meaning too subtle to be clearly expressed." He cites Karl Popper's observation that "ordinary language is conservative ...although 'common sense' is often right, 'things get really interesting just when it is wrong.'" So James concedes, "An expository language pushing deep into originality might not necessarily sound readily intelligible; with the niggling corollary that a language which does not sound readily intelligible might conceivably be exploratory"...But James quickly lets this mighty counterargument drop and scurries back to mocking Sartre's "ponderous folderol" and Heidegger's "high-flown philosophical flapdoodle." (Ibid)

I cite this at some length because it seems to me that James's prejudice is widely shared and therefore important to confront head-on. No doubt there are moments when the writers he mocks are guilty of "rhetorical gas" but my view is that often what in their work doesn't "sound readily intelligible" is indeed "exploratory." And I think that's when "things get really interesting."

For the most part Lawrence writes in a style that is as simple, clear and unpretentious as anyone could wish. But as his use (in the passages I quoted a moment ago) of such words as "void," "the unknown" and the notion of "an advance-guard" all indicate, he does share certain interests with the so-called "continental" writers and seeing this may help some readers, at least, to take the passages in question with the kind of seriousness they deserve. With this in mind, it may be worth pausing for a moment to note the striking degree to which the opening of his *Study of Thomas Hardy* anticipates the language and thought of Georges Bataille.[20] Consider first, for example, Robert Hurley's explanation of the significance of Bataille's use of the word "*consumation*—a noun that doesn't exist in French" and that Bataille opposes "to *consommation*, or consumption proper." Translating this neologism as "nonproductive (or useless) consumption," Hurley claims both that it "recalls the etymological sense of consuming, as in a fire that utterly destroys" and also that it is Bataille's "own concept of fire, sacrificial consumption, with a sense of nobility, as opposed to the bourgeois consumption of production and accumulation."[21] Compare this to Lawrence's description of the poppy just when "his fire breaks out of him" and he "submits to the issuing of his flame and his fire." And think as well of how, urging us to try to emulate the poppy and the phoenix, Lawrence explains that both of them achieve their "maximum of being" (*STH* 11) in the form of a "red flame licking into sight" (8), which seems to the world like "flaunting vanity" (10). It is precisely, Lawrence notes, "[b]ecause the red of the poppy and the fire of the phoenix" can't be "stored up" or deposited in some "bank," "but are spent with the day and disappear, [that] we talk of vanity" (10). Nevertheless, he insists that this is exactly the kind of "excess" (11), of admittedly "wasteful" expenditure we should value most. And this is precisely the kind of "unproductive" or "unconditional" expenditure or consumption[22] that characterizes the "general economy"— as opposed to an economy restricted to commercial values[23]—that in his (aptly titled) *Visions of Excess* Bataille was to celebrate.

Also worth noting here is the fact that, for both Bataille and Lawrence, this kind of expenditure or consumption manages to be both sacrifice and gift. I'm thinking here of the linkage that Bataille establishes between these notions:

> Sacrifice is the antithesis of production, which is accomplished with a view to the future; it is consumption that is concerned only with the moment. This is the sense in which it is gift and relinquishment, but what is given cannot be an object of preservation for the receiver: the gift of an offering makes it pass precisely into the world of abrupt consumption.[24]

It is true that in his book *Given Time* we can find Derrida maintaining that "[s]acrifice will always be distinguished from the pure gift (if there is any)" by virtue of the fact that, though a "sacrifice proposes an offering," it does so "only in the form of a destruction against which it exchanges, hopes for, or counts on a benefit, namely, a surplus-value or at least an amortization, a protection, and a security."[25] Whereas a "pure gift" must be "gratuitous and gracious" (*GT* 137), which means that it must be unimplicated in "the logic of exchange" (76) and not be "prey to calculation and measure" (91). But while granting that the distinction Derrida makes here often (perhaps usually) applies, I don't think it does so in the kinds of nonproductive expenditure we've been considering. In particular, Lawrence's account of the poppy being not "afraid of giving himself forth" or of "giving himself away to the unknown" seems to me a splendid example of an action or gesture that clearly manages to be both sacrificial and gift-like without any expectation of reciprocal exchange or future gain entering in at all.

But to return to "the unknown." What is most importantly at stake here? My suggestion is that we may usefully understand the need Lawrence feels to be so emphatic by considering for a moment "the philosophical opposition to identity logic" that Ross Posnock maintains was in "the first third of the twentieth century...international in scope: William James, Dewey, Bergson, Simmel, Benjamin, and Adorno were among those who challenged its coerciveness."[26] In my view, this list can be extended to a later period to include such French writers as Bataille, Blanchot, Levinas and Derrida. But here, with reference to the two main subjects of his book (the novelist Henry James and his brother, the philosopher William), is how Posnock explains both identity logic and some reasons for opposing it:

> Each brother practices his own mode of what I call a politics of nonidentity, a phrase that cannot avoid the paradox of trying to label a strategy dedicated to disrupting the compulsion to fix identity. Any definition is identification, and identity logic is our normal mode of thought. By positing a transparent coincidence between concepts and their objects, this logic tacitly excludes ambiguity, as the flux of reality is converted into the fixity of concepts. Confronted by a social and political order seeking to dissolve difference into a monolithic American identity, William and Henry were united in their suspicion of the assimilating, homogenizing thrust of totalizing systems.

...

When the compulsion to identity is relaxed (if not removed), nonidentity thinking becomes a way to loosen emotional and sexual constrictions and abandon oneself to the shocks of experience. (*Trial* 16, 82).

In the light of this, I would say that Lawrence shared Henry and William's "suspicion of the assimilating, homogenizing thrust of totalizing systems" and that he too practiced a kind of nonidentity thinking. After all, when it is understood in this way, what is nonidentity thinking if not a means of giving us access to the unknown? And what does the latter offer us if not what many thinkers came to feel was denied by, for example, Hegel's totalizing system: namely, the prospect that there are still significant discoveries to be made, that we might still have something new to experience in life, that life might still be an adventure, that our next big step in life might be unpredictable.[27] As we shall shortly begin to see, these were also major concerns of Levinas and Derrida, neither of whom felt that they were things we could take for granted.

It's true, however, that alongside some intriguing affinities, there are also important differences between Lawrence, on the one hand, and Bataille, Levinas, Blanchot, Foucault and Derrida (all five of whom differ from one another in important respects too of course) on the other; and some of these differences are no doubt traceable to the fact that, like other English intellectuals of his time (and despite his indebtedness to Nietzsche, *Le Gai Savaire* being one of the titles he considered for the book we now know as *Study of Thomas Hardy*), Lawrence lacked access to the kind of common philosophical culture enjoyed by all five of the French intellectuals just mentioned.

It may be helpful to keep this last fact in mind as we now begin to explore, by means of a Lawrence-centered approach, the idea of a Thought from (and of) the Outside.

One last reminder before we move ahead. Though Blanchot is the intellectual most associated with a notion of the Outside (with Foucault announcing in 1966, in his essay "Maurice Blanchot: The Thought from Outside" ["*La pensée du dehors*"] that "for us he is that thought itself"[28]), I will have very little (almost but significantly not quite nothing) to say about Blanchot, Foucault and Bataille in this chapter. Instead, I will be discussing Lawrence in relation to Levinas and (to a lesser extent) Derrida. That Levinas can be considered to be a thinker of the Outside is suggested by such things as the subtitle of his book *Totality and Infinity* ("An Essay on Exteriority" [*Essai sur l'extériorité*]), the last chapter (entitled Outside [*Au dehors*]) of his *Otherwise than Being or Beyond Essence*, and the title (*Outside the Suject* [*Hors Sujet*]) of one of his essay collections.[29] As for Derrida, however we interpret the once-famous claim he made in his *Of Grammatology* that "[t]here is nothing outside of the text* [there is no outside-text; *il n'y a pas de hors-texte*],"[30] I will be maintaining that in his later work he too can be regarded as a thinker of the Outside.

(ii) The Outside as the out-of-doors

> It is very much easier to shatter prison bars than to open undiscovered doors to life.
> —D.H.Lawrence (*Virgin and the Gipsy* 19)[31]

> I prefer to open my doors to the coming of the tree.
> —D.H.Lawrence ("Pan in America")[32]

> In a violently poetic text, Lawrence describes what produces poetry: people are constantly putting up an umbrella that shelters them and on the underside of which they draw a firmament and write their conventions and opinions.
> —Deleuze and Guattari (1991)[33]

If asked about Lawrence's relation to the Outside, we might well think first either of his love of nature or, perhaps, of such passages as the following excerpt from his 1923 essay on "The Future of the Novel" (originally published as "Surgery for the Novel—Or a Bomb"):

> The novel has got...to break a way through, like a hole in a wall. And the public will scream and say it is sacrilege: because, of course, when you've been jammed for a long time in a tight corner, you get really used to its stuffiness and its tightness, till you find it absolutely stinkingly cosy; and then, of course you're horrified when you see a new glaring hole in what was your cosy

wall ... You back away from the cold stream of fresh air as if it was
killing you.
   But gradually first one and then another of the sheep filters
through the gap, and finds a new world outside. (*STHOE* 155)

Here, obviously, the "new world outside" is evoked in terms of the brac-
ing cold that we associate with the out-of-doors, and in sharp contrast to
the stuffiness we associate with being in-doors. We find similar imagery
in many of Lawrence's writings: in *The Virgin and the Gipsy*, for example,
where the prison-like, in-door setting takes the form of the Rectory; or in
"Introduction to These Paintings," where it alternates as the Cave and the
Tomb or Sepulcher.
   There can be no doubt but that in these and many other cases in Lawrence the Outside is given to us in terms of the world of non-human nature. Take, for example, what he has to say on the subject in the "Pan in
America" essay he wrote while living on a ranch in New Mexico. If the
"Great God Pan" turned at one point into "the Christian devil," this was
not, according to Lawrence, the end of him. On the contrary, "Pan keeps
on being reborn." For example, "in the eighteenth century he had quite
a vogue. He gave rise to an 'ism,' and there were many pantheists, Wordsworth one of the first. They worshipped Nature in her sweet-and-pure-
aspect, her Lucy Gray aspect" (23). Lawrence, on the other hand, finds
Pan in "a big pine tree [that] rises like a guardian spirit in front of the
cabin where we live" (24). And this is not Nature in its "sweet-and-pure
aspect": "I think," Lawrence tells us, "no man could live near a pine tree
and remain quite suave and supple and compliant. Something fierce and
bristling is communicated...I am conscious," he assures us, "that it helps
to change me, vitally" (25). Is it possible that this is true? Or do we have
to say that Lawrence is simply deluded here? "Of course," he tells us, "if
I like to cut myself off, and say it is all bunk, a tree is merely so much
lumber not yet sawn, then in a great measure I shall *be* cut off. So much
depends on one's attitude" 25-6). Either "[o]ne can shut many, many doors
of receptivity in oneself; or one can open many doors that are shut" (26).
Doors or windows. Lawrence knew of course perfectly well that we live in
"the mechanical conquered universe of modern humanity" but he insisted
that, while the machine doesn't have any windows, we do: "even the most

mechanized human being has only got his windows nailed up, or bricked in" (31).

Now while Levinas's great predecessor Martin Buber might have had understood talk of opening one's "doors to the coming of the tree" ("as I contemplate the tree," Buber once wrote, "I am drawn into a relation, and the tree ceases to be an It"[34]), it is difficult to imagine Levinas himself having much sympathy for it. As Hent De Vries has noted in his book *Minimal Theologies*, the exteriority that concerns Levinas "has nothing in common with...the world of *phusis* and of things." Indeed, De Vries claims that "nature (both in such obvious senses as natural beauty and as human internal or corporeal nature) is, for Levinas, neither a paradigm for alterity nor a medium in which the drama of the absolutely nonidentical—the unique, *das Besondere*, as Adorno would say—can unfold or be mediated."[35] But if this certainly marks one of the important differences between Levinas and Lawrence, it is possible to argue that on this point Lawrence has Derrida with him. As John Caputo puts it, Derrida too differs from Levinas in wanting "to attribute the radical and infinite alterity that theology has always reserved for God" *not only* "to each man or woman" because "this is a 'wholly other (*tout autre*) form of alterity: one or other persons but just as well places, animals, language' ([Derrida] *GD*, 71)."[36] From this point of view, 'God' can be taken (in Caputo's words) to be "the name of the absolutely other, a place-holder for the *tout autre*" (201). And Caputo argues that, "[l]ike negative theology, deconstruction turns on its desire for the *tout autre*" (3); that they "share a common passion and desire, a common *désir de Dieu*..." (51).

With this in mind let's briefly look at the form taken by the Outside in the 1929 "Chaos in Poetry" review[37] Lawrence wrote of Harry Crosby's *Chariot of the Sun*:

> Man fixes some wonderful erection of his own between himself and the wild chaos, and gradually goes bleached and stifled under his parasol. Then comes a poet, enemy of convention, and makes a slit in the umbrella; and lo! the glimpse of chaos is a vision, a window to the sun. But after a while, getting used to the vision, and not liking the genuine draught from chaos, commonplace man daubs a simulacrum of the window that opens on to chaos... (*Phoenix* 255–6)

Here again, "commonplace man" prefers to stay in-doors, living under a
kind of umbrella ("a house of apparent form and stability, fixity" [255])
and the Outside is again figured as the out-doors. But this time it is also
"chaos" and Lawrence's point is that "mankind" now faces "a momentous
crisis ... when we have to get back to chaos" (256). Not that we can hope to
live in it full-time or to entirely dispense with our "umbrellas." Indeed, the
latter "are a necessity of our consciousness" (258-9), presumably because
full exposure to the chaos can be terrifying. So that "when man became
conscious, and aware of himself, his own littleness and puniness in the
whirl of the vast chaos of God, he took fright, and began inventing God in
his own image" (258). That was understandable. "Now," however, "comes
the moment when the terrified but inordinately conceited human consciousness must at last submit, and own itself part of the vast and potent
living chaos" (258). Or at least, this (I take Lawrence to be implying), is
what we must do if we are honest. I think this is what he means when he
says that "never again shall we be able to put up The Absolute Umbrella,
either religious or moral or rational or scientific or practical" (259).[38] If
we do try to put it up again then we will be fooling ourselves, deliberately
cutting ourselves off from "the roving, uncaring chaos which is all we shall
ever know of God" (259).

What does this suggest if not that the wish we started out from—
Lawrence's wish, in effect, that we be prepared to traverse our "known
and come...to meet the unknown" (especially since he elsewhere makes it
clear that for him "the outside" *is* "the unknown"[39])—is a wish or desire
for (and perhaps of) God?[40]

I will have something more to say a bit later on concerning Lawrence's
reflections (which seem, typically for him, to be casually thrown off but
which are exceptionally important) on the umbrella, the "simulacrum of
the window" and "the roving, uncaring chaos" but for now I simply want
to note that, even though the Outside in the passages we've just considered is undeniably evoked in contrast to oppressive, prison-like, walled-in
interiors, it is clear that something more than the *literal* out-of-doors is at
stake. In other words, for Lawrence too it is a matter (in Levinas's words)
of a "[b]eyond" that is in some sense "more exterior than the outside of
the world—[the world of] landscapes, things, institutions" (qtd. from
Entre-Nous in De Vries's *MT* 348–9). And it may be possible for us to see

this more clearly if we turn aside for a few moments to consider Levinas's thought in slightly more detail.

(iii) Levinas and exteriority (or otherwise than being)

The resounding call of a vocation above the logic that still commands the individual through the necessities of the genus and
species, the awakening to a vigilance—original and ultimate—of
thought in which the other, still part of an objective world in
knowledge, is also outside the world.

—Levinas[41]

I am especially interested here in Hent De Vries's argument that Levinas should be seen (alongside Theodor Adorno) as having produced a minimal theology that attempts "to express transcendence—the nonidentical,
the particular, the singular, the other or Other—in a world that, [Levinas]
acknowledges, has become all too familiar with reasonable grounds for
atheism" (*MT* 347). By way of explaining the sense in which the theology in question is obliged to be minimal, De Vries maintains that in such
a world the absolute "no longer can or should resemble or represent the
highest being" (5). He claims, furthermore, that for Levinas the "absolute—the idea of the 'infinite' or 'in-finite,' in his idiom—is a significa-
tion or sense without (fixed) content, without (given) horizon, without
(ultimate) referent" (6).

    With two main and important exceptions (Plato's Good beyond Being
and Descartes's idea of the Infinite [see, for example, De Vries, *MT* 447]),
Levinas sees Western philosophy as having "most often been an ontology,"
which he understands as entailing "a reduction of the other to the same"
(*TI* 43). One of the ways in which Levinas has defined his own project is in
terms of how it differs from the most famous twentieth century attempt
to rethink ontology: Heidegger's. Thus in his *Totality and Infinity* (1961),
Levinas maintains that "[t]o affirm," as he thinks Heidegger does in his
Being and Time, "the priority of *Being* over *existents* is to already decide
the essence of philosophy; it is to subordinate" the ethical relation ("the relation with *someone*,...an existent") to a relationship of knowing (the kind
of knowing that, by "depriving the unknown being of its alterity" (42), or,

in other words, by permitting "the apprehension [and thus] the domination of existents ..., subordinates justice to freedom"[45]). I take it that
this is the kind of knowing Lawrence had in mind when he claimed that
"[t]o *know* a living thing is to kill it."[42] For Levinas, therefore, "[o]ntology
as first philosophy is a philosophy of power" (*TI* 46) and he associates it
with "possession" and "the imperialism of the same," "the same, produced
as egoism" (38-9). In Lawrentian terms, Levinas is talking here about
"the apotheosis of the ego," when "[t]hat which we *are* is absolute," when
"[t]here is no adding to it, no superseding this accomplished self" because
"[i]t is universal and final" and "every little ego is crowned with the false
crown of its own supremacy, every other ego...a false usurper, and nothing
more."[43]

Levinas's conclusion is that the "terms must be reversed" (*TI* 47). So
that for him, in other words, a religious (or more specifically, Judaically-
inflected) ethics replaces a (basically Greek-derived) ontology as first philosophy (*TI* 304), the core of which is now to be found in "the relation
to *someone*," rather than in the "relation to *Being*," someone *other*, whose
otherness is respected rather than being "reduced to the same." This gives
us, according to him, "a situation where totality [which for him takes
different forms, including, I would say, the one we've just seen Lawrence
describe] breaks up, a situation that conditions the totality itself. Such a
situation," he claims, "is the gleam of exteriority or of transcendence in the
face of the Other"[44] (*TI* 24); "transcendence" being understood here as a
"revelation of infinity" (*TI* 25) and "the epiphany of the face" constituting nothing less than "the origin of exteriority" (*TI* 261), which I take to
be Levinas's word for the Outside. So that whereas, in (Levinas's reading
of) Kierkegaard, for example, "resistance to system manifest[s] itself as the
egoist cry of the subjectivity, still concerned for happiness or salvation"
(*TI* 305), in Levinas resistance to, or the way out of, system or totality is to
be found in the relation with the (human) Other.

Now Lawrence also attached the utmost importance to this relation,
arguing as he did (in "Democracy") that "the fact upon which any great
scheme of social life must be based...is the fact of otherness," "the strange
reality of Otherness" (*RDP* 78). Lawrence could also be ironical at the expense of the conventional idea of "salvation," as we can see in the following
excerpt from his 1925 essay on "Morality and the Novel," where we find

him claiming that "our life *consists* in [the] achieving of a pure relationship between ourselves and the living universe about us":

> This is how I "save my soul," by accomplishing a pure relationship between me and another person, me and other people, me and a nation, me and a race of men, me and the animals, me and the trees or flowers, me and the earth, me and the skies and sun and stars, me and the moon; an infinity of pure relations, big and little, like the stars of the sky: that makes our eternity, for each one of us.[45]

And even if (unlike Levinas) Lawrence talks here of "an infinity of pure relations," he nevertheless tends to privilege the one relationship (between humans) that Levinas focusses on. Furthermore, we can certainly say of Lawrence what Jill Robbins at one point says about Levinas, that for him too the "habitual tendency of the self seeks to suppress alterity; first of all and most of the time my tendency is murderous toward the other. This is precisely," Robbins adds, "what the encounter with the face can be said to interrupt" (*Altered* 141). I'll say something about Levinas's notion of the "face" a bit later but for the moment I simply want to note that Lawrence's version of this encounter is the relationship in which, as he puts it in his essay on "Morality and the Novel," "each seeks only *the true relatedess to the other*" (my italics), a relationship he carefully distinguishes both from self-sacrifice (in which one "of the two parties...yields utterly to the other") and from a "fight to the death" (*STH* 174).

If we judge by this essay, we can perhaps say that for Lawrence, as for Levinas, when one *is* in "true relatedness to the other," then, paradoxically, one is in the state that Levinas describes in the title of one of his books as *Otherwise than Being or Beyond Essence* (*Autrement qu'être ou au-delà de l'essence*) (1974). This is one of the things I had in mind when deciding to start off from those two sentences in which Lawrence refers to "the firing line, where what *is*" comes into "contact with what is not."[46] But I'm thinking now of the opening of "Morality and the Novel" where the subject is Van Gogh painting sunflowers. Lawrence claims that Van Gogh's "painting does not represent the sunflower itself. We shall never know what the sunflower itself is. And the camera will *visualise* the sunflower far more perfectly than Van Gogh can." But in a way this is beside the point, which is that the painting or the "vision on the canvas" is "a revelation of the perfected relation, at a certain moment, between a man and a sunflower." This vision of perfected relation—or indeed, since the latter can only be found in the former, we could just say this perfected relation—"has no existence" in "dimensional space"; it is, rather, "in-between everything, in the fourth dimension." And it therefore has "the fourth-dimensional quality of eternity and perfection." Yet at the same time, "it is momentaneous" (*STH* 171). Lawrence describes the paradox as follows:

> Man and the sunflower both pass away from the moment, in the process of forming a new relationship. The relation between all things changes from day to day, in a subtle stealth of change. Hence art, which reveals or attains to another perfect relationship, will be forever new.
>
> At the same time, that which exists in the non-dimensional space of pure relationship, is deathless, lifeless, and eternal. That is, it gives us the *feeling* of being beyond life or death. We say an Assyrian lion or an Egyptian hawk's-head "lives." What we really mean is that it is beyond life, and therefore beyond death. And there is something inside us which must also be beyond life and beyond death, since that "feeling" which we get from an Assyrian lion or an Egyptian hawk's-head is so infinitely precious to us. As the evening star, that spark of pure relation between night and day, has been precious to man since time began. (171–2)

It is Lawrence's insistence that "that which exists in the non-dimensional space of pure relationship" is "beyond life," which makes me feel justified in saying that it must also be beyond being, or at least beyond any of the ways in which being is ordinarily understood.

But if we do say this, then we have a difficulty to confront. In "Reflections on the Death of a Porcupine" Lawrence refers to this fourth dimension as a dimension "of *being*."[47] What are we to make of this? [48]

It seems to me that here we have an interesting case in which, because they are using the same words very differently, Lawrence and Levinas seem to be saying very different things, whereas they are actually saying something similar. Let's take Levinas first. When he maintains, at the end of his "Ethics as First Philosophy" essay, that the key philosophical question is "how being justifies itself,"[49] he might well seem to be striking a most unLawrentian note. But among the things he is thinking of here are some lines that he likes to quote from Pascal's *Pensées*; Pascal's claim, for example, that "the I (*mon*) is hateful" (qtd. on 82) and that "the usurpation of the whole world" begins with the declaration: "This is my place in the sun."[50] With these lines in mind Levinas asks a question that helps to explain the question with which "Ethics as First Philosophy" ends:

> My being-in-the-world or my "place in the sun," my being at home, have these not also been the usurpation of spaces belonging to the other man whom I have already oppressed or starved, or driven out into a third world; are they not acts of repulsing, excluding, exiling, stripping, killing? (*LR* 82).

With these sentiments Lawrence might well have agreed. Except that what Levinas refers to as "[m]y being-in-the-world" and Lawrence thinks of as the realm of what he calls "my instrumental identity, my inferior I, my self-conscious ego" is, as Lawrence understands it, the realm we occupy when we are "part of nature" and of "the flux" and *when we are in this realm Lawrence thinks we have no being at all* ("Crown" *RDP* 272). This is because, having admitted that "you can't have being without existence, any more than you can have the dandelion flower without the leaves and the long tap root," Lawrence then goes on to somewhat idiosyncratically understand being as "a *transcendent* form of existence, and as much material as existence is. Only the matter suddenly enters the fourth dimension" (my italics, "Reflections," *RDP* 359). So that what Lawrence means by "being" is what Levinas means when he speaks of "transcendence." According to Lawrence, we are only fully in being when we are in blossom and "our blossoming is transcendent, beyond death and life" ("Crown" *RDP* 282). This is what he is saying when he claims, at the beginning of his *Study of Thomas Hardy*, that both the poppy and the phoenix achieve their "maximum of being" (*STH* 11) in the form of a "red flame licking into sight" (8).

Like Levinas, then, Lawrence also believes that, as *Levinas* understands the word, "being" *can't* justify itself. And of course Levinas doesn't think transcendence (what Lawrence oddly calls "being" or "blossoming") *needs* to justify itself, any more than Lawrence does. This is why I maintain that here they are actually saying something very similar and why (to repeat myself) I want to say that if, as Lawrence insists, "that which exists in the non-dimensional space of pure relationship" is "beyond life," then it must also be *beyond* being, *or at least otherwise than any of the ways in which being is ordinarily understood.*

Now it's true that to read the relevant passages in Lawrence in this way is, to some extent, undeniably, to read them against the grain. So that when (to take just one of countless possible examples) Birkin maintains that we have "got to learn not-to-be, before [we] can come into being" (WL 44), we must understand "come into being" as meaning something like "begin to blossom." If the cost clearly involves doing some violence to the text, what is the reward?

I think I can best answer by showing in some detail how thinking the relation to the Other (or to otherness) as something that "has no existence" in "dimensional space"— or as something that can only be characterised (awkwardly, but accurately) as being somehow outside of, or beyond, or at least otherwise than, being—can help us respond to a kind of scepticism that seems to me important to deal with, the kind that has recently been expressed by Amit Chaudhuri in his book on *D.H.Lawrence and 'Difference'.* Commenting on Lawrence's *Birds, Beasts and Flowers*, Chaudhuri notes that "[w]hat is agreed upon generally" by the book's critics "is that, to appropriate a term from linguistics, the 'signified' of the poem is undefinable, powerful, ineffable, but mysteriously transmissable and even paraphrasable. This 'signified,' which may be called 'otherness' or 'life,' lies outside the text, *out there* in the landscape or object described, while each signifier—bat, snake, eagle, tortoise, fish—makes a connection with the 'signified,' thus capturing, conveying, or evoking it."[51] Though Chaudhuri does refer to "the validity of this kind of reading," this seems disingenuous of him since what he himself wants to do is celebrate these poems for (what he sees as) their *refusal* to take us *"out there,"* for the way, for example, in which "the word or name—'bat' or 'snake'—remains, to a large extent, textual" (60).

Thus, with reference to the poem "Bat," Chaudhuri claims that what "is being written about, whether given the appellation 'bat' or 'swallow,' has, like Derrida's [characterisation of his term] *différance,* 'neither existence nor essence. It belongs to no category of being, present or absent.' It seems that 'there is no *name* for this, not even essence or Being'; whatever it is, it 'continually breaks up in a chain of different substitutions.' It is 'neither a *word* nor a *concept*,' and it is 'clear that it cannot be *exposed*. We can expose only what, at a certain moment, can become *present*, manifest,' and in the poem, contradictorily, there is no such moment. What we witness, then, in this reading, is *différance* itself, and the play of *différance*" (65). Here is Chaudhuri on the poem itself:

> [T]he bat in the poem ["Bat"] seems not so much a real one, but a facsimile, a puppet that, at its very moment of metaphoric creation, breaks down into its components and raw materials. This dummy bat is constantly elicited in terms of the materials its costume is made of: its components lie exposed. For instance, it is like "a black glove thrown up at the light,/And falling back." It has "Wings like bits of umbrella." It hangs itself upside down "like an old rag"; rows of sleeping bats become "rows of disgusting old rags." Is Lawrence concerned, in this poem, with "batness," with "otherness," or displaying the ordinary but ingenious materials out of which his dummy is constructed?...The dummy bat is made of old rags, a black glove, and bits of umbrella; unlike the real bat, it cannot decompose or die; within the space of the poem, which is the workshop in which it is made, it can be taken apart and sewn together again numberless times...(66)

In summary, then, Chaudhuri's argument is that Lawrence's poems return the reader "repeatedly from the magnificent world of the Mediterranean landscape where the 'real' beasts roam, to the textual world of the poems"(79) ; that they return us, in other words, from what I am calling the Outside to the inside of the artist's workshop.

It would be possible (but a mistake) to dismiss Chaudhuri's reading on the grounds that it is so obviously thesis-driven. I am thinking here of the insistent use of terms like "puppet," "costume" and "dummy" in the passage I've just quoted and (to my mind, even more revealingly) of the "lucky accident" he refers to in the following:

> Derrida, in distinguishing *écriture* from writing, calls words "black marks on white paper." Tellingly, and by lucky accident,

> Lawrence too often refers to his creatures as if he were describ-
> ing the printed or written word. The bat, for instance, he sees as
> either a "blot" or a "clot," two words as much suggestive of the vi-
> sual appearance of the word upon the page as of the bat observed
> from a distance. (79)

Why that "Tellingly," that "lucky accident" and that "too often," if not
that Chaudhuri thinks he has found here confirmation for his thesis?

Still, I have certainly not cited Chaudhuri here simply in order to dismiss him and his reading. I do, however, think he has missed the point,
which is that Lawrence's poem is no more intended to represent the bat
itself than Van Gogh's painting is intended to "represent the sunflower
itself." If, as Lawrence says, we "shall never know what the sunflower itself is," then nor will we ever know what the bat itself is. But we can say
of Lawrence's poem what Lawrence says of Van Gogh's painting, that it
reveals the "relation, at a certain moment, between a man and a sunflower
[or in this case, a bat]." And if (as seems to me the case) we can say about
an actual bat what (in "Democracy") Lawrence says (while discussing "the
fact of *otherness*") about "an actual man [being] present before us"—that it
is "an inscrutable and incarnate Mystery, untranslatable" (*RDP* 78)—the
point about the "materials" Chaudhuri has been so struck by (and that he
can help the rest of us see more sharply) is that they are the means the artist uses to do the impossible, to translate the untranslatable. So yes, they
do draw attention to the speaker but not, I would argue, at the expense of
the actual or real bat. The two words "blot" and "clot" may well suggest
"the visual appearance of the word upon the page" but they also powerfully evoke "the bat observed from a distance."

Two further points in this connection. (i) If we can say of the relation
between Lawrence and the bat what Lawrence says of the relation between
Van Gogh and the sunflower (that it "has no existence" in "dimensional
space"), then we can see that some of the things Derrida says about his
term *différance*—that it has "neither existence nor essence. It belongs to
no category of being, present or absent"—do seem oddly appropriate. (At
least to the way Lawrence speaks of "the fourth dimension" at the beginning of his essay on "Morality and the Novel.") (ii) And if I myself see Derrida as being much more open to the Outside than Chaudhuri sees him, in
all fairness I think it has to be said that this became easier to see in much

of the work Derrida produced after Chaudhuri wrote his book than it was in Derrida's earlier work.[52]

If we recall now the two paragraphs I quoted from the "Morality and the Novel" essay, my next suggestion is that the reference here to "something inside us which must also be beyond life and beyond death" might go some way toward justifying Ursula's concluding (in the microscope scene in *The Rainbow*) that "[s]elf was a oneness with the infinite"; that "[t]o be oneself was a supreme, gleaming triumph of infinity."[53] And I suggest that we might consider the exchange that occurs in *Women in Love* between Birkin and Ursula just before they write their resignations in the light of what Lawrence says in "Morality and the Novel" about that "perfected relation" that "has no existence" in "dimensional space":

> "But where can one go?" she asked, anxiously. "After all, there *is* only the world, and none of it is very distant."
>
> "Still," he said, "I should like to go with you—nowhere. It would be rather wandering just to nowhere. That's the place to get to—nowhere. One wants to wander away from the world's somewheres, into our own nowhere."
>
> Still she meditated.
>
> "You see, my love," she said, "I'm so afraid that while we are only people, we've got to take the world that's given—because there isn't any other."
>
> "Yes there is," he said. "There's somewhere where we can be free—somewhere where one needn't wear much clothes—none even..."
>
> ...
>
> "It isn't really a locality, though," he said. "It's a perfected relation between you and me, and others—the perfected relation—so that we are free together." (*WL* 315–16)[54]

But for this "perfected relation " to occur then, according to Lawrence (in "Morality and the Novel"), "[e]ach must be true to himself, herself, his own manhood, her own womanhood, and let the relationship work out of itself." And this requires both courage—the "[c]ourage to accept the life-thrust from within oneself, and then from the other person"—and discipline. (*STH* 174–5) What else might it require? Here again there are some interesting similarities between Lawrence's thought and Levinas's.[55]

(iv) Out of context and identity: the "face," visuality, and the "obscene beyond"

> We are only totally laid bare by proceeding without trickery to the unknown.
>
> —Bataille[56]

> He may find knowledge by retracing the old courses, he may satisfy his moral sense by working within the known, certain of what he is doing. But for real, utter satisfaction, he must give himself up to complete quivering uncertainty, to sentient non-knowledge.
>
> —Lawrence (*STH* 35)

I'm thinking first of their shared tendency to proceed by way of negatives. We can begin to get at this by asking what Levinas means when he uses the term "face." When asked by Philippe Nemo what his "phenomenology of the face...consist[s] in," Levinas replied that he doesn't know "if one can speak of a 'phenomenology' of the face, since phenomenology describes what appears" (*Ethics and Infinity* 85) and "what is specifically the face...cannot be reduced to [perception]" (86). In other words, Levinas refuses "the notion of vision to describe the authentic relationship with the Other" (88). As Levinas understands it, "the look is knowledge, perception," the problem with which is that "[y]ou turn yourself toward the Other *as toward an object* when you see a nose, eyes, a forehead, a chin, and you can describe them" (85, my italics). So that the "best way of encountering the Other [*as* an Other, rather than as an object] is not even to notice the color of his eyes!" (85) The point about the "face" is that it "cannot become a content, which your thought would embrace; it is uncontainable, it leads you beyond" (86-7). Finally, the "face" is the "way in which the other presents himself, exceeding *the idea of the other in me*" (*TI* 50).

All of this might well remind us of the comical (but still serious) exchange between Birkin and Ursula that follows on from the latter's mocking question ("But don't you think me good-looking?") in the "Mino" chapter of *Women in Love*:

> He looked at her, to see if he felt that she was good-looking.
> "I don't *feel* that you're good-looking," he said.
> "Not even attractive?" she mocked, bitingly.
> He knitted his brows in sudden exasperation.
> "Don't you see that it's not a question of visual appreciation in the least," he cried. "I don't *want* to see you. I've seen plenty of women, I'm sick and weary of seeing them. I want a woman I don't see."
> "I'm sorry I can't oblige you by being invisible," she laughed.
> "Yes," he said, "you are invisible to me, if you don't force me to be visually aware of you. But I don't want to see you or hear you."
> "What did you ask me to tea for, then?" she mocked.
> But he would take no notice of her. He was talking to himself.
> "I want to find you, where you don't know your own existence, the you that your common sense denies utterly." (147)[57]

Or think of the following passage from *The Rainbow*, describing Anna's dissatisfaction with Anton Skrebensky:

> His body was beautiful, his movements intent and quick, she admired him and she appreciated him without reserve. He seemed completed now. He roused no fruitful fecundity in her. He seemed added up, finished. She knew him all round, not on any side did he lead into the unknown. (*Rainbow* 439).

So much, then, for good-looks, for visual appreciaton; so much even for the beauty of the body. Elsewhere of course Lawrence often attaches great importance to the body but if a person is self-contained, "added up, finished" (to use Levinas's term, a Totality) then the beauty of his or her body is not going to be enough. What matters most is that a person "lead into the unknown" (Levinas's Infinity).

When Birkin tells Ursula he wants to meet her in the "beyond, where there is no speech and no terms of agreement," we might—if we have

Levinas in mind—see this as meaning that he wants to meet her out of "context." Here is Levinas responding again to Philippe Nemo:

> The face is signification, and signification without context. I mean that the Other, in the rectitude of his face, is not a character within a context. Ordinarily one is a "character": a professor at the Sorbonne, a Supreme Court justice, son of so-and-so, everything that is in one's passport, the manner of dressing, of presenting oneself. And all signification in the usual sense of the term is relative to such a context: the meaning of something is in its relation to another thing. Here, to the contrary, the face is meaning all by itself. You are you. (*EI* 86)

Out of context or, as Lawrence puts it at the end of his *Studies in Classic American Literature*, on the Open Road. "The leaving of the soul free unto herself, the leaving of his fate to her and to the loom of the open road." Lawrence says this is "Whitman's essential message" and he calls it "the bravest doctrine man has ever proposed to himself" (*Studies* 173). He maintains that it is also "Whitman's message of American democracy":

> The true democracy, where soul meets soul, in the open road. Democracy. American democracy where all journey down the open road, and where a soul is known at once in its going. Not by its clothes or appearance. Whitman did away with that. Not by its family name. Not even by its reputation. Whitman and Melville both discounted that. Not by a progression of piety, or by works of Charity. Not by works at all. Not by anything, but just itself. The soul passing unenhanced, passing on foot and being no more than itself. (176)

Far from being a thing of the past, and not likely to be mistaken for the "democracy" we have in the present, this, it might be said, is like an anticipation of Derrida's "'democracy to come,'" in which Derrida explains that "to come" signifies "a thinking of the event, of what comes. It's the space opened in order for there to be an event, the to-come, so that the coming be that of the other."[58]

It might be helpful here to note the explanation Levinas provided in a 1988 interview entitled "The Vocation of the Other" of the "two ways in which one can understand the identity of man":

> First, as a being who is particular in his genus. By genus, I mean every genus to which the individual human belongs: nation, profession, race, place and date of birth, etc....However, the other way of being identified is the one that permits us to say "I" or "me" without any consultation with regard to the genus to which one would belong, nor with regard to the differences that one will have constated within oneself in relation to others...Everything happens as if one were seized straightaway in one's irreducible uniqueness. (*Righteous?* 110)[59]

In other words, the identity that the face-to-face encounter takes us out of—when we are Out of Context or in the Open Road—is the former, an identity constructed in terms of the "genus" to which we belong, or in terms of our different "attributes" (Ibid 106).

By way of an example, consider what happens near the end of D.H.Lawrence's short story "The Horse-Dealer's Daughter." A doctor, Jack Fergusson, is walking in the countryside, paying the last of his house-calls for the day, when his quick eye detects "a figure in black" some distance away who is "passing through the gates of the field, down towards the pond."[60] He sees that it must be Mabel Pervin, whom he has got to know only very slightly while visiting her brothers but who is associated for him with "the innermost body of [the working people's] life," for which he has a "craving" (144). Having been intermittently and almost unconsciously aware of her throughout the day, he now stops to watch as (clearly intending to end her life) she wades slowly into the water until he loses sight of her "in the dusk of the dead afternoon" (145). Though he makes haste, it takes him several minutes to get to the pond, and then, since he can't swim and so is afraid, a while longer for him to wade out into the water, locate her beneath the surface and get her back to the bank. When she regains consciousness, and realizes that he has undressed her ("to bring you round"), she quickly concludes and immediately declares that he must love her. In response, he is initially "amazed, bewildered, and afraid":

He had never thought of loving her.... When he rescued her and restored her, he was a doctor and she was a patient...this introduction of the personal element was very distasteful to him, a violation of his professional honour. It was horrible to have her there embracing his knees...Yet her hands were drawing him towards her. He put out his hand quickly to steady himself, and grasped her bare shoulder. A flame seemed to burn the hand.... He had no intention of loving her: his whole will was against his yielding. It was horrible—and yet wonderful was the touch of her shoulder, beautiful the shining of her face...

With an inward groan he gave way, and let his heart yield towards her. A gentle smile came on his face...

He could not bear to look at her any more. He dropped on his knees and caught her head with his arm and pressed her face against his throat...

He felt the hot tears wet his neck and the hollows of his neck, and he remained motionless, suspended through one of man's eternities. Only now it had become indispensable to him to have her face pressed close to him, he could never let her go again. (148–49)

Notice that the transformation that occurs here does not take place easily (on the contrary) but that the major effort involved is of the paradoxical kind that has to do with yielding, giving up the protection provided by one's professional identity (doctor, in this case), abandoning control—the controlling power of one's will and the kind of control found in a viewing position that enables one to survey the other person in her entirety (which is what Jack relinquishes when he drops to his knees). So that it is not as if either Jack or Mabel consciously make what happens happen but, rather, "it had become indispensable." And what happens could be described as a kind of miracle, "The Miracle" being in fact the title Lawrence first thought of giving the story.[61]

Recall now what we earlier noted Lawrence saying about the umbrella that we erect between ourselves and chaos. I would say that one of the forms this umbrella can take is of the kind of identity we have just seen Jack Fergusson giving up. When we try to do without our umbrella/identity—when we allow ourselves to move Out of Context or onto the Open

Road—there is real risk and danger involved. And it may be, as Michael Bell suggests, that "Gazing into [Mabel's] eyes by the fireside puts [Dr Fergusson] at greater risk than following her into the pond" (xxvii). But in any case, pain is inevitable ("'You love me?' she said, rather faltering./'Yes.' The word cost him a painful effort. Not because it wasn't true. But because it was too newly true, the *saying* seemed to tear open again his newly-torn heart" [150][62]) and there is a sense in which we are indeed exposing ourselves to a kind of chaos. So it is important to note first that if this experience inevitably involves the death (sometimes perhaps permanent, more often, probably, temporary) of one's umbrella/identity, it also (at least as Lawrence imagines it) creates the possibility of rebirth into a different kind of identity, the kind (in Levinas's words) "that permits us to say 'I' or 'me' without any consultation with regard to the genus to which one would belong." And secondly, that if one is not prepared to risk exposing oneself to chaos then it is the latter, alternative kind of identity, that is in danger of perishing, or of being killed off.

In making that last point I'm thinking specifically of two things, the first of which is the following passage from Maurice Blanchot's essay on "Literature and the Right to Death":

> For me to be able to say, "This woman" I must somehow take her flesh and blood reality away from her, cause her to be absent, annihilate her. The word gives me the being, but it gives it to me deprived of being. The word is the absence of that being, its nothingness, what is left of it when it has lost being—the very fact that it does not exist ... Of course my language does not kill anyone. And yet: when I say, "This woman," real death has been announced and is already present in my language; my language means that this person, who is here right now, can be detached from herself, removed from her existence and her presence and suddenly plunged into a nothingness in which there is no existence or presence; my language essentially signifies the possibility of this destruction...[63]

"Reference, dedication, predication: Blanchot doesn't," Gerald Bruns notes, "hesitate to call it murder." And still commenting on the above passage, Bruns adds the following explanation: "To speak—that is, to predicate this of that, to bring things under the rule of identity—is to destroy their singularity or alterity as existing things by integrating them into the order of the same."[64]

If this sounds somewhat fanciful or exaggerated, a powerful example of the kind of murder predication ("bring[ing] things under the rule of identity") can achieve is to be found in the ending of Lawrence *Virgin and the Gipsy* (where the murder in question resembles unintentional suicide):

> And Yvette, lying in bed, moaned in her heart: Oh, I love him [the gipsy]! I love him! I love him! The grief over him kept her prostrate. Yet practically, she too was acquiescent in the fact of his disappearance. Her young soul knew the wisdom of it.
>
> But after Granny's funeral, she received a little letter, dated from some unknown place.
>
> "Dear miss, I see in the paper you are all right after your ducking, as is the same with me. I hope I see you again one day, maybe at Tideswell cattle fair, or maybe we come that way again. I come that day to say good-bye! And I never said it, well, the water give no time, but I live in hopes. Your obdt. Servant Joe Boswell."
>
> And only then she realized that he had a name. (90)

It isn't just the name: it's also, of course, the way in which the Gipsy's language reveals/betrays (in effect, places) him, stripping away the aura and glamour that Yvette had earlier associated both with him and the Outside that he inhabits.[65] (We have been told a bit earlier that if "he struck stealthily on the outside," she struck "more secretly on the inside of the establishment" [74]. And though she felt at times that "if she belonged to any side, and to any clan, it was to his," the fact is that "she was born inside the pale. And she liked comfort, and a certain prestige. Even as a mere rector's daughter, one did have a certain prestige" [75].) So what we have at the end of this novella is a Return to Context, a retreat from the Open Road back to the security of the inside. We might also think here of a couple of the ways in which Blanchot's idea of the Outside has been developed by some of his admirers. As Kevin Hart explains it, in *The Dark Gaze*, Blanchot has two versions of the Outside. "In its earlier form it denotes the sacred in its malign form (it is identified with Hades)...while in its later form (which does not replace the earlier), the infernal dimension is forgotten and it opens a postmetaphysical ethics of the other person."[66]

As I noted at the end of the last chapter, it would seem that in its earlier form Blanchot's Outside resembles the condition described in the title of Levinas's 1946 essay "There is: existence without existents." As he explains to an interviewer, Levinas's *il y a* is very different to "the Heideggerian *es gibt* [It gives]." Whereas the *es gibt* "is a generosity," with being giving "itself anonymously...like an abundance, like a diffuse goodness," "the *there is* is unbearable in its indifference" (*Righteous* 45). Not surprisingly, perhaps, Levinas associates the latter with "facelessness" (*TI* 190) and considers that "the true exit from the *there is* is in obligation, in the 'for-the-other,'" in the subordination of the I "to the other," this being, for him, "the ethical event," in which "someone appears who is the subject par excellence" (*Righteous* 45-6).[67]

But Hart suggests that it was the later version of Blanchot's Outside that attracted Michel Foucault and that what the latter "retained from Blanchot was the endless murmur of the Outside, of human beings on the streets escaping 'all authority, be it political, moral, or religious'" (Hart 159).[68] And I think it is the later version of Blanchot's Outside that John Paul Ricco is working with in his book on *The Logic of the Lure*. With reference to "what Blanchot and Foucault refer to as the *Outside*" (4) Ricco tells us that he is trying, in *The Logic of the Lure*, to describe a "[q]ueer erotic relationality" that will suggest "an ethics that is outside of, or more accurately, beside a 'system of interdictions'" (20). Ricco thinks we ought to be following the later Foucault in trying "to think beyond identities (categories of individuals) and acts (sexual practices), towards rather unspecified—and perhaps unspecifiable—forms of relationality and modes of pleasure. Persistently indeterminate and therefore largely unrecoverable, these are the forms and forces that...in their unworking of sexuality, in the evacuation of its content,...have the potential to make identities and acts irrelevant" (18). Ricco believes this is what John Rajchman is getting at when he writes (in his book *Constructions*) that as "indeterminate spatial bodies, we are thus something else than calculating individuals, members of communities, or even cheerful participants in a nice 'civil society'" (qtd by Ricco, 19). "This *something else*," Ricco maintains, "is the non-relational relation to the Outside, to whoever, whatever, wherever, and whenever, a relation ... in ... promiscuous erotic perversity" (19).

It is in the light of this that Ricco suggests we should understand "Foucault's notion of ethics as an aesthetics that would be the practice of *ascesis*" (20-1). This, Ricco claims, "would be less a mode of being than of becoming through a relinquishing or refusing of what today we often call our 'baggage.' Think of it," he urges us, "as a becoming of self that is an unbecoming of self, an *art of living* that is an *art of leaving*. One would no longer," he proclaims, "be the subject of the law but would be a subject unto the Outside, beyond even the status of an outlaw" (21).

My point is that this gives us one plausible interpretation of what *could* happen on the Lawrentian/Whitmanian Open Road. We might perhaps categorize it with a term Lawrence uses in *Women in Love*: "the obscene beyond" (*WL* 242). And since it could obviously be thought to carry some negative connotations, I should perhaps add that I am sure Lawrence intends it non-judgmentally, which is also how Ricco intends his description of "a relation...in...promiscuous erotic perversity" to be read.

At one point in his *Minimal Theologies*, Hent De Vries wonders if we can't speak of a secret relation in Levinas's work "between the amoral or even diabolical *il y a*, on the one hand, and divine illeity, revealed only in the ethical trace, on the other" (458).[69] In a similar way, we might also reflect on the sometimes close proximity of "the obscene" and other, more divine-like, kinds of "beyond" in Lawrence. For now, however, I simply want to turn to some examples of the latter, to what (with Levinas in mind) De Vries calls "ethical transcendence (the face and illeity)" (*MT* 458). But at the same time, this next section is where I want to draw attention to, and briefly reflect upon, a major difference between Levinas and Lawrence, the fact that the Other that Levinas invariably has in mind is usually the neighbour or needy stranger, and this is not usually the case for Lawrence.

(v) An "immanent transcendence": "God in the face of the other"

[W]e are...dealing here...with a certain quasi-mystic *deification*;... because the self becomes as other as the totally other for which

"God" is still the most exemplary—in a sense, the most substitut-
able—name.
                    —De Vries (*Philosophy and the Turn to Religion* 129)[70]

[T]he human is...the place where God *works*, where "God lives."
Hence, an immanent transcendence."
                    —Levinas (*Righteous* 148)

Myself, I believe in God. But I'm off on a different road.
                    —Lawrence ("On Being Religious," *Phoenix*, 730)

As we noticed at the beginning of the last section, both Levinas and
Lawrence refuse (in the words of the former) "the notion of vision to describe the authentic relationship with the Other" (*Ethics and Infinity* 88).
For another example of Lawrence refusing it we can recall the moment
near the end of the third ("Class-Room") chapter of *Women in Love* when
(arguing with Hermione in front of Ursula) Birkin insists on a crucial difference:

"There's the whole difference in the world...between the actual
sensual being, and the vicious mental-deliberate profligacy our
lot goes in for. In our night-time, there's always the electricity
switched on, we watch ourselves, we get it all in the head, really.—You've got to lapse out before you can know what sensual
reality is, lapse into unknowingness, and give up your volition...
You've got to learn not-to-be, before you can come into being."
(*WL* 44)

Much later in the novel, at the end of the twenty third ("Excurse") chapter, we find Birkin and Ursula lapsing out together as they make love in
the dark ("He extinguished the lamps at once, and it was pure night,
with shadows of trees like realities of other, nightly being") in Sherwood
Forest:

Quenched, inhuman, his fingers upon her unrevealed nudity
were the fingers of silence upon silence, the body of mysterious
night upon the body of mysterious night, the night masculine

and feminine, never to be seen with the eye, or known with the
mind, only known as a palpable revelation of living otherness.

She had her desire of him, she touched, she received the max-
imums of unspeakable communication in touch, dark, subtle,
positively silent, a magnificent gift and give again, a perfect acceptance and yielding, a mystery, *the reality of that which can never
be known, vital, sensual reality that can never be transmuted into
mind content, but remains outside,* living body of darkness and
silence and subtlety, the mystic body of reality. She had her desire
fulfilled, he had his desire fulfilled. For she was to him what he
was to her, the immemorial magnificence of mystic, palpable, real
otherness. (*WL,* my italics 320)

What is striking here is that in the complete absence of their umbrella-
identities, or of what Birkin earlier refers to as their "papier-mâché realised
selves" (*WL* 44), we find ourselves not with "Birkin" and "Ursula" making
love but with two amazingly abstract, impersonal, inhuman and anonymous entities ("the body of mysterious night upon the body of mysterious
night"). So it is essential not to overlook the fact that this is immediately
followed by Lawrence's account of what happens when they wake up the
next day:

> They looked at each other and laughed, then looked away, filled
> with darkness and secrecy. Then they kissed and remembered
> the magnificence of the night. It was so magnificent, such an
> inheritance of a universe of dark reality, that they were afraid
> to seem to remember. They hid away the remembrance and the
> knowledge. (Ibid)

It is interesting to note that, according to Derrida (in an early essay on
Bataille), something like this *has* to occur if humans are to achieve a kind
of sovereignty that would differ from Hegelian lordship: (264)

> For sovereignty has no identity, is not *self, for itself, toward it-
> self, near itself.* In order not to govern, that is to say, in order
> not to be subjugated...it must expend itself without reserve, lose
> itself, lose consciousness, lose all memory of itself and all the

interiority of itself; as opposed to *Erinnerung*, as opposed to the avarice which assimilates meaning, it must *practice forget-ting*, the *aktive Vergesslichkeit* of which Nietzsche speaks; and, as the ultimate subversion of lordship, it must no longer seek to be recognized.[71]

As if in keeping with this, consider the significance of the way in which, when they are leaving for Europe, they do *not* visit the Café Prompadour (unlike Gudrun and Gerald, who can't, it seems, resist: "Gudrun hated the Café, yet she always went back to it" [WL 380]), having no need for the recognition it is expressly designed to provide. Instead, we rediscover them on the channel boat seeking the reverse of recognition:

> They went right to the bows of the softly plunging vessel. In the complete obscurity, Birkin found a comparatively sheltered nook.... In the midst of this profound darkness, there seemed to glow on her heart the effulgence of a paradise unknown and un-realised... (*WL* 387, 388)

But the moment to which I have been leading up actually occurs before Birkin and Ursula leave for the Continent and before we turn to it it will be appropriate to recall Levinas's reference to "the gleam of exteriority or of transcendence in the face of the Other" and Lawrence's telling us (in the Ursula-at-the-microscope scene in *The Rainbow*) that to "be oneself was a supreme, gleaming triumph of infinity." Consider in the light of this Lawrence's description of how Ursula looks to Birkin in *Women in Love*, just after she has turned up on his doorstep in some distress because of the way her father has just reacted ("Father hit me") to her telling him, rather abruptly, that she and Birkin intend to get married:

> Now, washed all clear by her tears, she was new and frail like a flower just unfolded, a flower so new, so tender, so made perfect by inner light, that he could not bear to look on her, he must hide her against himself, cover his eyes against her. She had the perfect candour of creation, something translucent and simple, like a radiant, shining flower that moment unfolded in primal blessedness. She was so new, so wonder-clear, so undimmed. And

he was so old, so steeped in heavy memories. Her soul was new, undefined and glimmering with the unseen. (*WL* 368)

What is then interesting is Birkin's feeling that "the passion of gratitude with which he received her into his soul ... could never be understood by her." He is convinced that the fact that "[t]his marriage with her was his resurrection and his life" is something "she could not know." The following passage helps us to understand why he thinks this:

> She wanted to be made much of, to be adored ... How could he tell her of the immanence of her beauty, that was not form or weight or colour, but something like a strange golden light! How could he know himself what her beauty lay in, for him. He said "Your nose is beautiful, your chin is adorable." But it sounded like lies, and she was disappointed, hurt. Even when he said, whispering with truth, "I love you, I love you," it was not the real truth. It was something beyond love, such a gladness of having surpassed oneself, of having transcended the old existence. How could he say "I," when he was something new and unknown, not himself at all? This I, this old formula of the ego, was a dead letter. (*WL* 369)

What ought we to make of these two passages?

I will limit myself here to the simple observation that the language is hyperbolic[72] and of course this is also true of some of the other examples of Lawrence's language we looked at earlier ("excess," "unknown," "nakedness," "the horrific space of the void," "no standard," "no understanding," "outside the pale," "nothing known"). I intend no criticism, however. In the context, hyperbole seems appropriate, as appropriate as the "logic and rhetoric of exaggeration, hyperbole, and excess" (*MT* xvii) that De Vries finds operating in Adorno, Levinas and Derrida. And there is (in the passages we've just looked at) no mistaking its import: Birkin is resurrected by Ursula and she is resurrected by him—what we have here are unmistakable traces of the divine, '[t]he trace," according to Levinas, being "the proximity of God in the face of the other."[73]

But it has to be said that this is not the *sort* of example that springs to mind when one is reading Levinas. Think, for example, of how (in a 1973 piece on "Ideology and Idealism") he praises Plato for setting "forth a *beyond* of institutional justice, like that of the dead judging the dead (*Gorgias* 523e), as if the justice of the living could not pass beyond the clothing of men, that is, could not penetrate the attributes that in others, offer themselves to knowing, to knowledge, as if that justice could not pass beyond the qualities that mask men...In the social community," Levinas comments, "the community of clothed beings, the privileges of rank obstruct justice" (*Levinas Reader* 243-4). What I find this calls to mind are some moments in *King Lear*, when the King has been locked outside the castle walls and is on the heath in the middle of a storm. We might think first of part of Lear's great speech on justice and authority:

> Through tattered clothes small vices do appear;
> Robes and furred gowns hide all. Plate sin with gold,
> And the strong lance of justice hurtless breaks;
> Arm it in rags, a pigmy's straw does piece it. (IV, vi, 166–69)

And if we recall the concern Lear shows for the Fool and Poor Tom (Edgar in disguise), and more generally for "Poor naked wretches" (III,iv,28), in the fourth scene of the previous act, then we might well conclude that what Levinas has to say about the face in the Nemo interviews is very relevant here:

> There is first the very uprightness of the face, its upright exposure, without defense. The skin of the face is that which stays most naked, most destitute. It is the most naked, though with a decent nudity. It is the most destitute also: there is an essential poverty in the face; the proof of this is that one tries to mask this poverty by putting on poses, by taking on a countenance. The face is exposed, menaced, as if inviting us to an act of violence. At the same time, the face is what forbids us to kill. (*EI* 86)

And here is Richard Cohen's take on this:

> Ethical priority, according to Levinas, occurs as the moral height of the other person over being, essence, identity, manifestation, principles, in brief, over me.

There is more to being than being. The surplus of the Other's nonencompassable alterity...is the way ethics intrudes, disturbs, commands being—from height and destitution. (EI 10)

When Lear (the King) approaches Poor Tom (the apparently poor beggar) the roles are reversed. Lear relates to Poor Tom, the destitute Other, as if the latter is above him, which is also how Lear relates to his daughter Cordelia at the end of act 4, when he goes down on his knees before her, Cordelia seeming to him at this point "a soul in bliss" (IV,vii,46). In each of these examples, Lear's Other faces him from "a dimension of height, a dimension of transcendence" (*TI* 215), in a clearly assymetrical relationship.

On the whole, this isn't how the Other tends to be presented in Lawrence and the question is: what accounts for the difference? It isn't, as one might at first think, that the Lawrentian Other is never associated with height, as one realizes when reflecting on the significance of Lawrence capitalizing the word Mystery when claiming that "[t]he fact that an actual man present before us is an inscrutable and incarnate Mystery, untranslatable,...is the fact of *otherness*" ("Democracy" *RDP* 78). It is Levinas's reiterated emphasis on how "destitute" the face is, and on its "essential poverty," that strikes us as being radically unlike Lawrence.

The explanation for the difference may just be that, while both Levinas and Lawrence are deeply rooted in the biblical tradition, Levinas is much more content to remain within the Judaeo-Christian orbit,[74] while Lawrence was more persuaded of the need to move beyond it. And this can make one wonder about something Jill Robbins says concerning Levinas's frequent use of the term "God" in the interviews collected in *Is It Righteous To Be?* "Ultimately," she claims, "it can be argued that the term *God* is something of a placeholder, the name for responsibility within the interhuman. That God is a preeminently empty notion, that to subject God to thematization entails a destruction of transcendence, Levinas had established in the 1975 essay 'God and Philosophy,' which forms the core of *Of God Comes to Mind*" (*Righteous* 19). I have the impression that this may apply more to Lawrence than it does to Levinas.

Consider, on the one hand, Levinas's response to an interviewer's asking him to reflect on how his "thought is founded on the biblical tradition":

But truly, in the Bible, the essential moment in the development of ethical conscience and of the dignity of man consists in recognizing oneself as a son of God: the filiality of transcendence... There is a magnificent meditation of Jean Paul 11 relative to Christianity, teaching us that God would be incarnated not solely in Christ, but through Christ in all men. This divine filiality is nothing new for Jews: the divine paternity experienced by Jewish piety, as it has been formulated by Isaiah, should be taken literally. (*Righteous* 109)

And, on the other hand, the last two paragraphs of Lawrence's little essay on "Books":

I know the greatness of Christianity: it is a past greatness. I know that, but for those early Christians, we should never have emerged from the chaos and hopeless disaster of the Dark Ages. If I had lived in the year 400, pray God, I should have been a true and passionate Christian. The adventurer.

But now I live in 1924, and the Christian venture is done. The adventure is gone out of Christianity. We must start on a new venture towards God. (*Phoenix* 734)

To get some idea of how far this could take Lawrence from the Judaeo-Christian idea (or ideas) of God the Father, consider his claim in "The Crown" that "there is nothing for a man to do but to behold God, and to become God" (RDP 304). And where are we going to behold God? Here are two possibilities:

Every new gesture, every fresh smile of a child is a new emergence into creative being: a glimpse of the Holy Ghost...

And the still clear look on an old face, and the stillness of old, withered hands, which have gathered the long repose of autumn, this is the purity of the two streams ["the flux of life and the flux of death"] consummated, and the bloom, like autumn crocuses, of age. ("Crown" RDP 285–6)

Usually, it's true, Lawrence's examples are more dramatic than these but note, in what might seem a more characteristic Lawrentian passage (that is organized around an allusion to the burning bush in *Exodus* 111.2)[75], the inclusion not just of the poppy (again) but also of the dandelion:

> The flower is the burning of God in the bush...The true God is *created* every time a pure relationship, or a consummation out of twoness into oneness takes place. So that the poppy flower is God come red out of the poppy-plant. And a man, if he win to a sheer fusion in himself of all the manifold creation, a pure relation, a sheer gleam of oneness out of manyness, then this man is God created where before God was uncreate...It is true of a man as it is true of a dandelion or of a tiger or of a dove ... One by one, in our consummation, we pass...like the bushes in the desert, we take fire with God, and burn timelessly: and within the flame is heaven that has come to pass. Every flower that comes out, every bird that sings, every hawk that drops like a blade on her prey, every tiger flashing his claws, every serpent hissing out poison, every dove bubbling in the leaves, this is timeless heaven established from the flood... ("Crown" 303)

At the same time, Lawrence is careful to remind us that we can "no more *stay* in this heaven, than the flower can stay on its stem" (304). Nor should we try: the "desire for constancy, for fixity in the temporal world" is "evil." Furthermore, though "[w]e cannot know God, in terms of the permanent, temporal world," we *can*, according to Lawrence, "know the *revelation* of God in the physical world." And that ought to be enough, since "the revelation of God *is* God" (my italics), even if "it vanishes as the rainbow" (304).

In summary, then, though Lawrence believes that we can momentarily enter the version of the Outside that he is sometimes willing (as here) to call "heaven" (not just by beholding but also by temporarily becoming God), Lawrence is quite clear that heaven is timeless and that we necessarily live for the most part "within the flux of time" (303). Isn't this more or less what Levinas has to tell us about the face-to-face encounter (which is to say, in effect, about *his* "heaven" ["Height," he maintains, "is heaven. The kingdom of heaven is ethical" (*Otherwise* 183)])? And is Lawrence's urging us to "create a new revelation of God" (305) all that different, really, to Levinas's telling us that "infinity is produced in the relationship of the same with the other" (*TI* 26)?

This, then, our relation with the Other, is how both Levinas and Lawrence imagine peace: "the new, superfine bliss, a peace superseding knowledge" (*WL* 369) that Birkin experiences when Ursula comes to him soon after being rejected by her father; and the peace (admittedly a different modality of, but still clearly, peace) that Levinas associates with "my solicitation for the other person" (*Righteous?* 56). So that, if anyone is still wondering about the meaning of "the firing line," it is to be understood *not* as a place where one attacks others but rather as a place where one runs the risk of being attacked or fired on oneself—a bit like the "*no-man's land*" in which Levinas locates Derrida ("In reading him, I always see the 1940 exodus again") in his "Wholly Otherwise" essay.[76] With reference to which Simon Critchley nicely comments "that deconstruction both suspends the present in a no man's land...while at the same time allowing the trace of ethical peace to persist beneath the fact of war" (*Ethics* 153).

Finally, Lawrence and Levinas agree that the Other only remains incomparable so long as we are in one form or another of the face-to-face relationship. "When I stand with another man, who is himself, and when I am truly myself, then," Lawrence claims, "I am only aware of a Presence, and of the strange reality of Otherness ... There is no comparing or estimating. There is only this strange recognition of *present otherness*...Comparison enters only when one of us departs from his own integral being, and enters the material-mechanical world. Then equality and inequality starts at once" ("Democracy," *Phoenix* 715-16; and see *RDP* 359). In Levinas's account of this transition, there is, as he says, "always a third party in the world" and this fact in itself forces us, in the name of justice, to engage in "judgment and comparison, a comparison of what is in principle incomparable, for every being is unique" (*Righteous* 165-66; and see 12). Hence, the aporia. On the one hand, each self is, in Lawrence's words, "a single well-head of creation, unquestionable," which means that "it cannot be compared with another self, another well-head, because, in its prime or creative reality, it can never be comprehended by any other self" ("Democracy" 714). On the other hand, sooner or later, comparison is necessary. And it is here, with questions concerning (what Levinas refers to as) the "third," that justice comes into the picture, justice and politics—at the same time, as we must now see, that this simultaneously marks the entrance of *in*justice.

Chapter Five

Thought from (and of) the outside

Part Two: Abraham and Isaac: hospitality, the messianic turn, and the religious suspension of the ethical (Derrida, Kierkegaard, Leavis, Conrad, Agamben, and others)

> Yet it is only by persistently referring to the religious that the reelaboration of these ethico-political traits [of deconstruction] avoids becoming moralistic, complacent, predictable, and opportunistic...
>
> ...
>
> [T]he central task of philosophy is not to say something else, but to say the Same *otherwise* (*autrement*) or at least *to the Other* and thus, ever indirectly, *à Dieu.*
>
> —Hent De Vries (*PTR*, 23, 124)

(vi) The introduction of the third party: betrayal, guilt, sacrifice and infinite responsibility

> I am responsible to anyone (that is to say to any other) only by failing in my responsibility to all the others, to the ethical or political generality. And I can never justify this sacrifice ...
>
> —Derrida (*GD* 70)

The fact that the concern for justice that comes with the third party necessarily entails "a comparison of what is in principle incomparable," this means (for Levinas) that "[j]ustice is already the first violence" (*Righteous?* 166, 136).[1] When we become "a threesome" and find ourselves having to face "the political question: *who* is the neighbor?"—and therefore forced to "compare the incomparable" (133)—then "violence enters the

scene because justice's judgment is violence" (134). This is a necessary violence, however, and we shouldn't try to shirk it. We can't live forever in "a
society of two, outside the relations that regulate individuals who belong
by appurtenance to the same genus" (108). Or as Simon Critchley puts it,
"the anarchic ethical particularity of Jerusalem" needs to be supplemented by "the hierarchy and totality" Levinas associates with "the Athenian
democratic political order and the philosophical question that Socrates
raises about the legitimacy, or *archē*, of that order" (*Ethics* 240).[2] And for
those who are understandably puzzled by this reference to the anarchic,
here is Gerald Bruns's explanation:

> Anarchy...is to be understood in its original sense of that which is
> outside, on the hither side, of the concept of principle: *an-arche*.
> The anarchic is not opposed to order dialectically as a Dionysian
> project of overcoming or undoing; it is rather the refractory re-
> gion excluded by an integral rationality that disposes everything
> according to the rule of unity and identity. (*Maurice Blanchot* 6)

Though it is true that Bruns is primarily thinking of Blanchot here, he
makes it clear that he takes this to be the way Levinas understands anarchy too (see 124-25). But while I agree that this does seem to be the way
Levinas understands anarchy (he explains, after all, that for him "anarchy
is not disorder as opposed to order," that it rather "troubles being over and
beyond these alternatives" [*OB* 101]), I myself want to say that "the refrac-
tory region excluded by an integral rationality" gives us one perfectly sat-
isfactory definition of the kind of chaos Lawrence's umbrella is designed
to protect us from.[3]
    On the one hand, then, if and when we allow ourselves to move Out of
Context or onto the Open Road (or, I would add, into Chaos) in order to
enter the face-to-face relationship, we do so as anarchists; whereas, on the
other hand, when we enter into those other relationships that involve us in
reciprocal duties, rights and laws we do so as citizens. And sooner or later,
"the return of the unique [from the an-archic (and in some sense Jewish)
Outside, back in] to the community of genus" (*Righteous?* 108)—which
Levinas sees as "the Greek moment" (67; and see 133), the moment of politics—is both inevitable and desirable. Not that the one moment eclipses

the other. On the contrary, Levinas insists that "both the hierarchy taught by Athens and the *abstract* and slightly *anarchical* ethical individualism taught by Jerusalem are *simultaneously necessary* in order to suppress [or, as I would prefer to say, minimize] violence" (qtd. by Critchley [the last italics are his] 240; and see De Vries[4]).

It is at this point that I propose we turn to Derrida, to see what he makes of this. Responding to Richard Rorty's confession that he has "trouble with the specifically Levinasian strains in his thought" (in particular, with "Levinas's pathos of the infinite"[5]), Derrida unapologetically reiterates his position, which is that he shares Levinas's belief in "the infinitude of responsibility," and he explains what he means by this as follows:

> If I conduct myself particularly well with regard to someone, I know that it is to the detriment of an other; of one nation to the detriment of another nation, of one family to the detriment of another family, of my friends to the detriment of other friends or non-friends, etc. This is the infinitude that inscribes itself within responsibility ...[6]

If responsibility is "not limitable," then, as "a consequence, whatever choice I might make, I cannot say with good conscience that I have made a good choice or that I have assumed my responsibilities" (Ibid). Moreover, as Derrida sees it, another consequence of "a responsibility without limits"[7] is the inevitability of betrayal. "You wanted," he tells John Millbank in a roundtable discussion, "to avoid betrayal or urge me to avoid betrayal and unfortunately I think we are, that I am, constantly betraying."[8] This is so, he explains, "[b]ecause as soon as I relate to an irreducible singular one I am betraying another one, or I introduce a third one who disturbs or corrupts the singular relation to the other" (68). "So you cannot," Derrida tells Millbank, "prevent me from having a bad conscience, and that," he adds, "is the main motivation of my ethics and my politics" (69).

According to Derrida, the very fact that "the [Levinasian] third one is already comparison" means that "the betrayal...is already there" (67). Or to put it another way, it means that despite our best intentions we are always inevitably engaged in the sacrifice of someone or something. Thus, while claiming that he is "constantly against," and "trying to deconstruct[,] the logic of sacrifice," Derrida admits that, while he tries "not to be simply sacrificialistic," he "cannot deny that sacrifice is unavoidable" (67). But this isn't all. With reference to Kierkgaard's account in *Fear and Trembling* of the story about Abraham's willingness to obey God's command that he sacrifice his son, Derrida argues that "what *Fear and Trembling* says about the sacrifice of Isaac" is a truth that "possess[es] the very structure of what occurs every day" (*GD* 78). And the clear implication of this is strikingly summarized by Hent De Vries's claim that Derrida follows Kierkegaard and Levinas in reading "the testimony of Abraham's sacrifice and the violence it entails as the paradigm for what is at stake in every genuine ethico-political decision" ("Violence" 18).[9] Basically, Kierkegaard argues that when Abraham obeys God's command, he is sacrificing ethics, in the simple sense that from an ethical point of view he is agreeing to be a murderer. But Abraham is no longer looking at things from an ethical point of view: in effect, he is suspending the ethical. This is what Kierkegaard calls (in "Problema 1" of *Fear and Trembling*) the "teleological suspension of the ethical" and what (more recently) Slavoj Žižek refers to as "the religious suspension of the ethical," which Žižek provokingly maintains is "the *sine qua non* of an authentic ethical engagement."[10] As for Derrida, he summarizes his sense of the situation as follows:

> As soon as I enter into a relation with the other, with the gaze, look, request, love, command, or call of the other, I know that I can respond only by sacrificing ethics, that is, by sacrificing whatever obliges me to also respond, in the same way, in the same instant, to all the others. I offer [like Abraham] a gift of death [in Abraham's case, both the death of his son and, therefore, figuratively speaking, his own death], I betray, I don't need to raise my knife over my son on Mount Moriah for that. Day and night, at every instant, on all the Mount Moriahs of this world, I am...raising my knife over what I love and must love, over those to whom I owe absolute fidelity, incommensurably... (*GD* 68)[11]

This gives us the gist of what Derrida himself is happy to refer to (adopting Vladimir Jankélévitch's term) as his "hyperbolical ethics" ("To Forgive" 29),[12] which I take to be his way of inviting us to say of his thought what the editor of *The Levinas Reader* says of Levinas's, that, yes, its "challenge is an excessive one."[13] And perhaps we can also say of Derrida's expansion of the meaning of "sacrifice" what De Vries says of Levinas's "expansion of the meaning of 'violence,'" that while it *risks* trivializing the concept, it *actually* "intensifies its meaning" ("Violence" 17). In each case, at any rate, what it comes down to in the last analysis is the conclusion expressed in the sentence that Levinas cites so often from Dostoevsky's *The Brothers Karamazov*: "We are all guilty, the one toward the other, and I more than all the others" (qtd in *Righteous?* 112; & see 229). In view, in other words, of what Derrida calls "the aporia that renders me incapable of giving enough, or of being hospitable enough, of being present enough to the present that I give, and to the welcome that I offer, such that...I always have to...ask forgiveness for not giving, for never giving enough, for never offering or welcoming enough'; in view of this, Derrida declares that "*[o]ne is always guilty*" ("To Forgive," my italics 22).

It may be worth pausing here for a moment in order to note that over the last few decades other thinkers have of course reached a similar conclusion, while still others have hotly contested it. On the one hand, then, one of the forms the debate takes concerns such questions as whether or not people living today are in any way responsible for the sins or crimes committed by their forefathers (anti-Semitism in Germany, the slavery trade in the UK and the US etc.), especially in those cases where current prosperity seems to have been at least partially made possible by past injustice.[14] On the other hand, and at the same time, there is the question concerning the extent of our responsibility for new, present-day injustices we may be helping to commit without our intending to, or without even our being aware of. Here I want to note Mellisa Orlie's reflections on a 1970 watercolour print by the German artist Anselm Kiefer entitled "Every Human Being Stands beneath His Own Dome of Heaven." This is an allusion to a passage in Nietzsche's *Thus Spoke Zarathustra* in which Zarathustra announces that his "blessing" is "to stand over every single thing as its own heaven, as its round roof, its azure bell, and eternal security" (Third Part, "Before Sunrise" 277). Explaining how she recognized within herself a longing for her "own azure bell," Orlie goes on to meditate "upon our need to secure a home in the world (I mean a place to sleep and eat, not an ontological sense of belonging) and how this need implicates us in trespasses against others, specifically in processes that render others homeless" (*Living Ethically* 2).[15] As she interprets it, "Kiefer's print conveys the hidden and unexpected power of the apparently isolated individual: he has made the rest of the human world disappear" (4). Her point is that that (making others disappear) is what we tend to do as well and that we need to address "the harmful effects (what I call 'trespasses' and at once 'ordinary' and 'ordered' evil) that inevitably follow not from our intentions and malevolence but from our participation in social processes and identities" (5). In short, Orlie believes that "if we desire to be free, we must assume responsibility for our trespasses" (169), which I think means that in practice her sense of responsibility is also infinite (or close to it). [16]

We are always guilty, then, because we are always hurting, indeed sacrificing, others and it would seem that nothing, not even (*pace* Žižek) "the 'postsecular' Messianic turn of deconstruction" (*Puppet* 3), can prevent this from happening. But let's pause here and turn aside for a moment in order to briefly consider this messianic turn.

(vii) Waiting to welcome the Stranger

Face to face with the other within a glance *and* a speech which both maintain distance and interrupt all totalities, this being-together as separation precedes or exceeds society, collectivity, community. Levinas calls it *religion*. It opens ethics. The ethical relation is a religious relation...[17]

　　　　　　　　　　　　　　　　　　　　—Derrida (1964)

[T]he messianic ... would be the opening to the future or to the coming of the other as the advent of justice, but without horizon of expectation and without prophetic prefiguration. The coming of the other can only emerge as a singular event when no anticipation sees it coming, when the other and death—and radical evil—can come as a surprise at any moment.

　　　　　　　　　　　　　—Derrida (1996; 'Faith" 17)

Instead of an open-ended and essentially borderless sociality of expectation, it [Christianity] has become an institution with carefully policed frontiers. Is this an inevitable outcome of thinking that the messiah has already showed up in history, in advance?

　　　　　　　　　　　　—Theodore W. Jennings, Jr. (2006)[18]

In Zarathustra's dialogue with the fire-dog, Nietzsche says that
true events arrive on doves' feet, that they surprise us in the
moment of greatest silence. On this point, as on many others,
he should have acknowledged his debt to that same Paul upon
whom he pours out his scorn. First epistle to the Thessalonians
(5.2): "The day of the Lord will come like a thief in the night."
                                              —Alain Badiou (*Saint Paul* 111)

For every second of time was the straight gate through which the
Messiah might enter.
                                              —Walter Benjamin[19]

Building in 1994 on what almost seems like one of Levinas's asides—
Levinas's reference "to the relation with the Other, that is, to justice" (*TI*
89)[20]—Derrida claims that this offers us an admittedly "very minimal"
but nevertheless "really rigorous" "definition of justice" (which he tells us
he "love[s]"):

[J]ustice is the relation to the other. That is all. Once you relate to
the other as the other, then something incalculable comes on the
scene, something which cannot be reduced to the law or to the
history of legal structures.[21]

If we read this in the light of Derrida's tendency around the time he made
this claim to start defining deconstruction "as the thinking of the gift and
of undeconstructible justice"[22] then we will see that deconstruction is implicitly being defined here largely in terms of the relation to the other, or of
what Levinas refers to as the "metaphysical event of transcendence—the
welcome of the Other, hospitality" (*TI* 254). And if this is what Levinas
calls religion, it clearly has a religious dimension for Derrida too. As we
can see when he begins to talk about the "messianic" in terms of "the coming of the other as the advent of justice" ("Faith" 17). Even if Derrida explains that he "prefer[s] to say *messianic* rather than *messianism*, so as to
designate a structure of experience rather than a religion" (*Specters* 167-8),
there can be no doubt but that this "waiting for someone to come" ("Villanova," *Nutshell* 22) has religious resonance and that it practically invites
the reading John Caputo gives it:

The messianic future of which deconstruction dreams, its desire and its passion, is the unforseeable future to come, absolutely to come, the justice, the democracy, the gift, the hospitality to come. Like Elijah knocking on our door! The first and last, the constant word in deconstruction is come, *viens*. (*Nutshell* 156)

As Caputo and Yvonne Sherwood note, it is of course always possible that the stranger knocking at our door might be "a monster" ("Otobiographies" 219), which might well make us tremble. But then, as Derrida reminds us, according to St Paul we should *always* be in a state of trembling. At least this would seem to be the case if we place ourselves in the position of those disciples Paul tells to "work out [their] salvation with fear and trembling" (*Philippians* 2:12; qtd. in Derrida's *GD* 56) and to do so in his absence. And as Derrida notes, "there is something even more serious at the origin of this trembling," the fact that "God is himself absent, hidden and silent, separate, secret, at the moment he has to be obeyed" (*GD* 57). If, therefore, as Derrida says in his first essay on Levinas, "the thought of Emmanuel Levinas can make us tremble" ("Violence" 82), this would seem entirely appropriate. And in the light of this, it seems worth noting that if, for Levinas and Derrida, "justice is the relation to the other," D.H. Lawrence is saying something similar when he maintains (in "Morality and the Novel") that "morality is that delicate, *forever trembling* and changing *balance* between me and my circumambient universe, which precedes and accompanies a true relatedness" (*STH,* first italics mine 172). And again, a few lines further on: "Morality in the novel is the *trembling instability* of the balance" (Ibid, my italics).[23]

But to return to the stranger at the door. If someone is knocking, and if (like Sherwood and Caputo) we ask "Who will dare to say 'Welcome'?" (Ibid, 220), one answer is the author of the "Song of a Man Who Has Come Through." Here is the ending of Lawrence's poem:

> What is the knocking?
> What is the knocking at the door in the night?
> It is somebody who wants to do us harm.
>
> No, no, it is the three strange angels.
> Admit them, admit them.[24]

Or we might think in this connection of the essay "Life" in which Lawrence maintains that we "are not created of ourselves. But from the unknown, from the great darkness of the outside that which is strange and
new arrives on our threshold, enters and takes place in us. Not of ourselves,
it is...*of the unknown which is the outside*" (*Phoenix* 696-7, my italics). And
here too (for Lawrence) it is a matter of wondering "Who comes, who is it
that we hear outside in the night? Who knocks, who knocks again?" (696)
We are told that the "stranger will come" but only, it seems, if we "wait in
patience, wait and always wait up for the stranger" (697).

Yet even if we were to succeed in practising the unconditional hospitality that largely constitutes "the 'postsecular' Messianic turn of deconstruction" and that, at various times, Derrida, Lawrence and Levinas all
appear to recommend, even if we did this, we would still inevitably be
engaged in the sacrifice of others. This is so for the reason we noted at the
end of the last (sixth) section. Here it is again in slightly different form:

> [W]hat binds me...in my singularity to the absolute singularity of
> the other, immediately propels me into the space or risk of abso-
> lute sacrifice. There are also others, an infinite number of them,
> the innumerable generality of others to whom I should be bound
> by the same responsibility, a general and universal responsibility
> (what Kierkegaard calls the ethical order). I cannot respond to
> the call, the request, the obligation, or even the love of another
> without sacrificing the other other, the other others. *Every other*
> *(one) is every (bit) other [tout autre est tout autre]*, every one else is
> completely or wholly other. (*GD* 68)

What this means, according to Derrida, is that "in order to be just, I am
unjust and I betray. I must," therefore, "ask forgivenessness for (the fact
of) being just. Because it is unjust to be just. I always betray someone to
be just; I always betray one for the other ..." ("To Forgive" 49). There is, in
other words, no way of avoiding the fact that the attention I give to one
other must always be at the expense of the attention I might have given to
another other, or to many others.

This can also be understood in terms of the inclusion/exclusion opposition. It would seem that, even with the best of intentions, we can't avoid
excluding, in one form or another, someone or something. Let's briefly

consider two examples here, the first from Lawrence, the second from Derrida. I am thinking of a couple of things Lawrence says—(i) "It is no good casting out devils. They belong to us, we must accept them and be at peace with them" and (ii) "There is no hope in exclusion" (*RDP* 35)—in his essay on "The Reality of Peace." The point I want to make here is that, even if one makes a conscious effort (as Lawrence clearly thought he was doing)[25] to avoid "casting out" or excluding the things one abhors, one may still end up doing so. Nor, in Lawrence's case, should this surprise us, not when we consider, for example, what he has to say in his "Morality and the Novel" essay about love and hate:

> All emotions, including love and hate, and rage and tenderness, go to the adjusting of the oscillating, unestablished balance between two people who amount to anything. If the novelist puts his thumb in the pan, for love, tenderness, sweetness, peace, then he commits an immoral act: he *prevents* the possibility of a pure relationship, a pure relatedness, the only thing that matters: and he makes inevitable the horrible reaction, when he lets his thumb go, towards hate and brutality, cruelty and destruction. (*STH* 173)[26]

Here we have a case of what (to borrow a term) we might call an "*excluding* inclusion" since it takes the form of a person's right to express hate and rage and therefore *inevitably* results in certain exclusions; as we find, for example, in such deeply disturbing (and frankly ugly) passages as the following (written during the first world war):[27]

> For many who are born and live year after year there is no such thing as coming to blossom...Many are parasite, living on the old and enfeebled body politic...They are like the large green cabbages that cannot move on into flower...It is given us to devour them...So with very many human lives...They are like the sheep in the fields...Thank God for the tigers and the butchers that will free us from the abominable tyranny of these greedy, negative sheep. ("Reality of Peace," *RDP* 40–42)

Though I certainly don't intend to try to justify such passages, I do believe it is vitally important not to forget that they come from a writer who also wrote not just what Derrida rightly calls the "extraordinary scene of hospitality"[28] in the poem "Snake" but quite possibly, I would say, *more* extraordinary scenes of hospitality than can be found in any other modern writer.

As for the example from Derrida, I'm thinking first of the claim Gil Anidjar makes at the beginning of his Introduction to the *Acts of Religion* collection, that "when Derrida writes on religion, it is always on the Abrahamic"—a notion, Anidjar explains, that is "of Islamic origin" (*Acts* 3). And secondly, in relation to this, of something Cleo McNelly Kearns says about "the project of inclusion" in her contribution to the *Derrida and Religion* collection:

Many now—myself included—use the qualifier "Abrahamic" when they wish to bind Judaism, Christianity, and Islam into a common paradigm. But it must be noted that the term indicates a point of origin not only patriarchal, both in the literal and the extended sense, but based on a figure construed differently and with varying degrees of intensity in each of these three faith traditions in question. "Before Abraham was I am," Jesus is said to have said (John 8:57-59), and the Abraham of the Qur'an is less a primordial founder in the sense given him by the nation of Israel than primus inter pares of a number of individual men of faith stretching back to Adam.

There are similar difficulties with several proposed groupings and rubrics. To speak of the three "monotheisms," for instance, would do well were it not for [the fact] that this term takes as self-evident a theology never quite as monolithic as has often been presumed ... So, too, even with the apparently more neutral and more descriptive rubric "religions of the book." For while it is true that Judaism, Christianity, and Islam all have "Bibles" of a sort, the Torah, the gospels and the Qur'an have neither the same religious function nor the same theological status in each, and the implication that no other world religion is based on a revealed text is relevant only in a very limited sense.

Given these problems, it is as difficult to avoid...failures of inclusion...as it is necessary to keep on trying to do so.[29]

However, even if we accept (at least provisionally) that there may be no way for us to avoid (in our attempts at being just and doing the right thing) excluding and thus sacrificing others, even so, it may still be possible to adopt different attitudes towards this fact (if fact it is). Specifically, it may (arguably) still be possible (i) to hold on to a more limited concept of responsibility than the infinite kind espoused by Levinas, Derrida and Dostoevsky's Alyosha; and accepting this more limited form of responsibility may (ii) relieve us of the guilt that inevitably comes with infinite responsibility while also creating the possibility of a good conscience (a *good* "good conscience, as it were, "good" in the sense of being non-complacent).

I propose to demonstrate this possibility with the help of a text (Joseph Conrad's *The Secret Sharer*), and a particular reading of this text (by the literary critic, F.R.Leavis), that (I will argue) together work to support what Derrida claims is jointly demonstrated by the Biblical account of Abraham preparing to sacrifice his son Isaac and Kierkegaard's commentary on this in his *Fear and Trembling*: namely, that "the concepts of responsibility, of decision, or of duty, are condemned a priori to paradox, scandal, and aporia" (*GD* 68). But before discussing *The Secret Sharer* and Leavis's reading of it, I need to establish something of a context: first by saying a few words about Leavis, explaining why I find it necessary to introduce him into the discussion at this point; then by saying something about D.H.Lawrence's novel *The Rainbow* and Leavis's commentary on it; finally by glancing at some of Leavis's remarks on Blake, Dickens and T.S.Eliot. Both while setting up this context and also while examining Leavis's later reading of Conrad's novella one of my aims will be to bring out a number of no doubt surprising affinities between what (with the help of Lawrence, Conrad, Blake, Dickens and both the Eliots, George and T.S.) Leavis had to say about religion, judgment, responsibility, decision and ethics and what (with the help of Kierkegaard) Derrida has to say about these things.

(viii) Leavis and Derrida on a "religious" or messianic sense of responsibility

[U]nless it has a religious quality the sense of human responsibility can't be adequate to the plight of the world that so desperately

needs it—won't, in fact, be what is needed.... [T]here is no acceptable religious position that is not a reinforcement of human
responsibility.

—F.R.Leavis[30]

(a)F.R.Leavis: The phantom's return

We confuse the analogous with the identical: "Exactly the same
thing is repeating itself, exactly the same thing." No, a certain
iterability (difference in repetition) ensures that what comes back
nevertheless remains a wholly other event. A phantom's return is,
each time, another, different return, on a different stage, in new
conditions to which we must always pay the closest attention if
we don't want to say or do just anything.

—Derrida (1996)[31]

Derrida and Leavis? Admittedly, on first glance, a most improbable-
seeming pairing. On the one hand, the philosopher who happily concedes
that he is sometimes charged with "saying nothing, not offering any content or any full proposition. I have never 'proposed' anything," Derrida
admits, "and that is perhaps the essential poverty of my work."[32] On the
other hand, the literary critic who is best known for having said quite a lot.
As, for example, in the opening sentence of his book *The Great Tradition*:
"The great English novelists are Jane Austen, George Eliot, Henry James
and Joseph Conrad—to stop for the moment at that comparatively safe
point in history." Of course, Leavis was subsequently to revise this judgement in various ways. Leaving that aside, however, such a sentence is, as
Leavis goes on to note, open to all kinds of misunderstandings. But then,
in his view, the "only way to escape misrepresentation is never to commit
oneself to any critical judgment that makes an impact—that is, never to
say anything."[33]

What can two such very different figures possibly have in common?
It is true that they can both be described as tireless and eloquent defenders
of the university, and as steadfast foes of homogenization. When Leavis
wanted to summarize what his journal *Scrutiny* stood for he referred, furthermore, to "the creative work it did on the contemporary intellectual-
cultural frontier in maintaining the critical function."[34] And what better

way of locating Derrida than on "the contemporary intellectual-cultural frontier"? Not, to be sure, the same frontier as the one Leavis frequented but, as we shall now see, there are, nevertheless, certain similarities, not the least significant of which is the fact that for the most part they did their thinking by means of close readings of others. And in Leavis's case, since he was a literary critic, *his* thought was the product of his critical engagement with some of the great creative writers.

But before going any further I had perhaps better note the opening of a book that sounds by its title—Andrew Gibson's *Postmodernity, Ethics and the Novel: From Leavis to Levinas* (1999)—as if it might be of some relevance to our discussion. After opening the book with the claim that it "is time to go back to Leavis," Gibson's second sentence tells us that to "start a book on the novel in such a way is to court yawns of boredom or disbelief, wry smiles, ironical jeers." And his fourth sentence is clearly intended to reassure: "I mean the point, however, in one (qualified) sense only." [35] Here, then, we would seem to have a clear case of one of those "unwritten rules and prohibitions" (if you know what's good for you, stay away from Leavis!) that, Žižek has claimed, "today's self-professed 'radical' academia is permeated by" and, as he adds, "although such rules are never explicitly stated, disobedience can have dire consequences."[36] If ever there was an obvious case of one of those "positions one is [*not*] allowed to adopt" (*Puppet* 5), the one I seem to be adopting here is definitely it.

Nor, it seems, is Leavis the only critic we ought, if we know what's good for us, to be staying away from. Gibson makes it very plain that the kind of "literary ethics" *he* "want[s] to reaffirm" (*PEN* 1) is of the poststructuralist or postmodern (*PEN* 13) variety he associates primarily with the names of Levinas and Derrida. He has no room for such philosophers as Alasdair MacIntyre, Richard Rorty and Martha Nussbaum, all of whom made somewhat earlier moves in the direction of literary ethics. One *might* think that the advocates of the more recent turn would be grateful for these earlier initiatives, but they are not. Not, at any rate, those who think like Gibson. Here, as he sees it, is the problem:

> Rorty and Nussbaum are by no means ignorant of contemporary developments in literary theory ... Nonetheless, in their own accounts of the novel, they appear to turn away from later theory to

an earlier tradition as explicitly instanced by Rorty in the names of "Leavis, Eliot, Edmund Wilson, Lionel Trilling, Frank Kermode, Harold Bloom." (*PEN* 8)

The problem, then, is that "for all their knowledge of post-structuralism, Rorty and Nussbaum's effective sense of the novel and the ethics of fiction is rather pre-structuralist" (*PEN* 8-9)—like MacIntyre's. So that, according to Gibson, whereas the "*philosopher* may feel that he or she is on new ground ..., [m]ost literary theorists or critics will not" (my italics, *PEN* 9).

The implication would seem to be that because MacIntyre, Rorty and Nussbaum are thought to be pre-structuralist, they are no more worth listening to—not if we are seeking ethical enlightenment—than the literary critics (from Leavis to Bloom) singled out by Rorty. Whatever the differences between them, they all occupy old ground. The ground has shifted, and the result is that these two groups of critics (together with the approaches they represent) have been rendered largely irrelevant.

There are, to put it mildly, a number of ironies here. For one thing, the differences between these philosophers—between Rorty's brand of pragmatism and the two distinct brands of Aristotelianism practised by MacIntyre and Nussbaum—are significant. But the irony I want to focus on concerns Gibson's belief that the ethical position *he* advocates (and thinks of as postructuralist or postmodern) marks a complete break with earlier forms of ethics. Insofar as the position in question is the Levinasian-Derridean one, I intend to show that Gibson is mistaken about this. I plan to do so, however, by turning *not* to Rorty, MacIntyre and Nussbaum (though I will be keeping Aristotelianism in mind and bringing MacIntyre into the discussion a bit later) but rather to one of that older generation of literary critics.

The fact is that no other literary critic has made so powerful a case as Leavis has done for the importance of literature and of literary study. If, moreover, as Leavis observed when explaining the lecture format he used to compose *Nor Shall My Sword*, the "repeated adducing of certain decisive names—for instance, Blake, Dickens, Lawrence and Shakespeare—had, for a public exposed to the higher name-dropping and the practice of poly-intellectual smatter, its point" (*NS* 30), then it's worth noting that it is simply impossible to talk about Leavis for more than a sentence or two without adducing one or another of these (and other related) "decisive names"—and today this has, if anything, an even greater point.

The literature that matters to Leavis can be seen (in Alain Badiou's terminology) as being made up of a series of truth-events. As Badiou understands it, an "event" occurs when something happens that "compels us to decide a *new* way of being." Here is part of his explanation:

> Such events are well and truly attested: the French Revolution of 1792, the meeting of Héloïse and Abélard, Galileo's creation of physics, Haydn's invention of the classical musical style...But also: the Cultural Revolution in China (1965-67), a personal amorous passion, the creation of Topos theory by the mathematician Grothendieck, the invention of the twelve-tone scale by Schoenberg...[Badiou's ellipses]
>
> From which "decision," then, stems the process of a truth? From the decision to relate henceforth to the situation *from the perspective of its evental [évenementiel] supplement*. Let us call this a fidelity. To be faithful to an event is to move within the situation that this event has supplemented, by *thinking* (although all thought is a practice, a putting to the test) the situation "according to" the event...
>
> It is clear that under the effect of a loving encounter, if I want to be *really* faithful to it, I must completely rework my ordinary way of "living" my situation...Berg and Webern, faithful to the musical event known by the name of "Schoenberg," cannot continue with *fin-de-siècle* neo-Romanticism as if nothing had happened...
>
> I shall call "truth" (*a* truth) the real process of a fidelity to an event: that which this fidelity *produces* in the situation.[37]

If, in other words, Berg and Webern continued "with *fin-de-siècle* neo-Romanticism as if nothing had happened," then for them—since they were not faithful to it—"Schoenberg" did *not* constitute a truth-event. And for Leavis, who (with Badiou in mind, it seems important to point out) practiced and stated "the invariant traits of what can be called the militant figure" (*Saint Paul* 2),[38] much the same applies to those writers who came after T.S.Eliot and D.H.Lawrence.

So that in focusing on Leavis, I also plan to show that much more is at stake than the possible rehabilitation of one critic's reputation: most importantly, the question as to whether or not we are ready to start listening again to some of those poets and novelists to whom, according to both sets of the critics Gibson stigmatizes, we *ought* to be turning, or indeed returning.

One other thing. Gibson attempts to distance himself from Leavis by explaining that he (Gibson) uses "the word ethics...rather than [what he takes to be] his [i.e., Leavis's] preferred term, morality" (*PEN* 1). Gibson tells us that he wants "to insist...on the crucial distinction between ethics and morality," the gist of which he describes (with the help of Geoffrey Galt Harpham and others) as follows:

> Ethics ... operates a kind of play within morality, holds it open, hopes to restrain it from violence or the will to domination ... In the terms of Derrida's engagement with Kierkegaard in *The Gift of Death*—an engagement conducted partly *via* Levinas—the ethical recognition is not of the Kierkegaardian either/or, but of "the paradox of Abraham"... So, too, [Drucilla] Cornell associates ethics (as articulated by Adorno and Levinas) with the undetermined, and morality with deontology, with the determination of the undetermined, as duties, obligations, systems, rules, norms, "a right way to behave." (*PEN* 15–16)

But almost everyone who writes on the subject feels the need to make *some* such distinction as this one, if not necessarily between ethics and morality, then between the moral and the moralistic; or (as Thomas Keenan would have it) between the ethico-political and "the discourse of grounds, morality, and good conscience."[39] And what Gibson doesn't seem to realize is that Leavis is no exception to this. What Gibson also shows no sign of realizing is that the "encounter with alterity" that he tells us "is central to Levinas's thought" (*PEN* 25) is central to Leavis's thought too, at least from the publication of his first essay on D.H. Lawrence's *The Rainbow* onwards.[40]

But before looking at the relevant section of Leavis's discussion of this novel, it is worth pausing for a moment to note just how appropriate it is that he should have had his first major encounter with alterity while working on this work. Because if one work of literature anticipates more than any other the late twentieth-century interest in otherness (including much of the terminology in which it got expressed) it is probably *The Rainbow*.

(b) "The Rainbow" and Leavis's response to it

It's a queer thing is a man's soul. It is the whole of him. Which means it is the unknown him, as well as the known ... Why the soul of man is a vast forest, and all Benjamin [Franklin] intended was a neat back garden...
     Here's my creed, against Benjamin's. This is what I believe:

                    ...

   "That my known self will never be more than a little clearing in the forest."
   "That gods, strange gods, come forth from the forest into the clearing of my known self, and then go back."
   "That I must have the courage to let them come and go"
                              —D.H.Lawrence[41]

[B]etween man and woman, the ultimate anchorage of real alterity.
                              — Luce Irigaray[42]

[T]he notion of the "outside" is expressed in many European languages by a word that means "at the door" (*fores* in Latin is the door of the house, *thyrathen* in Greek literally means "at the threshold").
                              —Giorgio Agamben[43]

The novel follows the fortunes of three generations of the Brangwen family and it opens by making a distinction between the men and women of the first generation. While both the men and the women have "a look in the eyes...as if they were expecting something unknown," [44] and while they both have on them "the drowse of blood-intimacy" (10), the women are on the whole more drawn to "the world beyond," to the battle "being waged on the edge of the unknown," to "the wonder of the beyond" (11, 13) than their men are. Tom Brangwen is an important exception to this as the heading of the first chapter ("How Tom Brangwen Married a Polish Lady") indicates. But even in this case, it's worth noting that it is the woman, Lydia, who turns out to be stronger, just as, in later generations, Anna is stronger than Will and Ursula than Anton. Thus, for example, at the end of chapter three, Tom finds that Lydia is "again the active unknown facing him. Must he admit her?" (88) "I want you to know," she tells him, "there is somebody there besides yourself" (89). In other words, she wants him to recognize her otherness. But he finds this difficult to do: precisely because she is "other than himself," going "to meet her" means venturing into "the awful unknown," which is "awful" because he would (on some level) prefer to remain "himself, apart," he is "afraid" and wants "to save himself" (90, 89, 90). Nevertheless, they do come together and the result is described as follows:

> They had passed through the doorway into the further space... She was the doorway to him, he to her. At last they had thrown open the doors, each to the other, and had stood in the doorways facing each other, whilst the light flooded out from behind on to each of their faces, it was the transfiguration, the glorification, the admission. It is as if God has "passed through the married pair without fully making Himself known to them" (91).

Unfortunately, however, the kind of satisfaction Tom and Lydia achieve two years into their marriage (for Tom she is "the gateway and the way out" so that he is able to travel "in her through the beyond"; "When she called, he answered, when he asked, her response came at once, or at length" [91]) proves elusive to Anna and Will, and even more so to Ursula and Anton. It is true that, in each case, near the beginning of the relationship, there are moments when the man appears full of promise: "Sometimes, when he [Will] stood in the doorway, his face lit up, he seemed like an Annunciation to her" (158); "There had," after Anton turns up, "been a Visit paid to the house. Once three angels stood in Abraham's doorway, and greeted him, and stayed and ate with him, leaving his household enrichened for ever when they went" (271). But though each case is different, it seems fair to say that at a certain point what we are told about Anna (that she relinguishes "the adventure to the unknown" [182]) applies to both Will and Anton as well. Actually, I want to return to say one more thing about Anna in my Conclusion but for now I will content myself with a few more comments on Anton.

"Ah," Ursula thinks in the penultimate chapter, "if he had only remained true to her...[h]e would have been her angel...if he had remained true to her, he would have been the doorway to her" (406). But Anton does not remain true, either to her or to himself. In Alain Badiou's terminology, we can say that Anton refuses to become "a subject of truth," since this would have meant "exposing himself 'entirely' to a post-evental fidelity" and to "the problem of knowing what he [would] *become* through [such a] testing experience" (*Ethics* 46). Whereas, according to Badiou, the "ordinary behaviour of the human animal is a matter of what Spinoza calls 'perseverance in being,' which is nothing other than the pursuit of interest, or the conservation of self"; and whereas this "is the law that governs some-one in so far as he knows himself"; "the test of truth does not fall under this law"—it falls instead under "a *law of the not-known* [*de l'insu*]" (Ibid). Badiou tells us that "Lacan touched on this point when he proposed his ethical maxim: 'do not give up on your desire' ['*ne pas céder sur son désir*']":

> For desire is constitutive of the subject of the unconscious; it is thus the not-known *par excellence*, such that "do not give up on your desire" rightly means: "do not give up on that part of yourself that you do not know." We might add that the ordeal of the not-known is the distant effect of the eventual supplement...and that "do not give up" means, in the end: do not give up on your own seizure by a truth-process. (47)[45]

In effect, the difference between Ursula and Anton is that he gives up and she doesn't on that part of ourselves that we don't know. One of the ways Lawrence makes this plain is in terms of Ursula's resistance to the idea that "[w]e move and live and have our being within the light...the eternal light of knowledge" (*R* 406). She resists this because she sees "the eyes of the wild beast gleaming from the darkness, watching the vanity of the camp fire and the sleepers; she felt the strange, foolish vanity of the camp, which said 'Beyond our light and our order there is nothing'" (405). Ursula is among those who, "having given up their vanity of the light, having died in their own conceit, [have seen] the gleam in the eyes of the wolf and the hyena, that it was the flash of the sword of angels, flashing at the door to come in ..." (406). Whereas, although there are moments when Anton seems at home in "the universal night" and waiting for Ursula in "the other darkness" (416), and although he knows that "[n]o highest good of the community would...give him the fulfilment of his soul," in the last analysis he doesn't consider "the soul of the individual sufficiently important" and all that ultimately matters to him is "fill[ing] one's place in the whole, the great scheme of man's elaborate civilisation" (305, 304). In effect, Anton agrees with Hegel that "the whole is the true," while Ursula (and Lawrence) side with the Adorno who was to invert Hegel's dictum by proclaiming that '[t]he whole is the false" (*Minima Moralia* 50). "He [Anton] was always," we are told, "side-tracking, always side-tracking his own soul" (411).[46] And so after Ursula rejects him he decides, therefore, to marry someone else, "quickly, to screen himself from the darkness, the challenge for his own soul" (447).

We can now look at Leavis's discussion in the early 1950s of the passage in the opening chapter of *The Rainbow,* which begins with Tom Brangwen seeing the Polish lady, Lydia Lensky, for the first time and ends with his going to ask her to marry him.

Having earlier made the point that "Lawrence belongs to the same ethical and religious tradition as George Eliot,"[47] when Leavis moves into his discussion of the passage in question, he claims that a "great difference" between these two great writers is to be found in the fact that we can't say of Lawrence what "has been said of George Eliot, by way of a limiting judgment, that the word for her is 'ethical' rather than 'religious'" (*DHL: N* 110). What, he then explains, "strikes us as religious is the intensity with which his men and women, hearkening to their deepest needs and promptings as they seek 'fulfilment' in marriage, know that they 'do not belong to themselves,' but are responsible to something that, in transcending the individual, transcends love and sex too" (*DHL:N* 111). In the first instance, Leavis is drawing on the following paragraph:

But during the long February nights with the ewes in labour, looking out from the shelter into the flashing stars, he [Tom

Brangwen] knew he did not belong to himself. He must admit that he was only fragmentary, something incomplete and subject. There were the stars in the dark heaven travelling, the whole host passing by on some eternal voyage. So he sat small and submissive to the greater ordering. (*R* 40)

At the same time, Leavis is also referring here to the whole ten or eleven page sequence (29-44), in which Tom Brangwen might be said to be responding to the call of the Other—the Other as manifested primarily (i) in Lydia Lensky (whose "foreignness," as Leavis points out, "emphasizes the theme of 'otherness'" [*DHL:N* 114]) but also in both (ii) "the greater order" of the stars (*R* 40) and (iii) within Tom, "in the depths of his stillness" (41).

Or to put it another way, what this sequence dramatizes is (in Derrida's words) "a singular event," "the coming of the other" (*FK* 17); "an event, the sudden coming of the new, of that which cannot be anticipated or repeated...a surprise" (*GT* 146). Derrida insists, in fact, that the "coming of the other can only emerge as a singular event when no anticipation sees it coming" (*FK* 17). There is little we can do to bring it about, other than to make the paradoxical kind of "decision that can consist in letting the other come and that can take the apparently passive form of the other's decision: even there where it appears in itself, in me, the decision is moreover always that of the other, which does not exonerate me of responsibility" (Ibid).

My point, then, is that all of this seems strikingly relevant both to Lawrence's novel and to Leavis's commentary on it. As for the latter, we have only to think of what Leavis has to say about the presence of something "religious" in Lawrence ("the intensity with which his men and women...know that they 'do not belong to themselves,' but are responsible to something ..."). What is Leavis drawing attention to here if not the "structure of experience" that Derrida calls "messianic" and that Derrida too thinks of as in some sense "religious" (*Specters* 166-67)—while insisting that it doesn't refer to any particular religion?

The "apparently passive form" of the "decision" is significant too, especially in view of Derrida's claim that the "passive decision" is a (or the) "condition of the event" (qtd. in Žižek, *OB* 148).[48] Once again, if the event we have in mind is the one that brings Tom Brangwen and Lydia Lensky together, this seems especially suggestive. Think, for example, of the following excerpts:

> "That's her," he said involuntarily... (*R* 29)
>
> It was coming, he knew, his fate. The world was submitting to its transformation. He made no move: it would come, what would come... (32)
>
> He submitted to that which was happening to him, letting go of his will, suffering the loss of himself... (38)
>
> It happened she came down to the Marsh with the child whilst he was in this state ... And then it came upon him that he would marry her and she would be his life... (39)
>
> One evening in March, when the wind was roaring outside, came the moment to ask her.... And as he watched the fire, he knew almost without thinking that he was going this evening... (40)

According to Derrida, there can be "no event without the surprise of a gift" (*GT* 119). Judging by the way he has written this episode, Lawrence would seem to agree. And if we ask who or what *gives* the gift or gifts in question (of Tom to Lydia and Lydia to Tom), then Lawrence's answer ("It was coming," "It happened" etc.) is essentially the same as Heidegger's: "*It gives*" (qtd. in *GT* 20–21).[49]

If, therefore, as Leavis says, "it is the arduously achieved wholeness of resolution in him [Tom] that acts" (*DHL:N* 114), then this "resolution" ("He was a long time resolving definitely ..." [*R* 40]) is "something that entails the opposite of any assertion of will or of self" (*DHL:N* 116). Which is, I take it, another way of saying that the resolution is somehow passive.[50]

(c) On Blake, Lawrence, Dickens and T.S.Eliot

> Wonder ... constitutes an *opening* ...
>
> —Irigaray[51]

> Wonder is the welcoming apprehension of the new...
>
> —Leavis (*NS* 15)

What we can begin to see here—in his first engagement with this key passage in *The Rainbow*—is the emergence of a new definition of what was later to become a crucial term for Leavis, just as it is also a crucial term in the thought of Levinas and Derrida: responsibility. If so, however, it is, in Leavis's case, the kind of definition that draws heavily on a process he finds at work in certain novelists and poets when they take words (such as "life") that are "unsusceptible of what is ordinarily meant by definition" and give them "a potent definition in the concrete," which he also refers to as "definition by creative means."[52] Thus, for example, after claiming that "Lawrence might have said of his own works what Blake said of his paintings and designs: 'though I call them mine, I know that they are not not mine,' Leavis goes on to explain that it "is the Blake corroborated and reinforced by Lawrence that [he has] in mind when [he] contend[s] that what desperately needs to be emphasized in the present plight of mankind is the essential human creativity that is human responsibility ..." (*NS* 19). Leavis associates this "*new* sense of responsibility that we may reasonably see as the momentous gain accruing to the heritage ... from ...'Romanticism'" (my italics, *NS* 12) with the Blakean "identity,"[53] thus distinguishing it from another kind of responsibility that he associates with "the closed ego—Blake's 'selfhood'"[54]:

> For [Blake's] Urizen, who in *Hard Times* appears as Gradgrind, the important thing is that life shall be known, its possibilities determined, so that the human individual as selfhood—which is what is given in Urizen—can feel protected by known law (in both senses of the word) from the new, unprecedented and unplaced. "Louisa, never wonder!" says Mr Gradgrind sternly to his deplorably youthful daughter. Responsibility in this [Gradgrindian] sense means scrupulous deference towards the laws that limit possibility, and towards the formulated definitions that chart the actual and may be taken as the real reality. (*NS* 14-15)

As for the Blakean kind of responsibility, Leavis immediately follows the above with this:

> What "wonder" means is what is given us in that creative lapse, or escape, from Eliotic habit, the unique and lovely "Marina," which opens:

> *What seas what shores what grey rocks and what islands*
> *What water lapping the bow*

and, but for the brief recall of the opening that forms the three-line coda, ends

> *The awakenened, lips parted, the hope, the new ships.*
> Wonder is the welcoming apprehension of the new, the anti-Urizenic recognition of the divined possibility... (*NS* 15)

To put it simply, then, what distinguishes these two kinds of responsibility is that one is open and responsive to otherness and one is not. And, as we have just seen, one at least of the ways in which the new sense of responsibility is to be understood as manifesting itself is in the kind of welcoming apprehension of otherness that we more commonly think of as wonder. But though this is vitally important, it would be misleading to leave the matter here.

We need to get a clearer idea of just how *disturbing* this new sense of responsibility to otherness can sometimes be in practice. And the best way to start doing this is to note Leavis's insistence that there is an "immeasurable distance" between "the meaning of 'responsibility' in the profound Laurentian [or Blakean] sense of the word" and "anything suggested by 'duty'" (*TWC* 126). In the immediate context it is clear that Leavis is specifically thinking here of the case of Anton Skrebensky (of *The Rainbow*). But he does say "*anything* suggested by 'duty'" and so the point I want to make is that the distinction he insists on here (between responsibility and duty) becomes more worrying if we reflect on some of the characters doing their duty in, say, *Middlemarch*. Think, for example, of the endings of chapters 42 and 74 where we see first Dorothea and then Mrs Bulstrode standing by their husbands. In each case the epigraph from Shakespeare's *Henry V111* to chapter 42 ("How much, methinks, I could despise this man,/Were I not bound in charity against it!") applies directly to the situation. It is difficult, at these two junctures, *not* to despise Mr Casaubon and Mr Bulstrode but their wives nevertheless stand by them. Or think of Mr Farebrother's self-sacrificing mission[55] to the woman he loves, Mary Garth, on Fred Vincy's behalf in chapter 52 ("His heart," the chapter's epigraph from Wordsworth reads, "The lowliest duties on itself did lay"). In his *Reading Derrida/Thinking Paul*, Theodore Jennings devotes his fifth chapter to "Derrida's reflections on a duty beyond debt," which Jennings characterizes as "an attempt to think something like obligation beyond the economy of debt and exchange" (96). It seems to me that in all three of these examples we have something very much like this: an obligation, yes ("Were I not *bound* in charity"), but in each case, since it is so marked by the "excess and abundance" Jennings associates with "the gift character of grace" (91), it seems to go way "beyond the economy of debt and exchange."

Nevertheless, on the one hand, we have the "ethical" characterized by "duty," as exemplified, at its most impressive, let's say, by George Eliot's Dorothea Brooke and Daniel Deronda and much less impressively by Lawrence's Anton Skrebensky; while, on the other, we have the "religious" characterized by Blakean or Lawrentian "responsibility," as exemplified for the late Leavis most dramatically and challengingly by the young captain in Conrad's *The Secret Sharer.*

(d) Pure (unconditional) hospitality, the messianic, judgment and decision: On "The Secret Sharer"

Kierkegaard sees acting "out of duty," in the universalizable sense of the law, as a dereliction of one's absolute duty...The sacrifice of Isaac belongs to what one might just dare to call the common treasure, the terrifying secret of the *mysterium tremendum* that is a property of all three so-called religions of the Book, the religions of the races of Abraham. This rigor, and the exaggerated demands it entails, compel the knight of faith to say and to do things that will appear (and must be) atrocious. They will necessarily revolt those who profess allegiance to morality in general, to Judeo-Christian-Islamic morality, or to the religion of love in general. But as [Jan] Patocka will say, perhaps Christianity has not yet thought through its own essence ...The absolutes of duty and of responsibility presume that one denounce, refute, and transcend, at the same time, all duty, all responsibility, and every human law ... In a word, ethics must be sacrificed in the name of duty.

—Jacques Derrida (*GD* 63, 64, 66–7)

[In *The Secret Sharer*] the young Conrad-Captain [is] for us, in
the testing situation, the presence of life ... as human responsibility focused in the individual being, one who so patently knows
that he "does not belong to himself" ... he deliberately puts the
ship he commands in desperate hazard, and outrages the master
mariner's morality ... I think of Blake: "I tell you, no virtue can
exist without breaking these ten commandments." But Conrad
leaves it not for a moment in doubt that the *Conway* code isn't
merely something to be broken. That it isn't is necessary to the
paradox.... The *Conway* stands for the community...that gives
responsibility its collaboratively creative background...This community is figured by the Merchant Service ...

—F.R.Leavis (*LP* 46, 47, 48)

The essential character of messianism may well be precisely its
particular relation to the law. In Judaism as in Christianity and
Shiite Islam, the messianic event above all signifies a crisis and
radical transformation of the entire order of the law.

—Georgio Agamben[56]

Part of my aim in this section is to show how Joseph Conrad's *The
Secret Sharer* and F.R.Leavis's reading of it together work to support what
Jacques Derrida claims is jointly demonstrated by the Biblical account
of Abraham preparing to sacrifice his son Isaac and Kierkegaard's commentary on this in his *Fear and Trembling*: namely, that "the concepts of
responsibility, of decision, or of duty, are condemned a priori to paradox,
scandal, and aporia" (*GD* 68). On the face of it, my contention may well
seem highly improbable since Conrad's novella does *not* have a structure
at all similar to that of the story of Abraham and Isaac, nor of course is it
immediately obvious that it has any kind of religious resonance. I realise,
furthermore, that some are likely to be initially sceptical when I say that
the structure the novella *does* have is that of (what, with Derrida and Emmanuel Levinas in mind, we might call) the Hospitality narrative, more
specifically, the *kind* of Hospitality narrative that takes the form of Welcoming the Other or Stranger (who may just turn out to be the Messiah).
This too might seem unlikely since the best-known reading of this novella
is the one found in the Introduction to the Signet edition in which Albert

Guerard maintains that "*The Secret Sharer* is what is known as a 'double' story...our 'double' (Leggatt) is...the embodiment of [the young captain's] more instinctive, more primitive, less rational self."[57] But I don't deny that in one sense Leggatt is indeed the young captain's double; in fact, the reading I propose insists on this, as I argue (with the help of Giorgio Agamben's reflections on a "celestial double" or "angelic self" that "constitutes the supreme soteriological and messianic experience"[58]) that at the *same time* as Leggatt is the double he can and ought also, simultaneously, to be seen as the Other.

My larger aim, then, is to say something about the messianic and to do so by means of an interpretation of Conrad's *The Secret Sharer*. This being so, it seems to me appropriate to recall something Frank Kermode had to say back in 1979 about a "view of interpretation" that he called "an outsider's theory" and that "stems ultimately from a Protestant tradition, that of the devout dissenter animated only by the action of the spirit, abhorring the claim of the institution to an historically validated traditional interpretation. It may," Kermode reflected, "be the end of that tradition; for I do not see how, finally, it can distinguish between sacred and secular texts, those works of the worldly canon that also appear to possess inexhaustible hermeneutic potential. (Heidegger's own exegeses of Hölderlin treat the text exactly as if it were sacred.)"[59] With this in mind, I want to make it plain that I do not think of *The Secret Sharer* as a sacred text. But on the other hand, I admit that I *have* come to think of it as a kind of parable, one that is comparable in stature to the "famous parable in Kafka's *The Trial*" on which Kermode comments ("Before the Law" being "a good deal longer than any biblical parable" and thus reminding us "that in principle parable may escape restrictions of length" [27,28]). It seems to me that *The Secret Sharer* deserves a literary critical reading that will take it with the kind of seriousness that philosophers like Derrida and Agamben have brought to their readings of Kafka's "Before the Law," with, for example, Agamben seeing "this parable" as "an allegory of the state of law in a messianic age" ("Messiah" 172).

This is a story of how a young man prepared himself to take his first voyage as a sea captain. Since he was, therefore, at the time "untried...by a position of the fullest responsibility" and, "at the threshold of a long passage," there was a real question in his mind as to whether or not he would manage to measure up. In fact, having "been appointed to the command only a fortnight before," he tells us that he felt "a stranger to the ship" and "somewhat of a stranger to [him]self."[60] His decision "to take a five hours' anchor watch on [him]self" (*TSS* 22) meant that, without thinking about possible consequences, he started off by preventing things being "properly attended to" (24). As a result of this, "the rope side ladder...had not been hauled in as it should have been" and, given the captain's belief that "exactitude in small matters is the very soul of discipline," he found himself wondering if "it was wise ever to interfere with the established routine of duties" (23–4).

Since there would be no story if the rope side ladder had not been left out, we can begin by raising the question as to whether this mightn't be more than just a crucial plot device. I suggest that we consider the possible relevance here of the "well-known parable about the Kingdom of the Messiah" that Agamben tells us Walter Benjamin once recounted to Ernest Bloch:

> A rabbi, a real cabalist, once said that in order to establish the reign of peace it is not necessary to destroy everything nor to begin a completely new world. It is sufficient to displace this cup or this bush or this stone just a little, and thus everything. But this small displacement is so difficult to achieve and its measure is so difficult to find that, with regard to the world, humans are incapable of it and it is necessary that the Messiah come. (*CC* 53)

Agamben claims that the "tiny displacement" that radically transforms everything "does not refer to the *state* of things, but to their sense and their limits. It does not take place *in* things, but at their periphery" (my italics 54). If we take the ship to be the "thing" in question here, then the small displacement that is constituted by the ladder's being left out—and therefore where (at that time) it oughtn't to have been—this might well be said to occur at the ship's limit or periphery, in the same way that a door might be said to be at the limit or periphery of a house. Furthermore, leaving the ladder out is like leaving a door open, which means that—without realizing or having planned it—the captain has set the stage for the possible arrival of the Other. When he goes to haul the ladder in himself, he then discovers that the Other has in fact arrived, in the form of a swimmer who is "floating very close to the ladder" (*TSS* 24). It is true, of course, that this is not followed by "the reign of peace" and I am not claiming that what we have here is "that 'small adjustment' in which, according to the rabbi's saying told by Benjamin, the messianic kingdom *consists*" (Agamben, *Potentialities*, my italics 174). At this point I am merely suggesting that the story's opening *could* (not unreasonably) be construed as intended to alert us to the possibility that the Other might turn out to have certain things in common with the Messiah, including, for example, the fact that he does, after all, arrive "like a thief in the night" (*1 Thessalonians* 5:2).

Now it seems to me that we may be better able to appreciate what is at stake in the captain's encounter with the stranger at the end of the ladder if we consider it in the light of the concern Richard Kearney has expressed that deconstruction appears to "leave us open to all comers":

> Derrida acknowledges the terrifying riskiness of undecidable-un-identifiable "newcomers" when he concedes that we have no way of telling the difference between the demonic and divine other. "For pure hospitality or pure gift to occur there must be absolute surprise ... an opening without horizon of expectation ... to the newcomer whoever that may be. The newcomer may be good or evil, but if you exclude the possibility that the newcomer is coming to destroy your house, if you want to control this and exclude this terrible possibility in advance, there is no hospitality ... The other, like the Messiah, must arrive whenever he or she wants."[61]

In the exchange that followed Kearney's paper, Derrida responds to Kearney's concern first by admitting he is "not sure there is pure hospitality" and then by maintaining that "if we want to understand what hospitality means, we have to think of unconditional hospitality, that is, openness to whomever, to any newcomer."[62]

My point is that this is precisely what Conrad's story enables us to do. In effect, this is another good way of describing the subject (pure, unconditional hospitality) he too is exploring.

When the captain first sees the stranger in the water below, he has no way of knowing whether the man is good or evil. The captain nonetheless welcomes him on board, unhesitatingly. This is so striking that it will be worth pausing again for a moment to ponder the relevance of some sentences from Derrida's commentary on the "Cities of Refuge" chapter of Levinas's *Beyond the Verse*:

> When someone once expressed concern to Levinas about the "phantomatic character" of his philosophy, especially when it treats the "face of the other," Levinas did not directly object. Resorting to what I have just called the "Pascalian" argument ("it is necessary that the other be welcomed independently of his qualities"), he clearly specified "welcomed," especially in an "immediate," urgent way, without waiting, as if "real" qualities, attributes, or properties (everything that makes a living person into something other than a phantom) slowed down, mediatized, or compromise the purity of this welcome. It is necessary to welcome the other in his alterity, without waiting, and thus not to pause to recognize his real predicates. [63]

Of course, it is true that, after the captain has taken the stranger to his cabin, he quickly learns not only the latter's name but also that Leggatt has killed a man. At this point it is obvious what, from an ordinary or conventional moral or ethical point of view, the captain should do. He should hand Leggatt over to the law. But, instead of doing this, he helps Leggatt escape. This means that the captain is risking—if he is discovered—legal punishment himself, as well, of course, as the loss of his position as captain.

As Levinas has noted, the Bible "says that there are a variety of ways to kill" (*Righteous?* 132) and, in the circumstances, it seems appropriate to glance at one of Levinas's Talmudic readings (more specifically at a few sentences from his commentary on an excerpt from the Tractate Makkoth 10a that focuses on the idea of cities of refuge—"a biblical institution discussed in Numbers 35"):

> When a murder is committed as an unwitting act of homicide; when, for example—a biblical example—an axe-head comes away from its handle during the work of the woodcutter and deals a mortal blow to a passer-by, this murder cannot be pursued before the court of judgement. This "objective" murder is committed without intent to harm. However, a close relation of the victim,

called an "avenger of blood"—or, more exactly, a *go'el hadam*, a "redeemer of spilt blood," whose "heart is heated" by the murder committed (*ki yicham levavo*)—has the right to carry out an act of vengeance. A certain right, beyond the public right of the court, is thus recognized for the "heat of the heart"...But...[a]gainst this marginal right, there is the right proper to protect the manslayer. The law of Moses designates cities of refuge where the manslayer takes refuge or is exiled...The "avenger of blood" can no longer pursue the murderer who has taken refuge in a city of refuge; but for the manslayer, who is also a murderer through negligence, the city of refuge is also an exile: a punishment.[64]

As I see it, then, in *The Secret Sharer*, the skipper of the *Sephora* who comes looking for Leggatt functions a little bit like the "avenger of blood" from whose clutches the young captain saves Leggat. Except of course that the *Sephora's* skipper represents not just a "marginal right" but the full force of the law. And it's also true that the manner in which Leggatt kills is very different to the biblical example of the axe-head accidentally coming away from its handle. But let's look at what he himself has to say about the incident. First of all, by way of preparing the captain, Leggatt tells him that his victim "was one of those creatures that are just simmering all the time with a silly sort of wickedness. Miserable devils that have no business to live at all. He wouldn't do his duty and wouldn't let anyone else do theirs" (*TSS* 27). Leggatt then offers the following account:

> It happened while we were setting a reefed foresail, at dusk. Reefed foresail! You understand the sort of weather. The only sail we had left to keep the ship running; so you may guess what it had been like for days...He gave me some of his cursed insolence at the sheet. I tell you I was overdone with this terrific weather that seemed to have no end to it...It was no time for gentlemanly reproof, so I turned round and felled him like an ox. He up and at me. We closed just as an awful sea made for the ship. All hands saw it coming and took to the rigging, but I had him by the throat, and went on shaking him like a rat...Then a crash as if the sky had fallen on my head. They say that for over ten minutes hardly anything was to be seen of the ship—just the three masts and a bit

of the forecastle head and of the poop all awash driving along in a smother of foam. It was a miracle that they found us, jammed together behind the forebitts. It's clear that I meant business, because I was holding him by the throat still when they picked us up. He was black in the face. It was too much for them. (28)

Was this "an unwitting act of homicide"? Leggatt's "[i]t's clear that I meant business" does not, in my view, conclusively prove that it was not. As I understand it, his point is that that is how it *looks* and that, in the face of this, his chances of getting a fair trial are minimal. The captain obviously agrees with this and presumably also believes Leggatt when the latter adds the information that "that foresail saved the ship" and "it was I that managed to set it" (31). All of this helps explain why he decides to protect Leggatt and to save him for his punishment of choice. In effect, it is as if, for both the captain and Leggatt, the law is "*in force [but] without significance,*" which is, according to Agamben, "[Gershom] Scholem's formula for the status of law in Kaka's novel [*The Trial*]."[65] Thus, with reference to "[t]he 'brand of Cain' business," Leggatt tells the captain that he is "ready to go off wandering on the face of the earth—and [that] that was price enough to pay for an Abel of that sort" (*TSS* 32). So at the end the captain leaves him "to be a fugitive and a vagabond on the earth, with no brand of the curse on his sane forehead to stay a slaying hand" (60).

Or as Derrida puts it in his commentary on Levinas, on the one hand, "shelter must be given to one who is guilty of an involuntary act, immunity, at least a temporary immunity, must be granted to a murderer" (*Adieu* 112); while on the other hand "by limiting the time of asylum offered to the murderer it [the counter-right] allows asylum to be turned into exile—and hospitality into punishment" (108).

We can now turn first to the lecture Leavis devoted to this work in 1966 (and published the following year in *"Anna Karenina" and Other Essays*) before looking a little later at his subsequent reflections on it, first in *The Living Principle* (1975) and then (more briefly) in *Thought, Words and Creativity* (1976).

In the lecture's opening paragraph, Leavis suggests that the "young captain of *The Secret Sharer* faces in a protracted way the moral problem faced by the young captain of *The Shadow-Line* when appealed to by the sick mate, Mr Burns, not to leave him behind in hospital":

His duty as a ship's master is not to listen; not to burden further the over-burdened crew with another sick and helpless man. But the young captain finds himself compelled by a finer ethic, finds himself as a seaman so compelled, not to leave Mr Burns behind.... The equivalent is the main theme of *The Secret Sharer*.[66]

For Leavis, in other words, it is a matter of a conflict between two ethics that is resolved when the "finer ethic" is accepted. But it is precisely this "finer ethic" that is so disturbing.

In the event, as Leavis says, Conrad's "main emphasis...falls on the lengths to which the young captain, in response to his profoundest ethical sense, is prepared to go" to save Leggatt "from 'justice.'" In the end, he even "risks the ship" (*SS* 117).

Why does the captain do all of this for Leggatt? In large part, it is no doubt because he and Leggatt are "Conway boy[s]," which means that Leggatt is able to appeal to him as if their "experiences had been as identical as [their] clothes" (*TSS* 27-8). To use the captain's own word, it is as if they are "double[s]" of one another in a world that is uncomprehending and unappreciative of their distinction, a distinction that is obviously linked to class. "My father's a parson in Norfolk," Leggatt tells the captain before asking him if he sees Leggatt "before a judge and jury on that charge? For myself I can't see the necessity" (27). Neither, it turns out, can the captain, who "knew well enough the pestiferous danger of such a character [as the man Leggatt killed] where there are no means of legal repression. And I knew well enough also that my double was no homicidal villain" (28). There is good reason, it seems to me, to feel uneasy about this: it isn't difficult to see how the relationship between the two doubles *could* be interpreted as signifying nothing better than class privilege and the power of an old-boys' network. And of course Conrad's depiction of Leggat's mutinous crew *could* be taken to indicate a generally reactionary position.[67]

Underlying these legitimate concerns is a question concerning otherness, a question that gets sharpened when Leavis offers the following explanation for the captain's behaviour:

He sees in the double who killed a man an *alter ego*. "It might very well have been myself who had done it"—that is his attitude. He doesn't mean humbly that he might have been guilty; there's

no question of guilt by the ultimate criterion that's invoked in
Conrad's art. By which I don't mean that the spirit of it is *Jenseits
von Gut und Böse*. On the contrary, there is an insistence on the
inescapable need for individual moral judgment, and for moral
conviction that is strong and courageous enough to forget codes
and to defy law and codified morality and justice. (*SS* 114)

At first glance this might seem to settle the matter and in such a way as to
disqualify the reading I am proposing: far from being the captain's *Other*,
Leggatt firmly belongs to the category of the *Same* (which is precisely of
course what the word "double" suggested in the first place). It might be
tempting to look for support of this view in Drucilla Cornell's reminder
that, from Levinas's point of view, there "is always a trace of otherness that
cannot be captured by my 'identifying' with the Other in terms of mutual
recognition ... The basis of ethics," Cornell then claims, "is not identification with those we recognize as like ourselves, instead the ethical relation
inheres in the encounter with the Other, the stranger, whose face beckons
us to heed the call to responsibility."[68] But let's look at what (as he draws
on Derrida) John Caputo has to say about the *alter ego*:

> According to the paradoxical grammar and logic of an *alter ego*,
> which has to do with the alterity of a fellow human being, the
> otherness of something different, a mere thing or object, would
> not be nearly so other. So the other is "absolutely other" only if
> the other is the same. Otherwise the other will be *less* transcen-
> dent, not more, an animal or a thing, for example, the *tout autre*
> will make no sense, and "no ethics would be possible." (*Prayers
> and Tears* 22)[69]

I think this helps us to see how it is that—even if the captain does not
encounter Leggatt in anything like his *full* radical otherness and even
if he understands Leggatt much too quickly (the Conway boy being a
prime example of the kind of identity unmistakably constructed according to a sacrificial logic of opposition and exclusion)—even so, Leggatt
nevertheless still somehow manages to remain a version of (in Cornell's
words) "the Other, the stranger, whose face beckons us to heed the call
to responsibility."

I think there is a sense, then, in which we may have to recognize that Leggatt belongs *both* to the category of the Same *and* to that of the Other. But not only this: I also think that the form the Other in question takes can legitimately be seen as Messianic. To explain what I mean I will leave Derrida and Leavis aside for a moment as I turn for help to some texts by Giorgio Agamben; texts which I intend to take—indeed, as I see it, am forced by the additional, indispensable, illumination they throw on Conrad's novella to take—considerable liberties with.

(d.i.) Unfreezing the Messianic Event: Using Agamben to illuminate Conrad and Conrad to revise Agamben

What is an exception? The exception is a kind of exclusion. It is an individual case that is excluded from the general rule...[However] the exception is not simply excluded but is rather truly "taken outside," as is implied by the word's etymological root (*ex-capere*).
                       —Giorgio Agamben ("The Messiah and the Sovereign,"
                                                    Potentialities 162)[70]
Having struck with the law a lasting compromise, the [Christian] church has frozen the messianic event ...
                                                    —Giorgio Agamben[71]

The first of these texts occurs a quarter of the way into Agamben's "Walter Benjamin and the Demonic: Happiness and Historical Redemption" (*Potentialities* 138-59) and it begins with Agamben reflecting on an essay by Gershom Scholem entitled "Walter Benjamin and His Angel." More specifically, it begins with him reflecting on Scholem's brief reference to Benjamin's "personal angel," in which Agamben finds "a fusion of the ancient pagan and Neoplatonic motif of the *idios daimōn* of every man with the Jewish motif of the celestial image, *demuth* or *zelem*, in whose image each man is created" (145):

The Cabalists interpret the passage of Genesis 1:27, according to which "God created man in his own *zelem*, in the *zelem* of God created he him"...in the sense that the second *zelem* designates the originary angelic form (and, later, astral body) in the image of which each man is created ... The angel-*zelem* therefore constitutes a kind of alter ego, a celestial double and originary image in which each man existed in heaven and which also accompanies man on earth...(146)

What interests Agamben here should also be of interest to anyone trying to fathom the deeper significance of Conrad's novella: namely, "the link between this theme, which concerns, so to speak, the prehistory and pre-existence of man, and prophetic and redemptive motifs, which concern the destiny and salvation of man." As for the latter, Agamben eleborates on them as follows:

> In a Cabalistic anthology that dates from the end of the thirteenth century (*Shushan Sodoth*), prophecy appears as a sudden vision of one's own double...In another Cabalistic text (Isaac Cohen, c.1270), prophetic experience is described as a metamorphosis of man into his own angel ...
>
> This vision of one's own angelic self concerns not only prophetic knowledge. According to a tradition found in Gnostic, Manichean, Jewish, and Iranian texts, it consitutes the supreme soteriological and messianic experience. (146–7)

My suggestion is that we might try seeing Leggatt *both* as the captain's angelic self and also as his Messiah.

I say we should "try" to see him in this way because it is admittedly likely to require some effort. We first need to visit the ending of the brief thirteenth section of *The Coming Community*. This is the section on "Halos." It begins with the reflection we noted earlier on the "tiny displacement" in the parable about the Kingdom of the Messiah and it concludes with Agamben turning to St Thomas's treatise on angels in order to illustrate how we might understand the idea that this displacement takes place at the periphery of things, "in the space of ease between every thing and itself" (*CC* 54). "One can think of the halo," he suggests, "as a zone in which possibility and reality, potentiality and actuality, become indistinguishable":

> The being that has reached its end, that has consumed all of its possibilities, thus receives as a gift a supplemental possibility...

This imperceptible trembling of the finite that makes its limits indeterminate and allows it to blend, to make itself whatever, is the tiny displacement that every thing must accomplish in the messianic world. (56)

So where is there a halo in *The Secret Sharer*? There isn't one: not literally, at any rate. But it seems to me that the captain's description of what he sees in the extreme darkness when (perilously close to the land, with ship-wreck a real possibility) he desperately needs to see *something* (anything will do) that will show him whether the ship is moving; that what he sees then might reasonably remind us of a halo (at least if we can imagine a halo detached from a head):

> All at once my strained, yearning stare distinguished a white ob-ject floating within a yard of the ship's side. White on the black water. A phosphorescent flash under it. What was that thing?...I recognized my own floppy hat. It must have fallen off his head... and he didn't bother. Now I had what I wanted—the saving mark for my eyes. (*TSS*, Conrad's ellipses 60)

Of course, this makes it perfectly clear that what the captain is actually seeing is the hat he had given to Leggatt "to save his homeless head from the dangers of the sun" (60), the hat that now becomes "the saving mark" for the captain's eyes. And "now—behold—it was saving the ship" (60). In other words, just (to appropriate Agamben's language) when the cap-tain and his ship seemed to have "reached [their] end," to have "consumed all of [their] possibilities," at that precise moment the captain "receives as a gift a supplemental possibility," which enables him to prevent the ship from going through "the very gate of Erebus," "the gate of the everlast-ing night" (*TSS* 58, 60), and enables him instead to experience something we might not expect to find outside of "the messianic world" (Agamben again), namely, a "perfect communion," albeit, that "of a seaman with his first command" (*TSS* 61).

If Leggatt is arguably messiah-like insofar as he proves to be the cap-tain's salvation, it is also true that, for his part, the captain saves Leggatt, saves him from the prospect of imprisonment, trial by jury and legal sen-tencing. And if this is what the captain saves Leggatt *from*, what Leggatt is saved *for* ("to be hidden forever from all friendly faces, to be a fugitive and a vagabond on the earth, with no brand of the curse on his sane forehead to stay a slaying hand" [60]) is something remarkably similar to the kind of "bare life" that Agamben associates with "*homo sacer* (sacred man)," that "obscure figure of archaic Roman law, in which human life is included in the juridical order [*ordinamento*] solely in the form of its exclusion (that is, of its capacity to be killed)" (*HS* 8). Furthermore, though I don't recall Agamben making the connection himself, I, at least, am reminded (again) here of the famous passage (*Matthew* 25: 34-46) I quoted near the end of the opening chapter, the passage in which Christ claims that he has come (and by clear implication still comes) among us in the form of those who are hungry, thirsty, naked, imprisoned: in short, as "the least" socially impressive specimens of humananity.

But if Leggatt resembles the Messiah both in the way he saves the captain and also in the abjectness of his fate, what about the captain? Who does he resemble? It seems to me he is very much like Agamben's figure of the sovereign, the one who (in the words of Carl Schmitt) "decides on the state of exception" (qtd. in *HS* 11). According to Agamben, "the sovereign, having the legal power to suspend the validity of the law, legally places himself outside the law" (15). Even though Conrad's captain most certainly does not have the legal power to do so, he too of course "places himself outside the law" and he does so in order to make an exception for Leggatt. If, moreover, as Agamben claims, "the production of bare life is the originary activity of sovereignty" (*HS* 83), then we might say that this too effectively describes what the captain does for Leggatt.

One last point in this connection. As Agamben sees it, the condition in which we find ourselves today is one in which "everyone is bare life and a *homo sacer* for everyone else"; "today...we are all virtually *homines sacri*" (*HS* 106, 115).[72] I think this is a mistake. Even though the positioning in the world of almost all readers of this (and of thinkers like Agamben) is likely to be closer to that of the captain's crew than it is to the position of captain, it is also likely to be much closer to that of the captain than it is to the exiled condition of Leggatt at the end of the novella. And if there is indeed a sense in which it can be said that the captain *produces* the "bare life" that he has procured for Leggatt, there is another sense in which we need to recognize that Leggatt has in turn produced (in the sense of having made possible) the captain's newfound sovereignty. Dickens makes this clearer in the relationship that develops in *Great Expectations* between Pip (the blacksmith's apprentice who turns into a gentleman) and Abel Magwitch (the escaped convict who is responsible for bringing about Pip's transformation). After all, what is this great novel telling us if not that in 19th century England gentlemen and beggars (or convicts) are tied to one another by cords that normally remain invisible, cords that Dickens enables us to see? Most of us are much more fortunately positioned than Agamben's *homines sacri*—much closer to the positions occupied by Conrad's captain or Dickens's Pip than to those occupied by Leggatt (Conrad's Cain) or Abel[73]—but we may be more responsible for the fate of the latter than we are always ready to admit.

(d.ii.) Leavis, Derrida, Kierkegaard and Žižek on the religious suspension of the ethical

> Life is a travelling to the edge of knowledge, then a leap taken.
> —D.H.Lawrence ("The Crown," *RDP*, 262)

Back now to Derrida and Leavis, beginning with the latter's claim (in his 1966 lecture) that if the captain admits his responsibility for Leggatt he does not do so out of a (Levinasian) sense of guilt. Nor does he react in a (Nietzschean) spirit of being beyond good and evil. It is a matter of his assuming responsibility for making the kind of moral judgment that risks appearing *ir*responsible and *im*moral.

When Leavis returned to the story almost a decade later, in *The Living Principle*, he did so in order (among other reasons) to draw out the parallel between the young captain and the literary critic, which he had left more implicit in his first commentary. For our purposes here, what is especially striking about this is the extent to which what Leavis had to say about judgement anticipates what Derrida has to say about decision. Thus, having noted yet again the Blakean paradox ("Tho' I call them Mine, I know that they are not Mine"), and having claimed that one's "criterion for calling an artist major is whether his work prompts us to say it ... for him" (*LP* 44), Leavis makes the connection between Conrad's captain and the literary critic as follows:

My critical judgment is mine, in the sense that I can't take over anyone else's (if I did, it would cease to be a judgment). But it is not merely or possessively "mine"; my implicit assumption being that it is right, "I know that it is not mine"—and that my responsibility is to mean it as universally valid. Of course, it has a training behind it; one that has entailed a complexity of necessarily collaborative frequentation—a matter, most importantly, of exercising sensibility and responsive thought on the work of creative writers. Such a judgment seems to oneself a judgment of reality, and for arriving at it there are no rules, though there is active informing "principle."

The young Captain's instant judgment, or realization, that it is his responsibility to save the young Chief Mate—a Conway boy who has committed homicide—from justice also has a training behind it ... But for them too there are no rules; the reference to the Conway musn't suggest that their training reduces to discipline and a code ... [W]ithout a nuclear live presence of essential responsibility [which by its very nature is "uncodifiable"] discipline and code would be no better than mechanical habit, and the mechanical can only deal with the routine and the expected (*LP* 46–8)

In a similar vein, here is something Derrida has to say—in an exchange with Richard Kearney during a recent conference on "Religion and Postmodernism"—about the nature of (what constitutes) a decision:

If I had criteria, a set of norms, that I would simply apply or enforce, there would be no decision. There is a decision to the extent that even if I have criteria, the criteria are not determining, that I make a decision beyond the criteria, *even if I know what the best criteria are, even if I apply them, the decision occurs to the extent that I do more than apply them.* Otherwise it would be a mechanical development, a mechanical explicitation, not a decision. (*DRK*, my italics 134)

If we ask what is wrong with "a mechanical development," the context makes it clear that Derrida's answer is essentially the same as Leavis's: "the mechanical can only deal with the routine and the expected," which is to say that it can only deal with more of the same, as opposed to the unknown other, which is always new and different. And if Leavis insists that my judgment is simultaneously mine and not-mine, Derrida similarly claims that "a responsible decision, to be responsible, must not be mine. My own decision, my own responsible decision, must in myself be the other's; if it's simply mine, it's not a decision." In short, Derrida maintains that "we have, not to account for, but to experience the fact that the freest decision in myself is a decision of the other in myself" (*DRK* 134).

But, if so, what better way of experiencing this paradoxical fact than in our engagement with imaginative literature? And, in this particular case, it would be difficult to think of a more appropriate text than *The Secret Sharer*. When, furthermore, Derrida claims that it is "the one who invites, the inviting host, who becomes the hostage,"[74] he is thinking of Pierre Klossowski's *Robert ce soir* (*OH* 83); when he says that "the hostage is the one who is delivered to the other in the sacred openness of ethics,"[75] and that there "would be no hospitality without the chance of spectrality" (*Adieu* 111-12), he is thinking of Levinas; but in each case he might just as well have been thinking of the way in which the ghost-like Leggat's host becomes his hostage as well. And what better illustration of the claim that there is or can be "no event without the surprise of a gift" (*GD* 119) than the (to my mind, halo-like) hat that, as we have already noticed, was first given by the captain to Leggat and that ends up by "saving the ship" (*TSS* 60)!

In his account of Abraham's decision, Derrida insists that "the concept of the instant is always indispensable" (*Gift* 72; and see 77). And consider in this connection how uncannily relevant two of the connections De Vries makes—while reflecting on how Derrida thinks of decision-making as not allowing "one time to anticipate, project, mediate, or meditate" (*PTR* 411)—seem to *The Secret Sharer*. De Vries cites the following from Georges Bataille's *Inner Experience*:

> Without night, no one would have to decide.... Decision is what is born before the worst and rises above. It is the essence of courage, of the heart, of being itself. And it is the reverse of project (it demands that one reject delay, that one decide on the spot, with everything at stake ...) (26; qtd. by De Vries 411)

And he notes that "[a]ccording to Derrida's 'Force of Law' the process of making a decision can be described as an 'acting in the night of non-knowledge and non-rule" (*PTR* 411).

Of course the differences between the Biblical story of Abraham and Isaac and Conrad's *The Secret Sharer* are admittedly more obvious than any similarities and they are major. Thus, in order to bring home to us a sense of Abraham's suffering, Kierkegaard tells us he "would remind people that the journey lasted three days and well into the fourth" and that "those three-and-a-half days should be infinitely longer than the two thousand years separating [him] from Abraham."[76] This is radically different to the ordeal the narrator undergoes while he keeps the stranger's presence in his cabin a secret.

And when Kierkegaard says he wants us to see "how murderous a paradox faith is, a paradox capable of making a murder into a holy act well pleasing to God, a paradox which gives Isaac back to Abraham, which no thought can grasp because faith begins precisely where thinking leaves off" (*Fear* 82), we realize that we are not tempted to regard either the murder committed by Leggatt or the risk the captain takes on Leggatt's behalf as holy acts. Nor are we tempted to say of the captain what Kierkegaard says of Abraham when he claims that we approach "him with a *horror religiosus* [holy terror] like that in which Israel approached Mount Sinai" (90). But even so, we have seen that, in its own way, *The Secret Sharer* is also troubling, at least in Leavis's reading of it. And of course the point I am trying to make is that it is troubling in precisely some of the ways the Abraham/Isaac story and Derrida's reading of it are troubling. Let us quickly note two of them.

One of the ways in question is vividly brought out by Terry Eagleton's scandalized reaction to what he calls the "extravagant parody of an ethics of otherness" he thinks Derrida provides us with in such works as his *Gift of Death*:

> Ethics, for the later Derrida, is a matter of absolute decisions, which must be made outside all given norms and forms of knowledge; decisions which are utterly vital, yet which completely evade conceptualization. One can only hope that he is not on the jury when one's case comes up in court. Such ethical choices are at once necessary and "impossible," wholly mine yet "the decision of the other in me"...[77]

As opposed to this ethics, which he characterises as being Kierkegaardian ("a new-fangled version of the fideistic heresy that faith is merely some blind leap in the dark, quite impervious to reason" [156]), Eagleton himself favours "Aristotelian virtue ethics" (159). In response to this, I want to make two points. First, that blindness can be imagined operating quite differently here, as it does, for example, in Hent De Vries's description of Derrida's position:

> [A] judge cannot pass a just judgment if he blindly follows the letter of the law and applies its principles and rules in a merely mechanical way. The decision must to a certain extent, "suspend" (or even "destroy") and reinvent the law. For each case that presents itself to him will be other and therefore asks for an *epochē* followed by a decision "which no existing, coded rule can or ought to guarantee absolutely." And yet, conversely, we would not call the judge just if he stopped short "before the undecidable" or abandoned "all rules, all principles." In order not to be neutralized, a just decision would thus have to have it both ways—that is, go through the aporia and *perform the contradiction*. (*PTR* 413–14)[78]

Second, I think it is worth noting the distinction that Alasdair MacIntyre makes (MacIntyre being widely regarded as the most distinguished contemporary exponent of Aristotelian virtue-ethics) when he claims that "judgment has an indispensable role in *the life of the virtuous man* which it does not and could not have in, for example, *the life of the merely law-abiding or rule-abiding man*."[79]

Another, second, way in which the Biblical and Conradian texts (together with the Derridean and Leavisian readings) are troubling concerns the linkage between responsibility and secrecy. As Derrida reminds us, "[f]or common sense, just as for philosophical reasoning, the most widely shared belief is that responsibility is tied to the public and to the nonsecret, to the possibility and even the necessity of accounting for one's words and actions in front of others, of justifying and owning up to them." But in the story of Abraham and Isaac "it appears, just as necessarily, that the absolute responsibility of my actions...instead implies secrecy" (*GD* 60). Indeed, "[s]ecrecy is essential to the exercise of this absolute responsibility as sacrificial responsibility" (67).

We now come to what seems to me an astonishing discovery and the key point in all of this. According to Leavis, *The Secret Sharer* can help us to understand that "Lawrence's 'moral sense'"—"One writes," Lawrence once maintained, "out of one's moral sense" (qtd. in Leavis, *LP* 45)—"is something like the antithesis of what the anti-puritan enlightened think of as 'moral'" (*LP* 48). What ought now to be apparent is that much the same can be said about Leavis's own moral sense—and about Derrida's; and also, of course, about Conrad's.

To say this is to affirm one of the things these otherwise very different writers have in common: a moral sense that manifests itself in the religious suspension of the ethical. In Leavis's case, the key text here is obviously *The Secret Sharer.* (And it is interesting, in this connection, to note how he refers to this story in his last book on Lawrence. On the one hand, we find him saying that "Conrad's distinctive attitude and tone are such that, challenged to describe them as we have them in the work of his kindled imagination, one would hardly find oneself prompted to bring in, for any positive major use, the word 'religious'" [*TWC* 128]; while, on the other hand, he makes it plain that he himself understands "the profound, the ultimate human responsibility defined by Conrad's art in *The Secret Sharer*" [98] with reference both to Lawrence's invocation of God in *The Plumed Serpent* [through the character Ramón] and also to Lawrence's claim that "[a]t the maximum of our imagination we are religious" [98, qtd. on 99].)[80]

As I have been saying, it seems to me that Conrad's novella functions for Leavis in much the same unsettling way as the story of Abraham and Isaac functions for Derrida: so as to reveal that "the concepts of responsibility, of decision, or of duty, are condemned a priori to paradox, scandal, and aporia" (*GD* 68). Except for one crucial difference, the Abraham/Isaac story also functions in this way for Kierkegaard—the difference being that for Kierkegaard the religion, in the name of which the ethical gets suspended, is Christianity,[81] whereas for Leavis, Lawrence, Conrad and Derrida it is (again, in the words of the latter) a "religion without religion" (*GD* 49).[82]

It is important to add that, though Derrida does speak of the ethical as having sometimes "to be refused in the name of a responsibility that doesn't keep account" (*GD* 62), and though he does say that "ethics must be sacrificed in the name of duty" (67), it is nevertheless clear that, as he and the other writers I've been mentioning understand it, the religious suspension of the ethical does *not* mean its cancellation.

But if this comes as a relief, it seems only honest to note how worryingly relevant some of Žižek's recent provocations are in this connection.[83] As Sarah Kay notes in her recent book on him, Žižek's "religious turn" is evident in a number of his "most recent books."[84] And if, as she maintains, he remains "a staunch materialist and atheist" (103), he does so while asking us to think of Lacan as "an 'apostle' in the Kierkegaardian sense; that is, he is the bearer of a truth which is not necessarily available for rational testing." This means, as she immediately points out, "that the very capitol of psychoanalysis has been assimilated to religion" (112). Kay claims that Žižek is drawn to religious thinkers because the "extremity of religious thought, its willingness to explore beyond the limitations of human reason and self-satisfaction—in short, beyond morality—confers on it a radical understanding of belief, freedom and agency that might lay the foundations for Leftist political action" (123). In any case, it isn't too difficult to think of the final action taken by Conrad's young captain as an instance of the kind of "radical gesture of 'striking at oneself'" that Žižek claims is "constitutive of subjectivity itself."[85] Or even, for that matter, as an illustration of "the terrorism that," he maintains, "characterizes every authentic ethical stance" (*DSS* 91).[86]

In the next chapter I will offer a somewhat fuller explanation of what I had in mind when I suggested earlier that, even if there may be no way for us to avoid acting in such a way as to exclude and thus sacrifice others, it may still be possible for us to adopt different attitudes towards this fact. And if the next chapter will again draw heavily on Levinas, Derrida, Leavis, George Eliot, Nietzsche, Žižek and D.H.Lawrence, this is because the attitudes in question interest me much more when they get expressed by one or another of these major thinkers than they do in the abstract.

Chapter Six

Balancing as we go: slave or noble? Abrahamic or Hellenist?

Is Nietzsche a Yes-sayer, or would he rather say No? The answer is, I think, that at the deepest level even he (whom Freud described as the person who knew more about himself than anyone else ever had or ever would) didn't know, or couldn't make up his mind. Rightly he saw various fundamental attitudes to life as warring temptations, and was unexampled in his honesty in spelling out the reasons for and against adopting any of them. And as his feelings about life accelerated in their alternations and became ever more intense, he produced...[*Twilight of the Idols* and *The Anti-Christ*] the two greatest documents of basic ambivalence that we possess.
—Michael Tanner[1]

[A]ttitudes are incipient acts...
—Kenneth Burke[2]

Paradox, scandal, and aporia are themselves nothing other than sacrifice, the revelation of conceptual thinking at its limit, at its death and finitude.
—Derrida (*GD* 68)

[E]ven if it is grounded in knowledge, the moment I take a decision it is a leap, I enter a heterogeneous space and that is the condition of responsibility.
 This is not only a problem but the *aporia* we have to face constantly. For me, however, the *aporia* is not simply paralysis, but the *aporia* or the *non-way* is the condition of walking...path-breaking implies *aporia*.
—Derrida ("Hospitality, Justice and Responsibility" 73)

We must balance as we go.
—D.H.Lawrence ("Morality and the Novel" 173)

On the one hand, then, we find Leavis confidently maintaining that "there's no question of guilt"; on the other, we have Derrida insisting that "[o]ne is always guilty" and Levinas citing with obvious approval Alyosha's "We are all guilty" in Dostoevsky's *The Brothers Karamazov*. But as regards the latter, it's worth noting that, in the opening sentence of his Introduction to *The Levinas Reader*, the editor cites a different translation of Alyosha's declaration, which reads not "we are all guilty" but, rather, "We are all *responsible* for everyone else—but I am more responsible than all the others" (my italics). So which is it? Guilt or responsibility?

Let's quickly look at three of the many occasions on which Levinas quotes and briefly comments on Alyosha's "We are all guilty ..." Immediately after citing it in an essay on Buber, we find Levinas first assuring us that "[t]hat superlative degree of guilt does not, of course, refer to any personal history, nor to the character traits of the individual making that statement"; and then saying that he understands it as a "non-transferable responsibility, as if my neighbor called me urgently ..." (*Outside the Subject* 44). In an interview entitled "The Vocation of the Other," Levinas explains that it is "not in order to recognize itself as more guilty by specific acts committed that the [Dostoevskyan] I who speaks here accuses itself. It is as *me*, always the foremost one responsible, experiencing inexhaustible obligations, that the I is in the wrong, and recognizes in this wrong the identity of its 'I'" (*Righteous?* 112). And finally, in an interview entitled "Responsibility and Substitution," Levinas says that Alyosha's declaration expresses what he takes to be the "'originary constitution' of the I or the unique, in a responsibility for the neighbor or the other, and the impossibility of escaping responsibility or of being replaced. The impossibility of escaping is not a servitude, but rather a being chosen" (*Righteous?* 229).

Even if it can be said that on these occasions Levinas places the emphasis more on our responsibility than on our guilt, he leaves us in no doubt both that he very much does want to retain the notion of guilt and that, as he sees it, the I is always "in the wrong." This stands in stark contrast to Leavis's attitude and, even after we've allowed for the fact that when he insists on there being "no question of guilt" Leavis is of course referring specifically to *The Secret Sharer*, the difference seems worth pondering. After all, if *The Secret Sharer* may reasonably be said to be about unconditional hospitality or the coming of the Other, it has to be admitted that Leggat arrives with a lot of baggage, that he brings various thirds along with him, and that the young captain's judgment in Leggat's favour clearly risks sacrificing those others, reminding us therefore that (as we have seen Levinas say) "justice's judgment is violence" (*Righteous?* 134). Yet still, this is the context in which Leavis maintains that there is "no question of guilt."

Not only does Leavis dismiss in this context all talk of guilt; his stress falls on a deserved state of "peace," what he refers to in his last book as "the peace of basic responsibility fully accepted—'responsibility' as the young ship's-captain of '*The Secret Sharer*' so naturally assumed it as his" (*TWC* 128). With "Lawrence's art" specifically in mind, Leavis then immediately goes on to distinguish this particular sense of responsibility from the kind that Anton Skrebensky stands for (in *The Rainbow*):

> But we didn't create ourselves; and the sole access to the promptings to be gathered from the unknown—from which life and creativity enter us—is by the well-head, which is deep below our valid thought. Submission to the promptings is the escape from the ego and its will; but such submission is, of its nature, a very active matter, demanding self-knowledge, intensive cultivation of the most delicate intuitiveness, and the courage to arrive at conclusions the precision and finality of which are not guaranteed: the responsibility for them is ours, and where it is not taken up there is no genuine responsibility. "But Noah, of course, is always in an unpopular minority"—it doesn't occur to Skrebensky to belong to that; that is, he leaves responsibility to the Whole, or to the community, or to the greatest good of the greatest number. (Ibid)

The quoted reference to Noah is taken from one of Lawrence's essays, in which Lawrence points out that the Christians were also in an unpopular minority "when Rome began to fall," whereas now (that is, in the 1920s) they "are in a hopelessly popular majority, so it is [now] their turn to fall."[3] What Leavis stresses, in other words, is the risk involved in any acceptance of basic responsibility, the risk that one may find oneself in an unpopular minority (just as Leavis did himself). But on the other hand, if (as another militant, Alain Badiou, puts it) one is willing to "be in the exception," to "keep a distance from power" and to "accept the consequences of a decision, however remote and difficult they may be," then one's life might "have meaning"[4] and one might even, as a reward, attain the kind of "peace" Leavis mentions.

In these circumstances, then, we need to dig more deeply. We may be better able to understand what Leavis says here about guilt if we look more closely at his conception of responsibility, which I want to get at indirectly, however, by means of a short detour through Levinas and George Eliot. Recall first something we noted Levinas saying earlier on, that "there are a variety of ways to kill. It isn't always," he then went on, "just a matter of killing, say, with a knife. The everyday killing with a good conscience, the killing in all innocence—there is such a thing as well!" (*Righteous?* 132) Jill Robbins is surely right (in commenting on these lines) to claim that "[i]t is as if [for Levinas, and also, I would say, Derrida] the habitual economy were all about killing" (*Righteous?* 2). But I think there is a sense in which Leavis would have wanted to subscribe to this view as well, at least if we understand it (as I think we should) in the light of a passage in *Middlemarch* in which Eliot observes that while our writers "are not afraid of telling over and over again how a man comes to fall in love with a woman," they seldom tell us the story of the growth and decline of an "intellectual passion." Eliot is thinking specifically of her character Lydgate, but she generalizes the case as follows:

[I]n the multitude of middle-aged men who go about their vocations...there is always a good number who once meant to shape their own deeds and alter the world a little. The story of their own coming to be shapen after the average and fit to be packed by the gross, is hardly ever told even in their consciousness; for perhaps their ardour in generous unpaid toil cooled as imperceptibly as the ardour of other youthful loves, till one day their earlier self walked like a ghost in its old home and made the new furniture ghastly. Nothing in the world more subtle than the process of their gradual change! In the beginning they inhaled it unknowingly: you and I may have sent some of our breath towards infecting them, when we uttered our conforming falsities or drew our silly conclusions: or perhaps it came with the vibrations from a woman's glance.[5]

What is Eliot describing here if not one of the variety of ways in which it is possible for us to help kill something (and someone) without our fully realizing that that is what we are doing. The damage we can do when we utter "our conforming falsities," or draw "our silly conclusions"! And indeed, the clear implication is that we (men obviously every bit as much as women) are responsible not only for the words that come out of our mouths but also for the ways in which we look at one another (the vibrations from our glances). I take it that (understood in this sense, at least) Eliot would surely have agreed with the first (if not necessarily the second half) of the sentence from *The Brothers Karamazov* that we noted a moment ago: "We are all responsible for everyone else—but I am more responsible than all the others."

Leavis was one of George Eliot's greatest admirers and champions, and I have no doubt but that he shared the sense of responsibility she conveys in her passage on the death of "intellectual passion." Indeed, if he was widely known (and frequently resented) as a moralist, more often than not as an exceptionally stern one, it could be said that this was largely due to the lengths he was prepared to go to avoid uttering "conforming falsities," or drawing "silly conclusions." But if, like George Eliot before him, he clearly had an unusually developed sense of responsibility, it was nevertheless not the kind of *unlimited* or *infinite* responsibility that Derrida and Levinas both wrote about. And this being the case, I need to address the kind of objection we find Derrida raising when asked in a 1989 interview about "Heidegger's silence concerning the camps":

> [R]esponsibility is excessive or it is not a responsibility. A limited, measured, calculable, rationally distributed responsibility is already the becoming-right of morality; it is at times also, in the best hypothesis, the dream of every good conscience, in the worst hypothesis, of the petty or grand inquisitors. I suppose, I hope you are not expecting me simply to say "I condemn Auschwitz" or "I condemn every silence on Auschwitz." As regards this last phrase or its equivalents, I find it a bit indecent, indeed, obscene, the mechanical nature of improvised trials instigated against all those whom one thinks one can accuse of not having named or thought "Auschwitz." A compulsion toward sententious discourse, strategic exploitation, the eloquence of denunciation....

Of course, silence on Auschwitz will never be justifiable; but neither is speaking about it...in order to say nothing...that does not go without saying, trivially, serving primarily to give oneself a good conscience...(*Points* 286-87)[6]

What I hope to have made clear in my account of Leavis's reading of *The Secret Sharer* is that it is quite possible to object to the kind of "sententious discourse" and "good conscience" Derrida describes here while conceiving of a responsibility that is "limited" without its also being the kind of "measured, calculable, rationally distributed responsibility," which seems in the passage I've just quoted to be the only alternative to an "excessive" responsibility that Derrida is willing to admit. And if this is true, then it ought to be also possible to imagine that a person who has discharged this limited responsibility might well be able to experience the pleasure of a relatively guilt-free, good conscience.[7] Even if he has blood on his hands? (Not of course literal blood but still a kind of blood, the metaphorical kind that gets spilled in the sort of Blakean mental war the title of one of Leavis's books—*Nor Shall My Sword*—points us towards.) According to Leavis and Blake (and of course countless others, Lawrence, Badiou, Žižek etc., etc.), even then.

I take it, then, that Leavis would surely have rejected the idea that, as a general principle, it is healthy to consider oneself as being always "*more* responsible than [everyone else]." I think he would have disagreed with the attitude expressed in the form of Dostoevsky's sentence that Levinas seems to have used most often: "We are all *guilty* of all and for all men before all, and I more than the others" (my italics, *EI* 98). And as for (in Levinas's own words) such "extreme formulas" as "I am responsible even for the Other's responsibility" and "I am responsible for the persecutions that I undergo" (*EI* 99), my guess is that Leavis would have thought them perverse. Indeed (to turn now to Nietzsche), with these two extreme Levinasian formulas in mind, we might well feel that the answer to a question posed by Richard Cohen—"Is his yet another, perhaps subtler, return to slave morality...?" (*EI* 3)—can only be affirmative. This would surely have been Nietzsche's conclusion. Nor of course would Nietzsche have wanted to disagree if we were to argue that, perverse or not, Levinas's extreme formulas might be seen as both Christian and Jewish. (I'm thinking of

Levinas's citation from *Lamentations* 3:30 of the line "To give his cheek to the smiter and to be filled with insults," which he reads in terms of "pass[ing] from the outrage undergone to the responsibility for the persecutor, and, in this sense from suffering to expiation for the other" [*OB* 111; *LR* 101].) From Nietzsche's point of view, those, after all, are precisely the sources from which the "slave morality" grew; and which he vigorously opposed in the name of a "noble" morality.

As we have seen, Leavis immediately followed the emphatic claim made by his essay on *The Secret Sharer* (on there being "no question of guilt by the ultimate criterion that's invoked in Conrad's art") with what I take to be the distancing allusion to Nietzsche ("By which I don't mean that the spirit of it is *Jenseits von Gut und Böse*") that is in turn followed by this: "On the contrary, there is an insistence on the inescapable need for individual moral judgment, and for moral conviction that is strong and courageous enough to forget codes and to defy law and codified morality and justice." But whatever *Leavis* took to be the spirit of Nietzsche's *Beyond Good and Evil*, my own view is that this last sentence nicely embodies it. I'm thinking especially, for example, of the following question from the 9th section of that book's Part One: "Is living not valuating, preferring, being unjust, being limited, wanting to be different?"[8] And I should add that I agree here with Michael Tanner, whose comment on this question reads as follows: "In contrast to the 'resignation' of the Stoics ..., Nietzsche posits living as choosing—that is the force of 'Is living not valuating, preferring, being unjust?', etc. The answer to that question, an answer so obvious that Nietzsche doesn't deign to give it, is of course 'Yes.'"[9] Leavis might not have liked this reference to "being unjust," not even if we choose to understand it in the Derridean sense as something we can't avoid being, no matter how much we would like to. But the point I wish to make here is that, even if we were to leave that reference out, a life spent "valuating" and "preferring" (which is the way Leavis spent his) could be said to involve a good deal of "sacrificing," a word that seems every bit as appropriate here as Tanner's "choosing." As appropriate, I mean, both in Nietzsche's case and in Leavis's. I take, for example, Leavis's Blakean *Nor Shall My Sword* title to indicate his awareness of this fact. And as for Nietzsche, I'm thinking not only of what is most obvious, the ferocity of his criticism (and thus sacrifice) of others, but also of how, as Henry Staten puts it, he "often defines the richest, strongest, most noble soul as the one that echoes ['a spendthrift or potlatch economy, what George Bataille calls a "general" economy']. 'A gift-giving virtue is the highest virtue,' Zarathustra says to his disciples. 'This is your thirst: to become sacrifices and gifts yourselves ...'" (*Nietzsche's Voice* 10).[10]

But if the Nietzschean opposition between "slave" and "noble" moralities gives us one possible way of *starting*, at least, to get the alternative attitudes we are reflecting on here into clearer focus, I think we also need to reflect on the claim Matthew Arnold once made in the two sentences from his *Culture and Anarchy* that Derrida chose as the epigraph to his 1964 essay/monograph on Levinas:

> Hebraism and Hellenism—between these two points of influence moves our world. At one time it feels more powerfully the attraction of one of them, at another time of the other; and it ought to be, though it never is, evenly and happily balanced between them.[11] (qtd. by Derrida in "Violence and Metaphysics" 79)

Arnold's argument of course was that in the second half of the 19th century it was "time to Hellenise" (*CA* 27). I suggest that, in order to make this relevant again today, we substitute the "Abrahamic" for "Hebraism," so as to include Islam as well as the Christianity that already belongs (along with Judaism) to Arnold's definition of "Hebraism." Once we have done this, we can then raise the question for our own time. What do we most need now? Another dose of Hellenism? Or of Abrahamism?

Of course, our answers to the above will inevitably be influenced by the further question as to *where* we are located, both spatially but also in ideological terms (in a gross but perhaps necessary oversimplification: as believers or unbelievers, for example). According to Arnold, "Hebraism" sees the main difficulty in the way of Hellenism's quest for perfection as being—in one word—"*sin*; and the space which sin fills in Hebraism, as compared with Hellenism, is indeed prodigious." Arnold tells us that in a sermon he heard this "obstacle to perfection" memorably compared "to a hideous hunchback seated on our shoulders,...which it is the main business of our lives to hate and oppose" (*CA* 112). When it is put like this, it is easy, I suggest, for those of us who are "unbelievers," to agree with the clear implication, which is that we no longer need to make this the main business of our lives: "the long discipline of Hebraism, and the...centuries of painful schooling in self-conquest" have made us ready for Hellenism (172).[12] Maybe so, but perhaps we oughtn't to embrace this conclusion too quickly. For one thing, those of us who admire one or more of the three thinkers (Nietzsche, Heidegger and Wittgenstein) Stephen Mulhall writes about in his recent book on *Philosophical Myths of the Fall* might find some food for thought (and thus reason for hesitation) in his argument concerning their relation to the idea of original sin. Here is Mulhall on the latter:

> [A]t its core is the conception that human nature as such is tragically flawed, perverse in its very structure or constitution. Human beings are not only naturally capable of acting—even disposed to act—sinfully, but are always already turned against themselves, against the true and against the good, by virtue of their very condition as human. Hence, that sinful orientation will distort and ultimately invalidate any efforts they might make by themselves to alter that orientation; the only possible solution lies in their attaining a certain kind of orientation to the divine.[13]

And here is Mulhall on Nietzsche, Heidegger and Wittgenstein:

> [W]e might think of the[se] three philosophers...as wanting to preserve a recognizable descendent of the Christian conception of human nature as always already averting us from the relation to truth, comprehension, and clarity that is nevertheless our birthright—hence, as structurally perverse or errant and yet redeemable from that fallen state—but as refusing to accept that such redemption is attainable only from a transcendental or divine source. In other words, these philosophers want to keep a conception of human beings as in need of redemption (rather than, say, improvement or self-realization) and as capable of it, but to relocate the source of that redemption within (or at least on the borders of) the world of human experience. (11)

This suggests, as Mulhall notes towards the end of his book, that it might be worth taking "seriously the possibility that any sufficiently rigorous attempt to give an account of the human mode of being will find itself recurring to (even reiterating) the core tenets of Christianity precisely because those tendencies are genuinely responsive to something deep and determining in human nature" (121).

A moment's recollection of some of the horrors that largely define the century that followed Arnold's also ought surely to give us pause, when we are thinking that Hebrew-or Abraham-ism has outlived its usefulness. One thinks of the first World War that (to cite two of our main figures) marked so deeply both Lawrence and Leavis (the latter serving in an ambulance unit); of the dedication—to the memory of "the six million assassinated by the National Socialists, and of the millions on millions of all confessions and all nations, victims of the same hatred of the other man, the same anti-semitism"—found at the beginning of Levinas's *Otherwise than Being*; and, more recently, of the way our prosperous western societies have "*allow[ed]* to die of hunger and disease tens of millions of children," a sacrifice that Derrida urges us to see both as analogous to Abraham's sacrifice of Isaac and also as the abyss that ensures the smooth functioning of our way of life, the abyss that talk of a limited responsibility can in his view only serve to obscure, even as it displays its "good conscience" (*GD* 84-6).

What, among other things, this too rapid overview of the last century can perhaps remind us of is the fact that *over a sufficient course of time* a major thinker may reasonably find him or herself giving different answers to our reformulation of Arnold's question (Is it time for more Hellenism or for more Abrahamism?). I'm thinking first of the contrast Derrida drew in 1966 between "the saddened, *negative*, nostalgic, guilty, Rousseauistic side of the thinking of play whose other side would be the Nietzschean *affirmation*, that is the joyous affirmation of the play of the world."[14] And my point here is that—without wanting either to deny the extent to which in his late work Derrida insists on the affirmative nature of deconstruction, or to claim that the late Derrida lapses at any point into (Rousseauistic or any other kind of) nostalgia—we ought to recognize a shift in emphasis in his late work from "*joyous* affirmation" to something more closely resembling a mood that accompanies sadness and the acceptance of an unavoidable guilt.

I hope it will be obvious by now that I do not want that last point to carry even the slightest hint of censure. It seems to me that by the end of the last century our exposure through the mass media to suffering all over the world has made it much more problematic than it can ever have been before for anyone to adopt the attitude we saw Emerson manifesting earlier (in chapter two):

[D]o not tell me, as a good man did today, of my obligation to put all poor men in good situations. Are they *my* poor? I tell thee, thou foolish philanthropist, that I grudge the dollar, the dime, the cent I give to such men as do not belong to me and to whom I do not belong.

By the same token, I take it that these same changes have made it easier for some of us to take more seriously than we might have been willing to take it a few decades ago the kind of (Levinasian) sentiment we find Hent De Vries articulating as follows:

"What is above all invisible is the offense universal history inflicts upon particulars"' ([Levinas] *TI* 247/225). On this *minimal morality* with *maximum effect* hinges the fate of the universe, of the sacred history that runs, as [Franz] Rosenzweig knew, parallel to—or in the interstices, the *entretemps* of—the other and whose dimensionality escapes the levelling horizon of History's linear course. (*Minimal Theologies* 474).

I will be explaining in my next book why I take "sacred" to be a term every bit as problematic—and in need of rethinking—as "religion." But this aside, the possible existence of such an alternative and largely hidden history as De Vries refers to seems to me crucially important. It will, furthermore, inevitably remind some of us of the last sentences of George Eliot's *Middlemarch*:

Her full nature...spent itself in channels which had no great name on the earth. But the effect of her [Dorothea Brooke's] being on those around her was incalculably diffusive: for the growing good of the world is partly dependent on unhistoric acts; and that things are not so ill with you and me as they might have been, is half owing to the number who lived faithfully a hidden life, and rest in unvisited tombs.

I am not, however, saying that it is now time for us to actually opt *for* the "slave"[15] or "Abrahamic" and *against* the "noble" or Hellenist." In fact, before I say anything about the latter pair, I now need to explain that the "Abrahamic" or "slave" attitude seems to me most compelling and attractive when we stress that aspect of it that brings it more closely still into alignment with the attitude we find in Levinas and Derrida. And to help us do this let's recall the following (once-famous) passage from *Middlemarch*:

> That element of tragedy which lies in the very fact of frequency, has not yet wrought itself into the coarse emotion of mankind; and perhaps our frames could hardly bear much of it. If we had a keen vision and feeling of all ordinary human life, it would be like hearing the grass grow and the squirrel's heart beat, and we should die of that roar which lies on the other side of silence. As it is, the quickest of us walk about well wadded with stupidity. (ch. 20 207)

Insofar, then, as we can say that Levinas and the later Derrida share an "Abrahamic" or "slave" attitude to life, it is one that is preoccupied with what lies "on the other side of silence"; it is concerned not so much (as Arnold had it) with sin as with the world's suffering and pain; for them it is the latter (and what they take to be our inescapable complicity with it) that (in Arnold's words) "fills the whole scene" (*CA* 112).

Here we might recall that traumatized body on the Cross that we briefly discussed near the end of the Preface. But then again, it might be more appropriate here to note the two sentences that come immediately before the ones I have just quoted:

> Nor can I suppose that when Mrs Casaubon is discovered in a fit of weeping six weeks after her wedding, the situation will be regarded as tragic. Some discouragement, some faintness of heart at the new real future which replaces the imaginary, is not unusual,

and we do not expect people to be deeply moved by what is not unusual. That element of tragedy which lies in the very fact of frequency, has not yet wrought itself into the coarse emotion of mankind; and perhaps our frames could hardly bear much of it.

What Eliot is drawing our attention to is the kind of tragedy (or tragic "element"), the kind of suffering and pain, that we fail to recognize simply because it is so common, so usual, so much a part of the ordinary ("of all ordinary human life").[16] The other Eliot (T.S.) presumably had this passage in mind when he wrote (a few lines from the end of the first section of "Burnt Norton") that "human kind/Cannot bear very much reality." In so far, then, as the "Abrahamic" or "slave" attitude can be understood as making it slightly less easy for us to ignore this reality, it seems to me to be accomplishing something important and I think it is worth noting here that for Nietzsche too there were times when the world's suffering and pain *almost* seemed to fill the whole scene.[17] He is of course best-known for his trenchant criticism of the Abrahamic or slave morality. But this is all the more reason why (as Henry Staten rightly insists) we should ponder such passages as the following (the first from his first book, *The Birth of Tragedy* in 1871, the second from *The Gay Science* in 1882):

> Suppose a human being has thus put his ear, as it were, to the heart chamber of the world will and felt the roaring desire for existence pouring from there into all the veins of the world...how could he fail to break suddenly? How could he endure to perceive the echo of innumerable shouts of pleasure and woe in the "wide space of the world night," enclosed in the wretched glass capsule of the human individual, without inexorably fleeing toward his primordial home?[18]
>
> ...
>
> Anyone who manages to experience the history of humanity as a whole as *his own history* will feel in an enormously general-ized way all the grief of an invalid who thinks of health, of an old man who thinks of the dreams of his youth, of a lover deprived of his beloved, of the martyr whose ideal is perishing, of the hero on the evening after a battle that has decided nothing but brought

him wounds and the loss of his friend. But if one endured, if one *could* endure this immense sum of grief of all kinds...[19]

Claiming that what in *The Birth of Tragedy* Nietzsche says about "the profound Hellene" (that he is "uniquely susceptible to the tenderest and deepest suffering"[sec. 7, 59[20]]) applies just as much to himself, Staten (whose discussion of these passages brought them to my attention) notes that "the 'enormously generalised' grief of an entire creation" is "what the later works call *pity*" (*Nietzsche's Voice* 214).[21] And here is part of what Staten has to say about Nietzsche's attitude towards the latter:

> What is so remarkable about Nietzsche's pity is the universality of its scope; it is a whole world of passion and suffering that he hears clamoring and to which he must in some way shut his ears (whether by artistic illusion as in *The Birth of Tragedy* or by "becoming hard," as repeatedly in the later work). "I know...that I need only expose myself to the sight of some genuine distress and I am lost. And if a suffering friend said to me, 'Look, I am about to die; please promise to die with me,' I should promise it; and the sight of a small mountain tribe fighting for its liberty would persuade me to offer it my hand and my life." [*Gay Science* sec. 338, 270].

From this Staten goes on to wonder if he isn't making Nietzsche sound too Romantic.[22] But for our purposes here what is rather more startling is the extent to which these passages (especially the first one about an ear being put "to the heart chamber of the world") seem uncannily reminiscent of the George Eliot who wrote about "that roar which lies on the other side of silence." After all, it would have seemed from the paragraph he devotes to her in his *Twilight of the Idols* that for her determination to hold on to "Christian morality" after having "got rid of the Christian God" (*Twilight*, section 5 of "Expeditions of an Untimely Man," 80) Nietzsche felt nothing but scorn. The scorn is real enough but it is perhaps an exaggeration to say that Nietzsche felt *nothing but* scorn. We might perhaps get a more accurate idea of his attitude to those things for which he (temporarily) makes Eliot stand if we try substituting "George Eliot" for "Romanticism" in the following two sentences (in which Staten addresses the question as to whether or not he is making Nietzsche sound too Romantic):

On the one hand, it is true that Nietzsche recognizes these impulses as something to be opposed and controlled; it could even
be said that his career-long opposition to Romanticism is his opposition to these impulses. On the other hand,...this Romanticism would not be something *external* to Nietzsche's project but
something that works it from within, as what has to be opposed
so strenuously because it is so intimate, so proper to Nietzsche's
own economy. (*Nietzshe's Voice* 215).

I should now note something Nietzsche immediately goes on to say in one
of the sections from which I have just quoted (the one that starts off with
his saying he is lost when he exposes himself to the sight of some genuine
distress). "All such arousing of pity and calling for help is secretly seduc-
tive," he says, "for our 'own way' is too hard and demanding ..." He then
tells us what his morality says to him:

Live in seclusion so that you *can* live for yourself...You will also
wish to help—but only those whose distress you *understand*—
your friends—and only in the manner in which you help yourself.
I want to make them bolder, more persevering, simpler, gayer. I
want to teach them what is understood by so few today, least of
all by these preachers of pity: *to share not suffering but joy.* (*Gay
Science*, Book 4, sec. 338, 271)

The first point I want to make here is that—whatever Nietzsche might
have thought—neither Levinas nor Derrida, nor George Eliot, are describable as "preachers of pity." But at the same time, as we have already seen,
Levinas and Derrida do believe that when it is properly understood our
responsibility is endless. According to Derrida (clearly speaking for himself
as well as for Levinas), the fact that "there is no real discontinuity between
voluntary and involuntary murder...forces us to infinitize our responsibility: we are also responsible for our lack of attention and for our careless-
ness, for what we do neither intentionally nor freely, indeed, for what we
do unconsciously—since this is never without significance" (*Adieu* 108).
Whereas, on the other hand, while far from being unaware of, or indifferent to, what "lies on the other side of silence," while agreeing that we are
responsible for the things Derrida mentions, Leavis would still not have

drawn the conclusion that our responsibility is therefore infinite; he (along with some others) would argue for a more limited concept of responsibility,[23] which not only leaves open the possibility of a relatively guilt-free good conscience but which even maintains a privileged space for play.

At this point it is worth reminding ourselves of the crucial importance Matthew Arnold attached to *play*; more specifically, to our being willing to follow "wherever the free play of our consciousness leads us" (*CA* ch. 6 167). In fact, to a large extent Arnold defined Hellenism (or as he put it, "the bent which we call Hellenising") precisely in terms of a "free play of consciousness" (*CA* "Conclusion" 176). And of course, as he explained in his classic essay on the subject, this was also how he understood one of the two key aspects of criticism, as being "essentially the exercise" of curiosity, a quality which his fellow citizens could only understand in "a rather bad and disparaging" sense but which he understood as "the free play of the mind"[24]; the other aspect being the making of the kind of distinctions ("between excellent and inferior, sound and unsound or only half-sound, true and untrue or only half-true") that "charlatanism"—because it stands for (what Kierkegaard calls) "the unhappy love of envy, instead of the happy love of admiration,"[25] which is what (at its best) I take criticism to stand for—would confuse or obliterate.[26]

As I too understand it, then, Hellenism stands for our need to find a space in which we can find time to play and practice criticism, a criticism that, in attempting to distinguish the "inferior" from the "excellent," and to discriminate among the "sound and unsound or only half-sound" and between the "true and untrue or only half-true," can't (and shouldn't try to) avoid having a sacrificial dimension to it. And when Hellenism is understood in this way, my feeling is that we need both it *and* Abrahamism: indeed, that what we need—*now as always*—is to try to find a balance between it and Abrahamism.

But since this is something that can be too easily said and too easily misunderstood, I want to try to make my meaning a bit clearer with reference first to another recent intervention by Žižek and then back to D.H.Lawrence's great 1925 essay on "Morality and the Novel."

First, then, a moment near the end of Žižek's contribution to the 2005 volume *The Neighbor: Three Inquiries in Political Theology*. On the basis of passages in which Che Guevara speaks, on the one hand, of a necessary and "relentless hatred of the enemy that...transforms us into... cold killing machines" while, on the other hand, claiming that "the true revolutionary is guided by strong feelings of love," Žižek asserts that, "in their love/hatred, revolutionaries are pushed beyond the limitations of empirical 'human nature,' so that their violence is literally *angelic*."[27] For Žižek this recalls "Christ's scandalous words from Luke" which we noted earlier (the ones enjoining us to hate our parents etc.) and he draws the following conclusion:

> This Christian stance is the opposite of the Oriental attitude of nonviolence, which—as we know from the long history of Buddhist rulers and warriors—can legitimize the worst violence. It is not that the revolutionary violence "really" aims at establishing a nonviolent harmony; on the contrary, the authentic revolutionary liberation is much more directly identified with violence—it is violence as such (the violent gesture of discarding, of establishing a difference, of drawing a line of separation) which liberates. Freedom is not a blissfully neutral state of harmony and balance, but the violent act which disturbs this balance. (186)

Like the essay in which it appears, this passage arouses mixed feelings in me. On the one hand, I take Žižek to be reacting against those who would stress the violent or sacrificial nature of any ethical decision or act of criticism[28] and I agree with him that we need the latter, even if it is violent. I agree, in other words, that any ethical decision or act of criticism can legitimately be seen (and certainly experienced as) an act of violence, if only because it frequently entails sacrifice; or in Žižek's words, a "violent gesture of discarding, of establishing a difference, of drawing a line of separation." In this sense, therefore, I sympathize with Žižek's desire to make (in his essay's subtitle) "A Plea for Ethical Violence." But on the other hand, I think he is making a mistake when he calls this "*violence as such*." I see this as a failure to make some crucial distinctions,[29] as a result of which we oughtn't perhaps to be *too* surprised to find him coming up with the appalling idea that we ought to be emulating Benny Morris, in whom he claims to find "the concealed obscene supplement to Levinasian ethics." According to Žižek, Morris's "ruthlessness," "his cold acceptance of the fact that we have to kill others in order to survive," "should be practiced in all domains today. For example, it is not enough to oppose the U.S. military presence in Iraq—one should condone the taking and killing of Western civilian hostages" (157).

This, I would suggest, is what can happen when the idea of "balance" is simply *rejected*, out of hand. So that, while I would agree that a certain way of invoking balance (sometimes, for example, Arnold's; as in his idea that the world "ought to be, though it never is, evenly and happily balanced between [Hellenism and Hebraism]") may well seem unreal and therefore make us impatient with it, I think that the solution is not to reject the term but rather to turn to a more effective way of invoking and using it. Though the following reflections by D.H.Lawrence were made with the novel in mind, their application is much wider:

> All emotions, including love and hate, and rage and tenderness, go to the adjusting of the oscillating, unestablished balance between two people who amount to anything. If the novelist puts his thumb in the pan, for love, tenderness, sweetness, peace, then he commits an immoral act...and he makes inevitable the horrible reaction, when he lets his thumb go, towards hate and brutality, cruelty and destruction.
>
> Life is so made, that opposites sway about a trembling centre of balance. The sins of the fathers are visited on the children. If the fathers drag down the balance on the side of love, peace, and production, then in the third or fourth generation the balance will swing back violently to hate, rage, and destruction. We must balance as we go. (*STH* 173)

Crucial here is the recognition that "balance" is not something we should try to fix;[30] that the "opposites" *should* be "sway[ing]" about a "centre" that *should* be "trembling"; and that, when it is properly understood, the process of "adjusting" the balance—a balance that *should* be "oscillating, unestablished" and unstable ("[m]orality in the novel [being] the trembling instability of the balance" [*STH* 172])—is seen to be endless. And sometimes (as, for example, when it allows for the expression of such emotions as hate or rage) the adjusting is likely to involve a certain violence, which may be the only way of avoiding worse forms of "brutality" and "cruelty," what Žižek calls "the worst violence."

For me, then, the idea that "[w]e must balance as we go" means that we must assume responsibility for making the kind of extremely difficult decisions Derrida talks about. And while it might seem nice to be able to promise that when, for example, one insists on taking time out to play, one will do so without entirely closing one's ears to human misery, it may be more honest to admit that this is probably not possible, nor even desirable. Nietzsche may have been right to insist that our ability to forget may be as essential to our well-being as our ability to remember. "It requires," he claimed, "a good deal of strength"—not insensitivity, notice, nor (as we have seen George Eliot put it) our being "well wadded with stupidity"—"to be able to live and to *forget* the extent to which to live and to be unjust is one and the same thing" (my italics).[31]

Chapter Seven

Driv[ing] to the edge of the unknown, and beyond

We are not created of ourselves. But from the unknown, from the great darkness of the outside that which is strange and new arrives on our threshold, enters and takes place in us.
— D.H.Lawrence ("Life" 696–7)

Neither do men light a candle, and put it under a bushel, but on a candlestick; and it giveth light unto all that are in the house.
— Matthew (5:15)

"What in the Sam Hill is going on here?"

Let us return, just for a second, to H.H.&D; specifically, to two moments in Hitchens's *God Is Not Great*. We have already noticed the first: it forms the end of the sentence in which Hitchens assures us that "[r]eligion comes from the period of human prehistory where nobody—not even the mighty Democritus who concluded that all matter was made from atoms—had the smallest idea what was going on" (64). Here is the second:

But there is a great deal to be learned and appreciated from the scrutiny of religion, and one often finds oneself standing atop the shoulders of distinguished writers and thinkers who were certainly one's intellectual and sometimes even one's moral superiors. Many of them, in their own time, had ripped away the disguise of idolatry and paganism, and even risked martyrdom for the sake of disputes with their own coreligionists. However, a moment in history has now arrived when even such a pygmy such as myself can claim to know more—through no merit of his own—and to see that the final ripping of the whole disguise is overdue. (151)

In their books, too, Dawkins and Harris convey the impression that they would also be happy for us to think of each one of them as the pygmy Hitchens describes himself as being. But of course it is false modesty. They genuinely believe that they can legitimately "claim to know more," that *they* know what is "going on."

Let's keep this in mind as we turn next to Annie Dillard's *Holy the Firm*. At the beginning of the second, middle part of this book, Dillard tells us of a plane crash that occurred in the woods not far from where she was living at the time. A man and his seven year old daughter were in the plane and the exploding fuel "burnt off her face."[1] The third section begins with Dillard telling us she "know[s] only enough of God to want to worship him, by any means ready to hand" (55). A few pages further on, aware of the fact that the girl, Julie Norwich, is "in the hospital, burned," Dillard says she read once that "[p]eople released from burn wards ...have a very high suicide rate" (59-60). We then get this:

> They had not realized, before they were burned, that life could in-
> clude such suffering, nor that they personally could be permitted
> such pain. No drugs ease the pain of third-degree burns, because
> burns destroy skin: the drugs simply leak into the sheets. His dis-
> ciples asked Christ about a roadside beggar who had been blind
> from birth, "Who did sin, this man or his parents, that he was
> born blind?" And Christ, who spat on the ground, made a mud
> of his spittle and clay, plastered the mud over the man's eyes, and
> gave him sight, answered, "Neither hath this man sinned, nor his
> parents: but that the works of God should be made manifest in
> him." Really? If we take this answer to refer to the affliction it-
> self—and not the subsequent cure—as "God's works made mani-
> fest," then we have, along with "Not as the world gives do I give
> unto you," two meager, baffling, and infuriating answers to one
> of the few questions worth asking, to wit, What in the Sam Hill
> is going on here?
>
> The works of God made manifest? Do we really need more
> victims to remind us that we're all victims?...Do we need blind
> men stumbling about, and little flamefaced children, to remind
> us what God can—and will—do? (59–61)

Coming as it does from someone whose belief in God it is impossible to doubt, this passage seems to me astounding (even more so when taken together with the references to Julie Norwich in the book's final paragraphs; for example:"She is preserved like a salted fillet from all evil, baptized at birth into time and now into eternity, into the bladelike arms of God" [73]). It isn't that Dillard's reflections make me wish I shared her belief in God but they do make me feel I'm in the presence of a kind of seriousness that H.H.&D seem unable to come close either to mustering or appreciating.

As Annie Dillard can help us to see, when it comes to "one of the few questions worth asking, to wit, What in the Sam Hill is going on here?" H.H.& D *don't* know, *none* of us do.

Hence the importance of keeping up (or open) some kind of relationship with the unknown; or (to use one of D.H.Lawrence's phrases) of participating in some way in "the adventure to the unknown." And with this in mind I now want to move towards a close by considering two questions, one Lawrence raises in the opening of his book-length "Study of Thomas Hardy" and one that Birkin asks Gerald Crich in the "In the Train" chapter of *Women in Love*. Both of these questions—"What is it that really matters?" and "What do you live for?"—have a religious dimension (expressing as they do forms of ultimate concern) and (being a literary critic) I plan to address them indirectly, by means of Lawrence's own attempts at doing so.[2]

What really matters in life? What do we live for?

I will begin with the first of these two questions, which Lawrence raises (in the form "What is it that really matters?") four paragraphs from the end of the opening chapter of his "Study." Lawrence's answer is dramatically simple but also provocative. We act most of the time as if we believe that what most matters is self-preservation (*STH* 7) and all the things we do (in particular, all the work we do) to ensure it: the efforts we make (through our work especially) to protect ourselves and our property, to save up so that we will have enough to eat and to wear and so that we will be safe. But to live like this, "without ever bursting the bud, the tight economical bud of caution and thrift and self-preservation" (10) is to rot and stagnate. The most important thing, the "final aim of every living thing, creature or being[,] is the full achievement of itself" (12). And if we ask, reasonably enough, how we are meant to fully achieve or become ourselves, Lawrence's advice is that we should look, in the first instance, to "the gaudy, fleeting poppy" and to the phoenix, both of which he thinks achieve themselves in the "red flame licking into sight," which seems to the world like "flaunting vanity" (8, 10). With the poppy and phoenix in mind, Lawrence says he wishes "we were all like kindled bonfires on the edge of space" (18). Or as he also puts it (with reference to Matthew), "what matters is the light under the bushel" (17), the light that we need to have available to us outside of the bushel, the light that we need to live by. We can now turn to consider Birkin's question.

"Tell me," Birkin asks Gerald, "What do you live for?" "I suppose," Gerald replies, "I live to work, to produce something..." Birkin presses Gerald further on this and then, moments later, still not satisfied with the way Gerald falls back on "the plausible ethics of productivity" (*WL* 56), he rephrases the question: "What do you think is the aim and object of your life, Gerald?" This time Gerald has no answer: "'At the moment, I couldn't say off-hand,' he replied, with faintly ironic humour." So Birkin begins to explain what *he* thinks. While admitting that he doesn't have it at the moment, Birkin says that what he wants is "love" (57), "the finality of love" with "one woman." When Gerald then confesses that he doesn't "believe a woman, and nothing but a woman, will ever make [his] life," we get the following exchange (which Birkin opens):

> "Then wherein does life centre, for you?"
> "I don't know—that's what I want somebody to tell me.—As far as I can make out, it doesn't centre at all. It is artificially held together by the social mechanism."
> Birkin pondered as if he would crack something.
> "I know," he said, "it just doesn't centre. The old ideals are dead as nails—nothing there. It seems to me there remains only this perfect union with a woman—sort of ultimate marriage—and there isn't anything else."
> "And you mean if there isn't the woman, there's nothing? said Gerald.
> "Pretty well that—seeing there's no God." (58)

Here, then, Lawrence implicitly raises another fundamental question. In the absence of God (in any of the ways, at any rate, in which God used to be known), what, if anything, performs one of the main functions that religion is supposed to perform, that of holding the world (or "life") together? This, in effect, is one of the key questions we find Birkin reflecting on throughout much of *Women in Love*. And it is clear from the overtures he makes to Gerald and Ursula that this (holding the world together in a more convincing way than it is held together by the social mechanism) is one of the principal functions the relationships he wants to enter into are intended to perform.

This is the point of the reiterated emphasis on the crucial significance of the bond, the pledge, the oath ("swear[ing] a *Blutbrüderschaft* [206]) and the "binding contract" (289). After all, as Derrida puts it in his essay on "Faith and Knowledge," *religio* begins with the "promise" (30).[3] This can perhaps help us to understand what is at stake when Birkin tells Ursula that "if we are going to know each other, we must pledge ourselves for ever" ("Mino" 145). And also, incidentally, when in the same chapter he explains that he thinks "the world is only held together by the mystic conjunction, the ultimate unison between people—a bond. And the immediate bond is between man and woman" (152). Similarly, in the sixteenth ("Man to Man") chapter, we find him claiming that "two exceptional people make another world. You and I," he tells Gerald, "we make another, separate world" (205). Or, as we are surely meant to feel, this *would* be the case if only (as we are told in chapter twenty-five, "Marriage or Not?") Gerald could "accept Rupert's offer of love, to enter into the bond of pure trust and love with the other man, and then subsequently with the woman [Gudrun]. If he pledged himself with the man he would later be able to pledge himself with the woman: not merely in legal marriage, but in absolute, mystic marriage" (353).

But Gerald is unable or unwilling to do this. He believes, as we have seen, that life "is artificially held together by the social mechanism." More specifically, we are told in the eighth ("Breadalby") chapter that Gerald believes that the "unifying principle was the work in hand. Only work, the business of production, held men together. It was mechanical, but then society *was* a mechanism" (102). And later, near the end of the seventeenth ("Industrial Magnate") chapter, we find Gerald concluding

that "[w]hat mattered was the great social productive machine. Let that
work perfectly" (227) and everything will be fine (or at least as good as
can be expected). The problem, however, is that as soon as Gerald has
"converted the industry [he is responsible for running] into a new and
terrible purity," he finds himself redundant—the "whole system was now
so perfect that Gerald was hardly necessary any more"—and he no longer knows "what to do" (231-2). As a result of which, his answer to the
question posed in the "Study of Thomas Hardy"—what really matters is
the great social productive machine—no longer sounds persuasive, not
even to himself. And the dilemma he found himself expressing to Birkin
much earlier (in "Breadalby")—"I wish you'd tell me something that *did*
matter" (96)—becomes acute.

I take it that, like Gerald Crich, most of us these days more or less
(happily or resignedly) "accept the established order," even if we don't
"livingly believe" in it ("Marriage or Not?" 353)—accept it, I mean, as
constituting reality. By the same token, when we ordinarily think of the
"real world," most of us are probably thinking, like Gerald, of the "world
of work" ("Industrial Magnet" 232). After all, as Lawrence noted in his
"Study," "the conscious mind has unanimously decreed" that our lives
are not to be spent in the "sheer play of being free": they are rather "to be
utilized for work, first and foremost" (*STH* 32). Or as Hannah Arendt
was later to put it in her book *The Human Condition*, "[w]hatever we do,
we are supposed to do for the sake of 'making a living': such is the verdict
of society." And the result, according to Arendt, is that "all serious activities...are called labor, and every activity which is not necessary either
for the life of the individual or for the life process of society is subsumed
under playfulness."[4] She points out, furthermore, that the "danger that
the modern age's emancipation of labor" might force "all mankind for
the first time under the yoke of necessity" was "clearly perceived by Marx
when he insisted that the aim of a revolution...must consist in the emancipation of man from labor" (130).

When one form of religion disappears (like, for example, the kind
of Christianity associated with Gerald Crich's father), other forms will
emerge to take its place: like Birkin's attempt to reimagine and recreate
friendship and marriage, on the one hand, and (to stay within *Women in
Love*), on the other, the kind of modernization for which "the machine

is the Godhead, and production or work is worship" ("Industrial Magnet" 225).

The fundamental choice we face is not between religion and non-religion but rather between religions. And this being the case, I think it is important that we pause for a moment to try to gain some historical perspective on the growing hegemony of the second of these two religions (the religion of Work); more specifically, I think we need to see this in the perspective provided by André Gorz in his *Critique of Economic Reason*.

Arguing that regular work for wages or for a salary—as distinct from housework, artistic work or the work of self-production—is "a modern invention," Gorz claims that it "was invented, then subsequently generalized only with the coming of industrialism."[5] But it wasn't just invented; it was first resisted and then imposed by force:

> [F]or workers at the end of the eighteenth century, "work" meant the application of an intuitive know-how that was an integral part of a time-honoured rhythm of life and they would not have dreamt of intensifying and prolonging their efforts in order to earn more ...
>
> The unwillingness of the workers to do a full day's labour, day after day, was the principal reason why the first factories went bankrupt. The bourgeoisie put this reluctance down to "laziness" and "insolence." They saw no other means of overcoming this problem than to pay the workers such meagre wages that it was necessary for the latter to do a good ten hours' toil every day of the week in order to earn enough to survive... (21)

If "work" as it has come to be understood in modern bourgeois society was invented and imposed by force so, Gorz argues, was the concept of "unemployment." But the invention and imposition of this latter category took place much later. As Gorz notes, "the right to intermittent work was perceived as an important freedom right up to the period in the 1910s when the notion of 'unemployment' was invented" (196). Here is Gorz's explanation as to *why* the category of "unemployment" was invented and what its invention meant in practice:

The notion of unemployment...was invented expressly to combat the practice of discontinuous work and to eliminate those
intermittent workers who often preferred to lose wages to "gain
independence from the employer and, more generally, from the
condition of wage-labour." The aim of the national network of
public labour exchanges, the creation of which was advocated in
1910 by William Beveridge, was "quite simply to destroy a category of the population," the category of intermittent workers:
they had either to become regular full-time wage-earners or else
be completely unemployed... (196-7)[6]

In case anyone thinks Gorz might be misrepresenting Beveridge, here is
the latter in his own words:

For the man who wants to work once and lie in bed for the rest of
the week the labour exchange will make their wish unrealisable.
For the man who wants to get a casual job now and again the exchange will gradually make his mode of life impossible. It will take
that one day a week he wanted to get and give it to another man
who has already four days a week and so will enable that other man
to get a decent living. Then the first man will be thrown on your
hands [Beveridge is replying here to a question by Professor Smart]
to be trained and disciplined into better ways. (qtd. 213-14)[7]

The upshot is that the danger foreseen by Arendt—"that the modern age's
emancipation of labor" might force "*all* mankind for the first time under
the yoke of necessity"—has largely been realized.[8] Working hours today
are generally longer, job security is weaker and the threat of unemployment is greater than was the case twenty or thirty years ago. Just think, for
example, of the pressures on the French (which is to say, on a society that
succeeded for a while in reducing the working week to under forty hours)
to get back into line, to work longer, just like the rest of us. Today (as we
rapidly approach the end of the first decade of the twenty-first century),
the dominant attitude around the world is once again summarized in Benjamin Franklin's (the would-be liberator's) whip-cracking "'*Work, you free
jewel, WORK!*' And the sad fact is that, for the overwhelming majority
of us, neither Lawrence's retort here ("Benjamin, I will not work" [*SCAL*

25]) nor Birkin and Ursula's solution in the "Excurse" chapter of *Women in Love* (when they send in their resignations from the world of work) are options. The days when it was sometimes possible to earn enough to survive comfortably on casual, discontinuous and intermittent labour have long gone. Those who are *forced* to try to get by on it are likely to find themselves in dire straits, wishing that they too could get into Weber's iron cage, the one in which the rest of us are, much of the time, only too willing to spend our lives. After all, where else could we possibly find the kind of security, comfort and entertainment that we have grown to depend on and that we now find it almost impossible to imagine living without? So to recall what Lawrence says about Gerald Critch's "acceptance of the established world," we may not "*livingly* believe" in the religion of Work that effectively constitutes this world *as* a (kind of gilt-lined) cage but, judging by both our actions and our inaction, it might seem that we give it the only kind of credence of which, these days, we may be capable.

Possibly. There is, in any case, an important sense in which it has to be admitted that the "world" in question is indeed "real" and it would, in the present circumstances, be irresponsible to encourage anyone to try to get by without establishing and maintaining at least some foothold in it. Anyone trying to do that would probably be making a fatal mistake.[9] But at the same time, we should certainly be trying to find ways of loosening its grip upon us because it would also be a terrible and fatal mistake to take this world of work for the *whole* of reality; or to effectively settle for it as the only religion we need. As I see it, that would be to *guarantee* catastrophe: on two counts.

First, on a global scale: in the sense that current forms of economic growth (which inevitably means current patterns of work or job structures) seem to be leading us inexorably towards ecological disaster. And secondly, on the personal level. I'm thinking here of the following exchange between Birkin and Gerald:

> "I suppose you are conducting the business as successfully as ever, and ignoring the demands of the soul."
> "That's it," said Gerald; "at least as far as the business is concerned. I couldn't say about the soul, I'm sure." (ch. 16, "Man to Man" 202)[10]

As I understand it, the religion of Work makes it more and more difficult for its adherents to attend to (and increasingly easy for us to ignore the existence of) the "demands of the soul."

Hence the need for the alternative proposed by Birkin in *Women in Love* and advocated by Lawrence in his "Study." At first glance, it might seem that we have not one but two alternatives here: on the one hand, entering into a "sort of ultimate marriage" or friendship; on the other, achieving oneself. Looked at more closely, however, we can see what they both have in common: both are ways of adventuring into the unknown; in Birkin's words, of "deliver[ing] *myself* over to the unknown" (*WL*, "Mino" 147);[11] in the words of the "Study," of traversing one's "known" and coming "to meet the unknown" (*STH* 19). And whatever *else* might be entailed in attending to the demands of the soul, I take it that, as Lawrence understands it, this hospitality to the stranger or openness to (or adventure into) the unknown must always be a key part of it.[12] So, in summary, I would say that here we have essentially one religion that not only forms an alternative to the religion of Work but that does so in radically different fashion to that often attributed to so-called *other-worldly religion*: instead of devaluing this world, it revalues it; instead of depreciating our sense of reality, it opens it up and enlarges it. As, for example, in its attempt to rescue the idea of "vanity": "Yet we call the poppy 'vanity'" (*STH* 12; and see 10). It seems to me that the far-reaching implications of this are hinted at in the following reflection of Hannah Arendt:

> The melancholy wisdom of *Ecclesiastes*—'Vanity of vanities; all is vanity .... There is no new thing under the sun,...there is no remembrance of former things; neither shall there be any remembrance of things that are to come with those that shall come after"—does not necessarily arise from specifically religious experience; but it is certainly unavoidable wherever and whenever trust in the world as a place fit for human appearance, for action and speech, is gone. (Arendt's ellipses, *Human Condition* 204)[13]

But "vanity" is only one of countless possible examples here: one could equally well reflect on the rescue operation Lawrence performs on such terms as "excess," "waste," adventure, play, laziness etc.

Two further points in this connection, the first of which concerns
motherhood and "the adventure to the unknown," something I promised
back in chapter five (in section viii.b) that I would return to here. At the
very end of the sixth ("Anna Victrix") chapter of *The Rainbow*, Lawrence
tells us that "[w]ith satisfaction she [Anna] relinquished the adventure to
the unknown. She was bearing her children" (*R* 182). This seems to me
worth drawing attention to here for a number of reasons. First because
it offers the opportunity to challenge the prejudice that some readers
today often bring to their reading of Lawrence, one that leads them to
expect to find his treatment of relations between the sexes tainted by sex-
ism. Sometimes it is, but not here.[14] To begin with, then, I suggest that
these two sentences should be read first in the light of the fact that the
preceding chapter has shown Anna to be a much bolder adventurer into
the unknown than her husband Will. (Among other things, one thinks,
for example, of her dancing, when she is naked and big with child "lifting
her hands and her body to the Unseen" [170].) But secondly I suggest that
when we read of Anna's relinquishing the adventure we should also have
in mind the following sentences from the opening of the sixth chapter of
The Study of Thomas Hardy:

> That she bear children is not a woman's significance. But that she
> bear herself, that is her supreme and risky fate: that she drive on
> to the edge of the unknown, and beyond. (*STH* 52)

In other words, as Lawrence understands it (as he understood it here, at any
rate), it is incumbent just as much upon women as it is upon men to "drive
on to the edge of the unknown, and beyond." And from this point of view
motherhood provides, as it were, no excuse for hanging back. But in her
essay on "Mary, Maternity, and Abrahamic Hospitality in Derrida's Reading of Massignon," Cleo McNelly Kearns reminds us that there is another
point of view that needs considering here too. Kearns points out that for
Derrida hospitality "is very much like a difficult pregnancy, that is to say an
experience fraught with expectations, perils, and contradictions":

> Welcomes to babies, like welcomes to strangers, are ambivalent,
> at once necessary and disconcerting, for by a progression of inten-
> sification hard to contain, they often involve both violence and

vulnerability; they fracture existing relationships and often call for self-abnegation or sacrifice, if only the abnegation of sheltering another within. The mother is both host and hostage to her unborn child... (*Derrida and Religion* 76-7)

It might well be said, then, that maternity "captures something of the ambiguity, the combination of desire, risk, promise, and messianic expectation inherent in entertaining another" *as nothing else can*, simply because the entertaining in question takes place "within the self" (78).[15]

The second point concerns Lawrence's idea that what really matters in life is that we should all become—or (better still) manage "the full achievement of"—ourselves (*STH* 12).[16] This might remind us of a number of things. First, perhaps, of the subtitle—"How One Becomes What One Is"—of Nietzsche's *Ecce Homo*,[17] which Alexander Nehamas uses as a chapter heading in his book *Nietzsche: Life as Literature* (1985) and which James Miller invokes at the beginning of his book *The Passion of Michael Foucault*, which he tells us is "a narrative account of one man's lifelong struggle to honor Nietzsche's gnomic injunction, 'to become what one is.'"[18] Secondly, it might also remind us of the little story about Reb Zusya:

> He was worried about his prospects in the world to come, and he said, "The Recording Angel won't ask me *Why weren't you Abraham?* Or *Why weren't you Moses?* He will ask me *Why weren't you Zusya?*"[19]

And finally (for our purposes here), it can remind us of something we noted at the beginning of the fourth chapter; namely, Lawrence's description of "the first great purpose of Democracy":

> that each man shall be spontaneously himself–each man himself, each woman herself, without any question of equality or inequality entering in at all; and that no man shall try to determine the being of any other man, or of any other woman. ("Democracy" 716)

What I think now needs to be emphasized, however, is what Lawrence has made clear just before he offers this description, which is that he thinks *being spontaneously oneself is "the most difficult thing of all"* (my italics, 714). It's interesting, furthermore, to note[20] that Lawrence's own explanation of this difficulty is in terms of what he calls "the fall of man" (715), which encourages us to think that our being spontaneously ourselves is his version of Paradise.

The idea that being spontaneously oneself may be the most difficult thing of all seems to me so important that I will be devoting one of the other two volumes in my attempt at *Rethinking Religion* to examining it, something I plan to do by means of an extensive, novel-based, engagement with René Girard's theory of mimetic desire.

Finally, one last thought.

From "the standpoint of redemption"

Like every generation that preceded us, we have been endowed with a *weak* Messianic power, *a power to which the past has a claim.*

—Walter Benjamin[21]

This brings me to the last paragraph of Theodor Adorno's *Minima Moralia: Reflections from Damaged Life.* It starts as follows:

The only philosophy which can be responsibly practised in face of despair is the attempt to contemplate all things as they would present themselves from the standpoint of redemption. Knowledge has no light but that shed on the world by redemption: all else is reconstruction, mere technique. Perspectives must be fashioned that displace and estrange the world, reveal it to be, with its rifts and crevices, as indigent and distorted as it will appear one day in the messianic light. To gain such perspectives without velleity or violence, entirely from felt contact with its objects—this alone is the task of thought.[22]

Notice the verb tenses: how we are first asked "to contemplate all things as they *would* present themselves from the standpoint of redemption"; then told, in effect, that enlightenment comes only from the light that is "shed on the world by redemption" and that "the task of thought" is to fashion perspectives that will reveal the world to be "as it *will* appear one day in the messianic light." After four more sentences that explain how simultaneously necessary ("the situation calls imperatively for such knowledge") and impossibly difficult ("because it presupposes a standpoint removed, even though by a hair's breadth, from the scope of existence") a task this is, we get the paragraph's final sentence: "But beside the demand thus placed on thought, the question of the reality or unreality of redemption itself hardly matters."

I find this compelling.[23] I can't myself think of philosophy having any more important undertaking than, in one form or another, the task Adorno describes and assigns to the would-be thinker (or philosopher) in each of us.[24]

Notes

Notes to Preface

1. Norman Mailer, "An Evening with Jackie Kennedy" (1962), *The Presidential Papers*, London: Corgi, 1965, 98.
2. Stanley Cavell, "An Emerson Mood" (1980), in *The Senses of Walden* (1972), expanded edition, San Francisco: North Point P, 1981 (141-160): 159.
3. E.P.Thompson, "An Open Letter to Leszek Kolakowski," *The Socialist Register* 1973, ed. Ralph Milliband and John Saville, London: The Merlin P, 1974 (1-100): 14.
4. Slavoj Žižek, *The Puppet and the Dwarf: The Perverse Core of Christianity*, Cambridge, MA.: MIT P, 2003, 3. Before Žižek reverses it, the thesis in question ends as follows: "The puppet called 'historical materialism' is to win all the time. It can easily be a match for anyone if it enlists the services of theology, which today, as we know, is wizened and has to keep out of sight." See Walter Benjamin, "Theses on the Philosophy of History" (1940), in *Illuminations*, ed. Hannah Arendt, Trans. Harry Zohn, London: Collins/Fontana, 1973 (255-66): 255.
5. Jacques Derrida & Maurizio Ferraris, *A Taste for the Secret* (1997), Trans. Giacomo Donis, Cambridge: Polity, 2001, 86.
6. Adam Phillips, *Promises, Promises: Essays on Psychoanalysis and Literature*, New York: Basic Books, 2001, xi.
7. Margaret Wente & Camille Paglia, "Interview," *Globe and Mail*, Sept. 15, 2007, F4.
8. See E.P.Thompson, "The Poverty of Theory or An Orrery of Errors" (1978), in *The Poverty of Theory and Other Essays*, New York & London: Monthly Review P,, 1978, 1-205.
9. Jean-Luc Nancy, "The Unsacrificeable." Trans. Richard Livingston. *Yale French Studies 79. Literature and the Ethical Question*, ed. Claire Nouvet. 1991. (20-38): 37.
10. Peter Hallward, *Out of this World: Deleuze and the Philosophy of Creation*, London and New York: Verso, 2006. 57.
11. Michael Foucault, "Maurice Blanchot: The Thought from Outside" (1966), in *Foucault/Blanchot*, New York: Zone Books, 1990 (7-58): 16.
12. Philip Goodchild, "Why is philosophy so compromised with God?," in Mary Bryden ed., *Deleuze and Religion*, London and New York: Routledge, 2001 (156-66), 161, 164.

13. Giorgio Agamben, "Absolute Immanence" (1996), in *Potentialities: Collected Essays in Philosophy*, Ed. & trans. Daniel Heller-Roazen, Stanford: Stanford UP, 1999 (220-39): 238-9.

14. Emmanuel Levinas, "Intention, Event, and the Other," Trans. Andrew Schmitz, in Jill Robbins ed., *Is It Righteous To Be? Interviews with Emmanuel Levinas*, Stanford: Stanford UP, 2001 (140-57): 148. See too Eric Santner's argument that "Freud and Rosenzweig are...among our most important thinkers of this immanent transcendence" (*On the Psychotheology of Everyday Life: Reflections on Freud and Rosenzweig*, Chicago: U of Chicago P, 2001, 10.

15. Giorgio Agamben, "Bartleby, or On Contingency" (1993), in *Potentialities* (243-71) 243.

16. But for those in danger of forgetting, there is, as Levinas reminds us, "a participation in Holy Scripture in the national literatures, in Homer and Plato, in Racine and Victor Hugo, as in Pushkin, Dosteovsky or Goethe, as of course in Tolstoy or in Agnon" (*Ethics and Infinity* [1982], Trans. Richard A. Cohen, Pittsbugh: Duquesne UP, 1985, 117). The English writers I have named certainly belong on this list.

17. Stanley Cavell "Kierkegaard's *On Authority and Revelation*" (1966), in *Must We Mean What We Say?: A Book of Essays* (1969). Cambridge: Cambridge UP, 1976, (163-79): 176.

Notes to Chapter One

1. Jacques Derrida, "Faith and Knowledge: The Two Sources of 'Religion' at the Limits of Reason Alone," trans. Samuel Weber, in *Religion*, eds. Jacques Derrida and Gianni Vattimo. Stanford: Stanford UP, 1998. (1-78): 3. Hereafter abbreviated FK. This lengthy essay has now been reprinted in a collection of Derrida's writings assembled together under the title *Acts of Religion*, ed. Gil Anidjar (New York and London: Routledge, 2002).

2. The sentence immediately following this reads as follows: "It is even the meaning that Benveniste believes obliged to retain with reference to the 'proper and constant usages' of the word during the classical period." This is a reference to Emile Benveniste's *Indo-European Language and Society*, Trans. Elizabeth Palmer, London: Faber & Faber, 1973, and Derrida footnotes it with his extract from Benveniste:

> This is where the expression *religio est*, "to have scruples," comes from...This usage is constant during the classical period...In sum, *religio* is a hesitation that holds back, a scruple that prevents, and not a sentiment that guides an action or that incites one to practice

a cult. It seems to us that this meaning, demonstrated by ancient usage beyond the slightest ambiguity, imposes a single interpretation for *religio*: that which Cicero gives in attaching *relgio* to *legere*. (Benveniste 521; qtd. by Derrida 71, n. 20)

3. Brian Bethune, "Is God Poison?," *Maclean's*, April 16 2007 (38-44) 39. The cover of this issue informs us that "A growing movement blames religion for all the world's ills, from the war on terror to AIDS in Africa to child abuse" and in larger letters asks the question "IS GOD POISON?" This effectively publicized Hitchens' *God Is Not Great*, which was due to come out the following month.

4. Anthony Gottlieb, "Atheists with Attitude: Why do they hate Him?," *New Yorker*, May 21 2007, 1-5 (on line); Michael Kinsley, "In God, Distrust," *The New York Times Book Review*, May 13 2007, 1, 8-9.

5. Ronald Aronson, "Faith No More? Against the Rising Tide of Rejuvenated Religion a Number of Writers Make the Case for Disbelief," *Book Forum*, 12:3, Oct./Nov. 2005, 16-19. As it happens, this review was also announced—in the words "Is God Still Dead? Ronald Aronson on the New Atheism"—on the cover. And to ensure maximum dramatic impact, the question "IS GOD STILL DEAD?" is printed in red, against a black background, a clear allusion to the April 8 1966 cover of *Time* magazine (that has the question "IS GOD DEAD?" in red on black). Aronson notes that Harris keeps alive atheism's "image as dogmatic, fanatically rationalistic" (18).

6. Marilynne Robinson, "Hysterical Scientism: The Ecstasy of Richard Dawkins," *Harper's*, November 2006, 83-8.; Terry Eagleton, "Lunging, Flailing, Mispunching," *London Review of Books*, 28:20, 19 October 2006, 32-4.

7. Thus, for example, in a second, more recent, piece, Ronald Aronson claims in his opening sentences that what we have here is "a remarkable intellectual wave. No fewer than five books by the New Atheists have appeared on bestseller lists in the past two years" ("The New Atheists," *Nation*, June 25, 2007 and on web at http://www.thenation.com/doc/20070625/aronson). He is referring to the four books I discuss here and also to Daniel Dennett's *Breaking the Spell*.

8. Michael Polanyi, *Personal Knowledge: Towards a Post-Critical Philosophy* (1958), Chicago: U of Chicago P, 1962, 286.

9. Sam Harris, *Letter to a Christian Nation*, New York: Knopf, Borzoi, 2006, 87.

10. Christopher Hitchens, *God Is Not Great: How Religion Poisons Everything*, Toronto: McClelland & Stewart, 2007, 283.

11. Sam Harris, *The End of Faith: Religion, Terror, and the Future of Reason* (2004), London: The Free Press, 2006, 281.
12. Richard Dawkins, *The God Delusion*, Boston & New York: Houghton & Mifflin Co., 2006, 250.
13. See, for example, Catherine Madsen's fine "Editorial," *CrossCurrent*, Fall 2006 and on web at
http://www.crosscurrents.org/Madseneditorialfall2006.htm
14. Thus, in "The New Atheists," Aronson writes: "Until now the most vocal left-of-center response to the Christian right, for example by Sojourners, has been to call for more religion in politics, not less. In early June the group organized a nationally televised forum at which John Edwards, Barack Obama and Hilary Clinton testified to their faith, talking about the 'hand of God' (Edwards), forgiveness (Obama) and prayer (Clinton)." Like Aronson, I too would prefer to see less rather than more, in fact ideally none at all, of this kind of thing.
15. In the following passage, for example, Harris sounds to me like a parent patiently explaining the way things are to a not too bright child:

> Consider: every devout Muslim has the same reasons for being a Muslim that you have for being a Christian. And yet you do not find their reasons compelling. The Koran repeatedly declares that it is the perfect word of the creator of the universe. Muslims believe this as fully as you believe the Bible's account of itself .... The truth is, you know exactly what it is like to be an atheist with respect to the beliefs of Muslims. *Isn't it obvious* that Muslims are fooling themselves? *Isn't it obvious* that anyone who thinks the Koran is the perfect word of the creator of the universe has not read the book critically? *Isn't it obvious* that the doctrine of Islam represents a near-perfect barrier to honest inquiry? *Yes, these things are obvious.* Understand that the way you view Islam is precisely the way devout Muslims view Christianity. And it is the way I view all religions. (*Letter*, my italics 7)

Of course, if you believe like Hitchens that religious folk are infants, this is precisely the right tone to adopt. But for a different way of looking at the problem Harris thinks he has solved so easily, consider this excerpt from D.H.Lawrence's "On Being Religious" (in *Phoenix: The Posthumous Papers of D.H.Lawrence (1936)*, ed. Edward McDonald, New York: Viking, 1972 [724-30]: 729):

From time to time, the Great God sends a new saviour. Christians will no longer have the pettiness to assert that Jesus is the only Saviour ever sent by the everlasting God. There have been other saviours, in other lands, at other times, with other messages.

16. Roland Barthes, *Criticism and Truth* (1966), Trans. Katrine Pilcher Keuneman, Minneapolis: U of Minnesota P, 1987, 50, 51.

17. Terry Eagleton, "Lunging, Flailing, Mispunching," *London Review of Books*, 28:20, 19 October 2006 (32-4): 32.

18. By way of example, Gottlieb immediately provides this: "A large survey in 2001 found that more than half of American Catholics, Episcopalians, Lutherans, Methodists, and Presbyterians believed that Jesus sinned—thus rejecting a central dogma of their own churches" (2). But as Gottlieb goes on to admit, polls can be misleading and it may be a mistake to take them (as Harris especially tends to do) at face value.

19. Frances Fitzgerald, "The Evangelical Surprise," *New York Review of Books*, LIV:7, April 26 2007 (31-4) 31. The surprise is that, "[d]uring the last two years, a half-dozen prominent evangelicals have published books denouncing the religious right .." One of these books, by Reverend Gregory Boyd is made up of a collection of sermons he gave that "caused a fifth of his congregation to leave the church," sermons in which "Boyd challenges the idea that the United States was, and should be, a Christian nation...There can be no such thing as a Christian nation, he argues" (33).

20. Jacques Derrida, *Aporias*, Trans. Thomas Dutoit, Stanford: Stanford UP, 1993, 20.

21. The tone of this passage reminds me of Monty Python but I think Hitchens is clearly not reproducing it intentionally. On the other hand, Dawkins tells us that what he considers the following "richly comic idea"—"To my naïve eyes, 'Thou shalt have no other gods but me' would seem an easy enough commandment to keep: a doddle, one might think, compared with 'Thou shalt not covet thy neighbour's wife.' Or her ass. (Or her ox.) Yet throughout the Old Testament, with the same predictable regularity as in bedroom farce, God had only to turn his back for a moment and the Children of Israel would be off and at it with Baal, or some trollop of a graven image"—"was suggested to [*him*] by Jonathan Miller who, surprisingly, never included it in a *Beyond the Fringe* sketch" (244). Most of the readings offered by Dawkins, Hitchins and Harris seem to me to be on this level (another example would be that of "Abraham setting out to barbecue Isaac" [Dawkins 251]. And all of this despite Hitchens' dismissal of religion for being childish. I recommend here what Raymond Williams has to say about "the boys" in his "Gravity's

Python" (1982), in *What I Came To Say*, Ed. Neil Belton, Francis Mulhern and Jenny Taylor, London: Hutchinson Radius, 1990, 108-12.

22. Dawkins expresses a similar concern when referring to Jesus's "somewhat dodgy family values" (250).

23. In a similar vein, after praising the Sermon on the Mount, Harris tells us "Islam appears to offer no such refuge for one who would live peacefully in a pluralistic world" (*End* 138)

24. Notice as well the hint that just possibly the psalmist might have known about the fool's unbelief because he might have been interrogating him, possibly under torture (the next sentence speaks of dissidents locked up in Soviet lunatic asylums).

25. Friedrich Nietzsche, *The Genealogy of Morals* (1887), Trans. Francis Golfing, in *The Birth of Tragedy* and *The Genealogy of Morals*, New York: Doubleday Anchor, 1956, 296-97.

26. Terrible and problematical but also most hopeful. It's worth pondering in this context what Alenka Zupančič identifies as "Nietzsche's oscillation between, on the one hand, the depreciation of truth as an enemy of life and, on the other, a kind of ethical imperative to pursue the truth, advocating (or, at least, valuing) a certain heroism of truth" (*The Shortest Shadow: Nietzsche's Philosophy of the Two*, Cambridge MA: MIT Press, 2003, 91; see too 93, 94, 95, 189).

27. A few sentences before the passage I've just quoted we find this: "Honest and intransigent atheism (the only air breathed today by the elite of this world), is thus not opposed to asceticism, all appearances to the contrary. Rather it is one of the last evolutionary phases of that ideal, one of its natural and logical consequences. It is the catastrophe, inspiring of respect, of a discipline in truth that has lasted for two millenia and which now prohibits the lie implicit in monotheistic belief" (*Genealogy* 296). The translation used by Zupančič has "we more spiritual men of this age" instead of "the elite of this world" (*The Shortest Shadow* 63).

28. I'm quoting here from the back cover of the paperback edition of Eric Santner's *On the Psychotheology of Everyday Life: Reflections on Freud and Rosenzweig*, Chicago: U of Chicago P, 2001; henceforth *Psychotheology*.

29. For example: "Christians seldom realize," according to Dawkins, "that much of the moral consideration for others which is apparently [only apparently?] promoted by both the Old and New Testaments was originally intended to apply only to a narrowly defined in-group. 'Love thy neighbour' didn't mean what we now think it means. It meant only 'Love another Jew'" (*God Delusion* 253). Maintaining that he is calling attention here "to one particularly unpleasant aspect of [the Bible's] ethical teaching," Dawkins explains that he is follow-

ing "the American physician and evolutionary anthropologist John Hartung" whom he credits ("The point is made devastatingly by [him]") with this insight (253). Moreover, Dawkins tells us that "Hartung puts it more bluntly than I dare: 'Jesus would have turned over in his grave if he had known that Paul would be taking his plan to the pigs'" (257). Here is Marilynne Robinson on the two objections she sees to the Dawkins/Hartung reading:

> First, the verse quoted here, Leviticus 19:18, does indeed begin, "You shall not take vengeance or bear a grudge against any of your people," language that allows a narrow interpretation of the commandment. But Leviticus 19:33-34 says "When an alien resides with you in your land, you shall not oppress the alien...You shall love the alien as yourself." In light of these verses, it is wrong by Dawkins's own standards to argue that the ethos of the law does not imply moral consideration for others...Second, Jesus provided a gloss on 19:18, the famous parable of the Good Samaritan. With specific reference to this verse, a lawyer asks Jesus, "And who is my neighbor?" Jesus tells a story [Luke 10: 30-7] that moves the lawyer to answer that the merciful Samaritan—a non-Jew—embodies the word "neighbor." That the question would be posed to Jesus, or by Luke, is evidence that the meaning of the law was not obvious or settled in antiquity. In general, Dawkins's air of genteel familiarity with Scripture...dissipates under the slightest scrutiny. (87)

30. Alain Badiou, *Saint Paul: The Foundation of Universalism* (1997), Trans. Ray Brassier, Stanford: Stanford UP, 2003, 1,2,108.

31. Slavoj Žižek and Glyn Daly, *Conversations with Zizek*, Oxford: Polity, 2004, 162.

32. Jacques Derrida, "Epoché and Faith: An Interview with Jacques Derrida," in *Derrida and Religion: Other Testaments*, Ed. Yvonne Sherwood and Kevin Hart, New York & London: Routledge, 2005 (27-50): 46, 47.

33. Dawkins reasons as follows: "Progressive ethicists today find it hard to defend any kind of retributive theory of punishment, let alone the scapegoat theory—executing an innocent to pay for the sins of the guilty. In any case (one can't help wondering), who was God trying to impress? Presumably himself—judge and jury as well as execution victim" (253). Not surprisingly, he finds this "barking mad, as well as viciously unpleasant" (253).

34. René Girard, "On Mel Gibson's The Passion of the Christ," *Anthropoetics* 10, no. 1 (Spring/Summer 2004), (1-6) 4. see http://www.anthropoetics. ucla.edu/ap1001/RGGibson.htm

35. Jacques Derrida, *The Gift of Death* (1992), Trans. David Wills, Chicago: U of Chicago P, 1995; henceforth *GD*. Patočka quoted on p. 30. Patočka was a Czech philosopher and a spokesman for the Charta 77 movement. He died as a result of police interrogations. His *Heretical Essays in the Philosophy of History* seems to me a major work and an exciting one.

36. Jacques Derrida, *Given Time* (1991), Trans. Peggy Kamuf, Chicago: U of Chicago P, 1992, 7. See in this connection the opening pages of Richard Kearney's "Deconstruction, God, and the Possible," the 18th chapter of *Derrida and Religion*, 297-307.

37. Simone Weil, *Gravity and Grace* (1947), Trans. Emma Craufurd, London: Routledge, 1972, 79. For Slavoj Zizek's reflections on this biblical verse see *The Puppet and the Dwarf* (especially pp. 15, 101, 126) and also the "Religion" section of the "Foreword to the Second Edition" of his *For They Know Not What They Do*, London & New York: Verso, 2002, (xi-cvii): l-lvii.

38 René Girard, *Things Hidden Since the Foundation of the World* (1978), Trans. Stephen Bann and Michael Metteer, Stanford: Stanford UP, 1987, 232-3.

39. Not that God appears *only* in this way. In *Mark* 14, 1-7, we learn of the disciples' indignation when a woman pours "an alabaster box of ointment of spikenard very precious" over Jesus's head. This seems to them a "waste" for "it might have been sold for more than three hundred pence, and have been given to the poor." But Jesus tells them to leave her alone for "she hath wrought a good work on me. For ye have the poor with you always, and whensoever ye will ye may do them good: but me ye have not always." Or *Luke* 10, 38-42: Martha's criticism of Mary who sits at Jesus's feet and hears his word instead of helping her sister Martha "who is cumbered about much serving." Jesus tells Martha that "one thing is needful: and Mary hath chosen that good part, which shall not be taken away from her."

40. Simone Weil, "Letter to Joe Bousquet," in George A. Panichas (ed.), *The Simone Weil Reader*, New York: David McKay, 1977 (86-93): 87-8; "The Love of God and Affliction," *The Simone Weil Reader*, (439-68) 440. I cite and comment on these lines in the chapter of my book on *The Cinema of Mike Leigh: A Sense of the Real* that is devoted to his film *All or Nothing*. I take the chapter's title ("In the messianic light") from Theodor Adorno. I try here and there throughout the book to make use of Eric Santner's *On the Psychotheology of Everyday Life*.

41. Over the years I have published a number of essays in which I bring Girard's theory to bear on different subjects: on the work of D.H.Lawrence (in *English*, Summer 1985 and in *Cambridge Quarterly*, XXV1:2 1997), on

the work of Conrad and Melville (in *Conrad, James, and Other Relations,* ed. Carabine et al., 1997) and on the Western (in *Cineaction,* June 1998). My other book on religion, the one I have almost but not quite finished and that I hope to publish after this one, makes extensive use of Girard.

42. René Girard, "An Interview with René Girard" (1978), in *"To double business bound": Essays on Literature, Mimesis, and Anthropology,* Baltimore: John Hopkins UP, 1978, (199-229) 226.

43. "Our everyday idiom is quite sound," Hitchens reports (as if anticipating disagreement), "in regarding 'scapegoating' with contempt"(211).

Notes to Chapter Two

1. D.H.Lawrence, "Books," *Phoenix: The Posthumous Papers of D.H.Lawrence (1936),* (731-34): 732, 734.

2. Luce Irigaray, "Women, the Sacred, Money" (1984), in *Sexes and Genealogies,* trans. Gillian C. Gill (1987), New York: Columbia UP, 1993, (73-88): 75. I should note here that the "Therefore it is crucial that we rethink religion" sentence continues with this: "and especially religious structures, categories, initiations, rules, and utopias, all of which have been masculine for centuries" (75). I have moved this to a footnote not because I disagree with it (I don't) but because if I had left it in the epigraph some readers might reasonably have assumed that I was going to say much more about the specifically masculine nature of "religion" than I actually do. But I do have a chapter on "Sacrifice as Matricide, " one that makes extensive use of Julia Kristeva, Mary Douglas and Martha Reineke, in my next book on religion.

3. Jill Robbins, "Introduction: 'Aprés Vous, Monsieur.'" *Is It Righteous To Be? Interviews With Emmanuel Levinas,* (1-19): 19.

4. Eric Voegelin, *Science, Politics and Gnosticism.* Chicago: Henry Regnery Co. (Gateway ed.), 1968: 107-08.

5.. Blaise Pascal, *Pensées,* trans. A.J.Krailsheimer. Harmondsworth: Penguin, 1977: 62.

6. In his "When Not Seeing Is Believing," *Time* October 9, 2006 (40-2), Andrew Sullivan notes how, in "today's unnerving, globalizing, sometimes terrifying world,...religious certainty is a balm more in demand than ever." He points out that "Muslims are not alone in grasping the relief of submission to authority...The new Pope...represents a return to a more authoritarian form of Catholicism...[and in] Protestant Christianity, especially in the U.S., the loudest voices are the most certain and uncompromising." What, in the face of this, Sullivan argues, we therefore

need to understand is something the 16th century writer Michel de Montaigne (who "lived in a world of religious war, just as we do") understood, which is "that complete religious certainty is, in fact, the real blasphemy." (This article is adapted from Sullivan's book *The Conservative Soul.*)

7. James Wood, "The Sickness Unto Life." *The New Republic.* November 8, 1999, (88-96): 88. This is a piece on the tradition of atheism and agnosticism with particular reference to the thought of Albert Camus. "The deepest struggle with Christianity may well," Wood argues, "be bloodily intramural. Thus the fiercest objectors to Christianity are often themselves believers; their belief is doubt-intoxicated, while by contrast the atheists are merely drunk on certainty" (88). Harris, Dawkins and Hitchens would seem to be the best, most recent examples of such atheists.

8. Eric Voegelin. *The New Science of Politics.* Chicago: U of Chicago P, 1952, 122.

9. Giles Gunn, "On Edward W. Said." *Raritan.* XX111: 4. Spring 2004, (71-78): 71.

10. Edward Said, *The World, the Text, and the Critic.* Cambridge MA: Harvard UP, 1983, 290.

11. William D. Hart, *Edward Said and the Religious Effects of Culture.* Cambridge: Cambridge UP, 2000, 7.

12. Jonathan Culler, "Comparative Literature and the Pieties," *Profession* 86, (30-32): 32.

13. A decade and a half later, in *The Human Stain* (2000), New York: Vintage, 2001, Philip Roth was to claim that "the ecstasy of sanctimony" is "America's oldest communal passion" (2).

14. Jonathan Culler, "A critic against the Christians," *TLS.* November 23, 1984, (1327-28): 1328.

15. For an interestingly different assessment of Empson's attitude towards Christianity see Eric Griffith's review of the second volume of John Haffenden's biography: "Cruelty of Worship," *TLS* October 26, 2007, 3-5, 7.

16. Thus, for example: "Marx and Freud, who lie behind militant literary theories of today, began powerful critical analyses of religion, but their followers have neglected to pursue this. Critics have abandoned the historic mission of education: to fight superstition and religious dogmatism" ("A Critic" 1328).

17. Paul Ricoeur, *Freud and Philosophy: An Essay on Interpretation* (1965). Trans. Denis Savage. New Haven: Yale UP, 1970, 32.

18. Régis Debray, *Critique of Political Reason* (1981). Trans. David Macey. London: Verso, 1983, 176.

19. Régis Debray, "The Indispensable Nation." Trans. Benjamin Storey and Donovan Hohn. *Harper's.* January 2004, (15-18): 16-17 (my italics).

20. Maurice Blanchot, *The Writing of the Disaster* (1980), Trans. Ann Smock, Lincoln: U of Nebraska P, 1986, 64. The rest of the sentence from which I have just quoted reads: "then what of the non-bond which disjoins beyond unity—which escapes the synchrony of 'holding together,' yet does so without breaking all relations or without ceasing, in this break or in this absence of relation, to open yet another relation? Must one be religious for that?" The closest I come to considering this particular possibility is (very briefly) in the second clarification at the end of chapter three and in the fourth section ("Out of Context and Identity") of chapter four.

21. Janice Valls-Russell, "Growing Up Muslim in France" ("A Community Divided.") *The New Leader*. March/April 2004, (6-8): 6.

22. Melissa A. Orlie, *Living Ethically, Acting Politically*, Ithaca and London: Cornell UP, 1997, 63. Orlie is drawing here on Max Weber's *Economy and Society*, ed. Guenther Roth and Claus Wittich (Berkely: U of California P, 1978), where we find the claim that "Whenever an organization is...genuinely an association of men, it has need of a god of its own" (411).

23. Charles Dickens, *Little Dorrit* (1855-7), Harmondsworth: Penguin, 1973, 673 (Book Second, ch. 16).

24. The individual's dependency on the mediator is one of the central points made by René Girard in his *Deceit, Desire, and the Novel* (1961; trans. 1965) but here I want to stay with Debray.

25. So much, then, for the young Marx's insistence that the "criticism of religion disillusions man...so that he will revolve about himself as his own true sun"—religion being "only the illusory sun about which man revolves so long as he does not revolve about himself" (Karl Marx, "A Contribution to The Philosophy of Hegel's 'Philosophy of Right'" [1843]. In *Critique of Hegel's 'Philosophy of Right,'* trans. Annette Jolin and Joseph O'Malley, Cambridge: Cambridge UP, 1970, [129-42]: 54).

26. Mark Taylor, Ed., *Critical Terms for Religious Studies*. Chicago & London: U of Chicago P, 1998, 8. Taylor tells us that "there appears to be little consensus [among scholars today] about precisely what religion *is* and how it can best be studied" (6, my italics).

27. George Grant, "Religion and the State," in *Technology and Empire: Perspectives on North America*, Toronto: House of Anansi, 1969, (41-60): 46. When he wrote this piece Grant was the Chair of the Department of Religion at McMaster University.

28. Alasdair MacIntyre, *After Virtue: A Study in Moral Theory*, Notre Dame, Indiana: U of Notre Dame P, 1981, 147.

29. Forster, E.M. *A Passage to India* (1924), Harmondsworth: Penguin, 1966, (ch. 4): 38.

30. At the end of *Violence and the Sacred* (trans. Patrick Gregory, Baltimore and London: John Hopkins UP, 1977; henceforth *VS*) Girard maintains that the attitude of "project[ing] upon religion alone the responsibility for a violent projection of violence that truly pertains to all societies including our own" can be "seen at its most flagrant in the writing of that gentleman-ethnologist Sir James Frazer":

> Frazer, like many another modern thinker, washed his hands of all the sordid acts perpetrated by religion and pronounced himself free of all taint of superstition. He was evidently unaware that this act of hand-washing has long been recognized as a purely intellectual, nonpolluting equivalent of some of the most ancient customs of mankind. (*VS* 317–18).

31. René Girard, "An Interview with René Girard," 226-27.

32.. This is of course precisely the charge I bring against H.H.&D in my Polemical Preface.

33. Wendy Steiner, *The Scandal of Pleasure: Art in an Age of Fundamentalism,* Chicago & London: U of Chicago P, 1995, 109.

34. Allison Weir, *Sacrificial Logics: Feminist Theory and the Critique of Identity,* London & New York: Routledge, 1996, 5.

35. Julia Kristeva, *Powers of Horror: An Essay on Abjection,* Trans. Leon S. Roudiez (1980), New York: Columbia UP, 1982, 106. Hitchens comes to mind here, his noting that William Lloyd Garrison "based his initial claim on the dangerous verse from Isaiah that calls on the faithful to 'come out, and be separated' (this is also the theological basis of Ian Paisley's fundamentalist and bigoted Presbyterianism in Northern Ireland)" (*God Is Not Great* 177).

36. I have taken a liberty here not only by reversing the order in which these two passages occur in the bible but also by running them together.

37. Søren Kierkegaard, *Fear and Trembling* (1843), Trans. Alastair Hannay, London: Penguin, 2003, qtd. on 99.

38. Julie Rak quotes this in her book *Negotiated Memory: Doukhobor Autobiographical Discourse,* Vancouver/Toronto: UBC Press 2004, qtd. on 34.

39. Quoted by Stanley Cavell in his "An Emerson Mood," in *The Senses of Walden,* San Francisco: North Point P, 1981, (141-60): 153.

40. Cavell goes on to note that "literal writing on the door-posts of one's house is more directly a description of the mezuzah (a small piece of parchment inscribed with two passages from Deuteronomy and marked with a name of

God, which may be carried as an amulet but which is more commonly seen slanted on the door frame of a dwelling as a sign that a Jewish family lives within)" (*Senses* 155). Though this and Cavell's subsequent comments on the mezuzah are important and illuminating, they seem to me not directly relevant to the point I am trying to make here.

41. Terry Eagleton, *The Illusions of Postmodernism*, Oxford: Blackwell, 1996, 67; see also 42, 95 and 127.

42. E.P.Thompson, *Zero Option*, London: The Merlin P, 1982, 170.

43. Hent De Vries and Samuel Weber, "Introduction" to *Violence, Identity, and Self-Determination*, Ed. De Vries and Weber, Stanford: U of Stanford P, 1997, (1-13): 1-2.

44. "On Forgiveness: A Roundtable Discussion with Jacques Derrida," in *Questioning God,* Eds. John D. Caputo, Mark Dooley, and Michael J. Scanlon, Bloomington and Indianapolis: Indiana UP, 2001, (52-72): 67.

45. Carl Schmitt, *The Concept of the Political* (1932), Trans. George Schwab, New Brunswick: Rutgers UP, 1976, 26.

46. Jacques Derrida, *Politics of Friendship* (1994), Trans. George Collins, London & New York: Verso, 1997, 83 (my italics). Derrida goes on to say that (from the same point of view) the loss of the enemy *could* result in something "worse: an unheard-of violence, the evil of a malice knowing neither measure nor ground, an unleashing incommensurable in its unprecedented—therefore monstrous—forms; a violence in the face of which what is called hostility, war, conflict, enmity, cruelty, even hatred, would regain reassuring and ultimately appeasing contours, because they would be *identifiable*" (83). It may be partly his awareness of this alarming possibility that leads Kenneth Reinhard to argue that "a political theology of the neighbor must come [*not* as a replacement for but rather] as a *supplement* to the political theology of the friend and enemy" (see "Toward a Political Theology of the Neighbor," in Slavoj Žižek, Eric L. Santner and Kenneth Reinhard, *The Neighbor: Three Inquiries in Political Theology*, Chicago: U of Chicago P, 2005, [11-75]: 14; see also 17 where Reinhard quotes Derrida). If, as Reinhard notes, the "political theology of the sovereign elaborated by Schmitt is based on the logic of the boundary," his (Reinhard's) hope is that "[Alan] Badiou's notion of the neighborhood, as a set where *no boundary* separates the set and its members and *no limit* is drawn between inside and outside, can contribute to the elaboration of a political theology of the neighbor" (67). In a somewhat similar vein, Santner speaks of a "passage to an entirely new sort of logic of being-with, one that no longer operates on the basis of membership in bounded sets or totalities set off against exceptions" ("Mir-

acles Happen: Benjamin, Rosensweig, Freud, and the Matter of the Neighbor," in *The Neighbor,* [76-133]: 129).

47. Susan Buck-Morss, *Thinking Past Terror: Islamism and Critical Theory on the Left,* London & New York: Verso, 2003, 19.

48. John Caputo, *Deconstruction in a Nutshell: A Conversation with Jacques Derrida,* Ed. and with Commentary by John Caputo, New York: Fordham UP, 1997; henceforth *Nutshell,* 158. Caputo now teaches at the University of Syracuse.

49. It seems worth mentioning, incidentally, if only because it would have been such an unlikely venue for the early Derrida, that in subsequent years he was to appear at two conferences held at Villanova, the first (in September 1997) on "Religion and Postmodernism" (proceedings later published as *God, the Gift, and Postmodernism,* 1999), the second a few years later on "Forgiveness" (proceedings later published as *Questioning God,* 2001).

50. Eduardo Mendietta, "Introduction: Religion as Critique," to *The Frankfurt School on Religion: Key Writings by the Major Thinkers,* Ed. Eduardo Mendietta, New York and London: Routledge, 2005, (1-17): 6.

51. Perry Anderson, "Arms and Rights: Rawls, Habermas and Bobbio in an Age of War," *New Left Review* 31, Jan-Feb 2005, (5-40): 17-18.

52. I should note that a significant contribution to this rethinking has come from within Religious Studies—as, for example, in Caputo's welcoming and Millbank's more critical responses to Derrida; and in the interaction between such theologians as Johann Baptist Metz, Helmut Peukert and Edmund Arens and Habermas (see *The Frankfurt School on Religion*).

53. Jacques Derrida, "Circumfession," in Geoffrey Bennington's *Jacques Derrida* (1991), Trans. Geoff Bennington, Chicago: U of Chicago P, 1993, (3-316): 154, 155.

54. Perhaps those working inside Religious Studies are much less likely to be surprised by this than the rest of us. A comment made by Yvonne Sherwood, one of the two editors of the *Derrida and Religion* collection, seems to me worth noting here. With reference to Derrida's use of the term "religion without religion," Sherwood confesses that she shares the reservations expressed by one of her contributors about how this phrase "may set off unintentional echoes in Protestant ears. As [Catherine] Keller warns in her essay in this volume, 'religion without religion' resonates all-too-easily with well-known Protestant hymns to pure faith, or faith alone. And it seems to come perilously close to Karl Barth's hugely influential distinction between Christian faith versus the earthbound, manmade idols and structures that constitute what he disparages as 'religion'" (Yvonne Sherwood and Kevin Hart, *Derrida and Religion: Other Testaments,* 236).

55. T.S.Eliot, *Four Quartets* (1944), London: Faber, 1970, ("Burnt Norton," V, 149-53): 19.

56. Julia Kristeva and Catherine Clément, *The Feminine and the Sacred* (1998), Trans. Jane Marie Todd, New York: Columbia UP, 2001, 105, 113.

57. Peter Tracy Connor, *Georges Bataille and the Mysticism of Sin,* Baltimore & London: John Hopkins UP, 2000, 110-11.

58. Hent De Vries, *Minimal Theologies: Critiques of Secular Reason in Adorno and Levinas* (1989), Trans. Geoffrey Hale. Baltimore and London: John Hopkins P, 2005, 610; henceforth *MT.* (See Adorno's "Meditations on Metaphysics" in *The Frankfurt School* 204.)

59. *Is It Righteous To Be? Interviews with Emmanuel Levinas,* 164. Levinas's point might remind us of the way in which Matthew Arnold uses the term Hebraism in *Culture and Anarchy.* Of course, Arnold thought that he and his readers were already Hebraic enough, so much so that they now needed to cultivate Hellenism. It's interesting to recall here the Arnoldian epigraph that Derrida chose for his first essay on Levinas.

60. Edith Wyschogrod and John D. Caputo, "Postmodernism and the Desire for God: An E-mail Exchange," in Wyschogrod's *Crossover Queries: Dwelling with Negatives, Embodying Philosophy's Others,* New York: Fordham UP, 2006, (298-315): 307.

61. "Against this background," Santner maintains in a footnote, "the claim that 'God is dead' comes really as something of a relief—a 'gentrification' of catastrophe—in that it effectuates a conversion of a far more disturbing, because nameless, loss into something we can mourn" (44).

62. T.S.Eliot, "The Perfect Critic," in *Selected Prose of T.S.Eliot,* Ed. Frank Kermode, London: Faber, 1975, (50-8): 55.

63. I'm referring here to the ending of a piece by Geoff Dyer entitled "Artificial Stupidity," which can be found in his *Anglo-English Attitudes: Essays, Reviews, Misadventures 1984-99,* London: Abacus, 1999, 257-60. Dyer maintains that "the whole idiom of discoursese has ossified to the extent that it is now [in Foucault's essay] actually insight-resistant: it is impossible to formulate interesting—let alone *original*—thought in these terms" (260).

Notes to Chapter Three

1. William James, *The Varieties of Religious Experience* (1902), New York: Vintage (Library of America), 1990: 108-9, 306.

2. D.H.Lawrence, "Which Class I Belong To," in *Late Essays and Articles,* Ed. James T. Boulton, Cambridge: Cambridge UP, 2004, (33-40):38.

3. In another interview we find Levinas saying this:

> "Thou shalt love the stranger"...is found in the Bible thirty-six times, exclusively in the Pentateuch—thirty-six times, according to a talmudic text which adds, "and maybe even forty-six"...This is a manner of saying that it is important to feel it, outside of any statistical interest in the tradition. And one ends up understanding this formula, "Thou shalt love the stranger," not as an anti-Le Pen politics, but as the audacious and true affirmation that love itself, affectivity itself, and feeling itself have their initial place in the relation with the other, with the stranger which every man is for every other man. After all, everyone is a stranger. "I am a stranger on earth," says a verse of the Psalms, "Give me your law" (Ps. 119:19). (*Righteous?* 63)

4. Jacques Derrida and Maurizio Ferraris, *A Taste For the Secret*, 27–8.
5. Marilynne Robinson, *The Death of Adam: Essays on Modern Thought*, New York: Picador, 2005, 178, 262. I am quoting from chapters entitled "Marguerite de Navarre" and "The Tyranny of Petty Coercion."
6. Forster, E.M. *A Passage to India* (1924), Harmondsworth: Penguin, 1966, (ch.4) 37-8.
7. Michael Ignatieff, *The Warrior's Honor: Ethnic War and the Modern Conscience,* New York: Henry Holt & Co., 1998, 19-20.
8. Charles Taylor, *Varieties of Religion Today: William James Revisited*, Cambridge, Mass.: Harvard UP, 2002, 97.
9. As Alan Wolfe puts it—in his "Higher Learning" *Lingua Franca*, 6:3. March/April 1996, (70-77): 70—universities "are hands down the most secular institutions in American society. This is a review of three books, George M. Marsden's *The Soul of the American University: From Protestant Establishment to Established Nonbelief,* Warren A. Nord's *Religion and American Education: Rethinking a National Dilemma* and Mark R. Schwehn's *Exiles from Eden: Religion and the Academic Vocation in America*. It's interesting to note that, if we judge by William James's book, it might seem that where the restricted realm of higher education is concerned things may not have changed very much over the last century. For example: "There is," he tells us, "a notion in the air about us that religion is probably only an anachronism, a case of 'survival,' an atavistic relapse into a mode of thought which humanity in its more enlightened examples has outgrown..." "This view," James then adds, "is so widespread at the present day" that he feels the need to "consider it with some explicitness" before passing on to his "own conclusions" (*Varieties* 439; see too 113).

10. Harold Bloom, *The American Religion: The Emergence of the Post-Christian Nation*, New York: Simon & Schuster, 1992. 37, 38-9, 45. It may be worth recalling here the claim Alexis de Toqueville made in 1835 to the effect that there "is no country in the world where the Christian religion retains greater influence over the souls of men than in America" (*Democracy in America* [1835], Trans. Henry Reeve, Ed. Phillips Bradley, New York: Knopf, 1945, vol. 1. 303). Louis Menand quotes this and comments that "when Tocqueville visited the United States, in 1831 and 1832, religious exuberance was at an unusual pitch...The Second Great Awakening, which had begun in New England at the turn of the century, had spread westward...It was a sectarian frenzy" (*The Metaphysical Club: A Story of Ideas in America*, New York: Farrar, Straus and Giroux, 2001. 80). It seems to me that in the US today religious exuberance is once again high; it is certainly far higher than in either Canada or the UK, the other two countries in which I spend most of my time.

11. See Julia Kristeva's discussion of "The Nobel Prize Affair" in *The Sense and Non-Sense of Revolt: The Powers and Limits of Psychoanalysis* (1996), Trans. Jeanine Herman, New York: Columbia UP, 2000, 150-56.

12. I learned about this in a piece by Jill Lawless ("Yes, sir") that discusses a list of 300 well-known people who have declined honours since 1945. The list was published by the *Sunday Times* in December 2003. See "Yes, sir: Britons promise to cast light on honors." *San Francisco Chronicle,* Friday December 26, 2003, D1, D8.

13. Though I don't think this is *simply* due to the fact that, like Davie, I too come from the UK, it seems to me that American academics in general tend to be far happier thinking of themselves as professionals than their colleagues (especially those of an older generation) from the UK. I'm pleased, at any rate, to note Derrida claiming in a 1981 interview that, since "deconstruction is, in itself, a positive response to an alterity which necessarily calls, summons or motivates it," "[d]econstruction is therefore vocation—a response to a call" ("Deconstruction and the Other," in *Dialogues with contemporary Continental Thinkers*," ed. Richard Kearney, Manchester: Manchester UP, 1984, [105-26]: 118).

14. Bruce Robbins, *Secular Vocations:Intellectuals, Professionalism,Culture*, London and New York: Verso, 1993, 23-4.

15. Frank Lentriccia, *After the New Criticism*. Chicago: U of Chicago P, 1980, 198, 196.

16. I'm drawing here on the material I first made use of in articles on "Frank Lentricchia and the Currently Paralyzed Debates" (*English*, XXXV11: 157,

Spring 1988, 1-38) and on "The Professionalization of the 'Intellectuals'" (*University of Toronto Quarterly* 58:4, Summer 1989, 498-507).

17. Trocchi was for a while a Situationist and a friend of Guy Debord. I remember reading his novel about heroin addiction, *Cain's Book* (1961), soon after it came out.

18. Tilda Swinton, Interview by Kevin Murphy, *Planet: Global Culture and Lifestyle*, Issue 6, Spring 2004, (040-043): 041.

19. The episode in question is called "Marine Life." It is number 215 in Season Ten and was first aired on 4/15/2003.

20. Ian Watt, *Conrad in the Nineteenth Century* (1979), Berkeley. Los Angeles: U of California P, 1981, 32 (my italics).

21. Quoted by Francis Mulhern in *The Moment of "Scrutiny,"* London: NLB, 1979, 327.

22. F.R.Leavis, *Letters in Criticism,* Ed. John Tasker, London: Chatto & Windus, 1974, 74.

23. Adam Phillips, "Looking at Obstacles," in *On Kissing, Tickling, and being Bored: Psychoanalytic Essays on the Unexamined Life*, Cambridge, Mass.: Harvard UP, 1993, (79-92): 89.

24. Darko Suvin, "Displaced Persons," *New Left Review* 31. Jan. Feb. 2005, (107-23): 122.

25. "In the Wilderness" was in fact the title of W.J.T.Mitchell's review (*London Review of Books*, 15:7, April 8 1993, 11-12) of Said's *Culture and Empire*. After pointing out that "Said's unswerving allegiance to what he calls 'secular' criticism, as opposed to religious hermeneutics" is made problematic by (among other things) his "claim that 'professionalism' has destroyed a sense of 'vocation'" ("religious vocation" being after all "one traditional grounding for ethical, political and even professional commitments"), Mitchell notes the way in which "Said's writing seems to vacillate between the professional tones of the immensely learned scholar, working collaboratively...and the voice of the prophet crying in the wilderness, alienated even from the community he has helped to create" (12).

26. Julie Rak explains that this event took place in three villages and that the "strongest authoritarian resistance to this act took place in Goreloye, where...[s]oldiers on horseback attempted to trample the Doukhobors, who huddled together and shielded those who were wounded, refusing to salute the authorities or to speak of the tsar in worshipful terms." According to Rak, the "Burning of Arms remains the single most important event in Doukhobor history, marking a return to the purity of Doukhobor pacifist practices" (*Negotiated* 37-8).

27. Joseph Conrad, *Nostromo* (1904), Harmondsworth: Penguin, 1974, 135.
28. Joseph Conrad, *Lord Jim* (1900), Harmondsworth: Penguin, 1973, 171.
29. Acknowledging that "Said knew this too," Suvin cites a sentence from "Reflections on Exile" in which Said says that "Exile, in the words of Wallace Stevens, is 'a mind of winter' ..." (qtd. in "Displaced Persons," 122).
30. D.H.Lawrence, Letter to Dr Trigant Burrow, 3 August 1927, in James T. Boulton & Margeret H. Boulton, with Gerald M. Lacy (eds.) *The Letters of D.H.Lawrence, Vol. VI 1927-28*, Cambridge: Cambridge UP, 1991, 113. John Worthen quotes this as one of two epigraphs to his biography *D.H.Lawrence: The Life of an Outsider* (2005). In a somewhat similar vein, we find Julian Young telling us that in section 9 of the second essay of his *Genealogy of Morals* Nietzsche "reminds us...of the 'benefits of community (*Gemeinwesen*),' peace, trust and safety, that are not available to the 'man *outside*.' 'Oh, what benefits!,' he continues, benefits we all too readily 'underestimate...today'" (*Nietzsche's Philosophy of Religion*, Cambridge: Cambridge UP, 2006, 155). With reference to Nietzsche's *Human, All-Too-Human*, Young writes this: "Of course, he himself is a free spirit. But a great deal of pain and nostalgia is involved in acknowledging this to be his destiny. Being, as a critic, unable to accept current social norms makes one *lonely* (HH ii Preface 3), turns one into a 'homeless' (HH ii b Introduction) 'wanderer' ..." (79). One more example, this one the ending of an interview with Philip Roth on the publication of his novel *Everyman*:

> "It's a horrible existence being a writer[,?] filled with deprivation. I don't miss specific people, but I miss life. I didn't discover that during the first 20 years, because I was fighting—in the ring with literature. That fight was life, but then I discovered that I was in the ring all by myself."
>
> He gets up. "It was the interests in life and the attempt to get life down on the pages which made me a writer—and then I discovered that, in many ways, I am standing on the outside of life. " (Martin Krasnick, "It no longer feels a great injustice that I have to die," Interview with Philip Roth, *Guardian* 14.12.05, (14-17): 17.

31. W.B.Yeats, "The Second Coming."
32. Emmanuel Levinas, "There is: Existence Without Existents" (1946), Trans. Alphonso Lingis, in *The Levinas Reader*, Ed. Sean Hand, Oxford: Blackwell, 2003, (30-36): 30-1.
33. Jill Robbins, *Altered Reading: Levinas and Literature*, Chicago: U of Chicago P, 1999, 97.

34. Gerald L. Bruns, *Maurice Blanchot: The Refusal of Philosophy,* Baltimore and London: John Hopkins UP, 1997, 52.

35. Emmanuel Levinas, *Totality and Infinity: An Essay On Exteriority* (1961), Trans. Alphonso Lingis, Pittsburgh: Duquesne UP, 1969. 261; henceforth *TI.*

36 George Eliot, *The Mill on the Floss* (1860), Harmondsworth: Penguin, 1979, (Book 4, ch. 3): 385-86.

37. John Paul Ricco, *The Logic of the Lure*, Chicago and London: Chicago UP, 2002, 19.

38. George Eliot, *Middlemarch: A Study of Provincial Life* (1871-72), London: Oxford UP, 1961, (Ch. 20): 207.

39. Nietzsche, *Thus Spoke Zarathustra*, Ed. and Trans. Walter Kaufmann, in *The Portable Niertzsche*, New York: Viking P, 1963, (Third Part, "The Convalescent") 329.

40. Henry Staten, *Nietzsche's Voice*, Ithaca and London: Cornell UP, 1993, 182.

41. Max Weber, *The Protestant Ethic and the Spirit of Capitalism* (1904-5), Trans. Talcott Parsons, New York: Charles Scribner's Sons, 1958, 181, 182.

Notes to Chapter Four

1. D.H.Lawrence, *Women in Love* (1920), Ed. David Farmer, Lindeth Vasey and John Worthen, Cambridge: Cambridge UP, 1987, 146; henceforth *WL.* Penguin edition has same pagination.

2. Raymond Williams, *Culture and Society: 1780-1950* (1958), New York: Harper, 1966, 336.

3. D.H.Lawrence, "Democracy" (1919), in *Reflections on the Death of a Porcupine and Other Essays*, Ed. Michael Herbert, Cambridge: Cambridge UP, 1988, (61-83): 80; henceforth *RDP.*

4. After telling us that Edward Said "became the concience of our profession," Giles Gunn claims that the "only other British or American critic and scholar and public intellectual who in different ways served a comparable function for his peers was Raymond Williams" ("On Edward W. Said" 71).

5. Edward Said, *Orientalism,* New York: Vintage, 1979.

6. Jane Tompkins, *West of Everything: The Inner Life of Westerns,* New York: Oxford UP, 1992, 203 (my italics).

7. Michael Foucault, "the ethic of care for the self as a practice of freedom" (1984), Trans. J.d.gauthier, s.j., in *The Final Foucault,* Eds. James Bernauer and David Rasmussen, Cambridge, MA: MIT Press, 1991, (1-20): 20.

8. I draw in this paragraph on the opening of my essay on "D.H.Lawrence (in *Women in Love*) on the Desire for Difference and 'the Fascism in Us All,'" *Cambridge Quarterly*, 26:2, (1997): 140-54.

9. The two most important of these emphases concern, *first*, a sentence Williams first quotes in full from Lawrence's essay on "Nottingham and the Mining Country" ("The industrial problem arises from the base forcing of all human energy into a competition of mere acquisition" [qtd. by Williams on 215]), and then cites on at least three more occasions (in the Lawrence section). And *secondly*, Williams's commentary on Lawrence's "interesting declaration of faith in democracy":

> So, we know the first great purpose of Democracy: that each man shall be spontaneously himself—each man himself, each woman herself, without any question of equality or inequality entering in at all; and that no man shall try to determine the being of any other man, or of any other woman.

"Our question," says Williams, "to those who would reject [this] must rest on the phrase 'no man shall try to determine the being of any other man.'" "Some of the most generous social movements have come to fail because, at heart, they have denied this [principle]" and "'to try to determine the being of any other man' is indeed, as Lawrence emphasized, an arrogant and base forcing" (224).

If we now return to the penultimate paragraph of *Culture and Society*, then, immediately after the sentence urging us to unlearn "the inherent dominative mode," we find Williams reflecting on "the struggle for democracy" and claiming that unfortunately "much that passes for democratic is allied, in spirit, with the practice of its open enemies. It is as if, in fear or vision, we are now all determined to lay our hands on life and force it into our own image ..." A few sentences further on, Williams warns that "[w]e project our old images into the future, and take hold of ourselves and others to force energy towards that substantiation." We need to understand, therefore, that if, on the one hand, "[t]here is the hostility to change of those who wish to cling to privilege," on the other hand, "[t]here is also the hostility to one's life being determined, in a dominative mood masked by whatever idealism or benevolence. This latter hostility is valuable...It is the chafing of any felt life against the hands which seek to determine its course ..." In addition, then, to "major material barriers to democracy...there is also this barrier in our minds, behind which, with an assumption of virtue, we seek to lay hands on others, and, from our own constructions, determine their course" (356).

232

10. D.H.Lawrence, "Foreword to *Women in Love*" (1919), Appendix 1, *Women in Love* (1920), (483-86): 485-6.

11. Of course, it might reasonably be pointed out here that if there is one aspect of Lawrence's work that may have received more than its fair share of attention, it is precisely its religious dimension. Thus, to mention just a few of the relevant titles: from 1932 (which saw the publication of Catherine Carswell's *The Savage Pilgrimage* and Frederick Carter's *D.H.Lawrence and the Body Mystical*) to the 1960s (George A. Panichas's *Adventure in Consciousness: The Meaning of D.H.Lawrence's Religious Quest* [1964]), through to the 1990s (Virginia Hyde's *The Risen Adam: D.H.Lawrence's Revisionist Typology* [1992], Paul Poplawski's *Promptings of Desire: Creativity and the Religious Impulse in the Works of D.H.Lawrence* [1993]) and the present decade (T.R.Wright's *D.H.Lawrence and the Bible* [2000], Fereshten Zangenehpour's *Sufism and the Quest for Fulfilment in D.H.Lawrence's "The Rainbow"* [2000], Charles Burak's *D.H.Lawrence's Language of Sacred Experience* [2005]).

12. D.H.Lawrence, "39. To Reverend Robert Reid, 3 December 1907," *The Letters of D.H.Lawrence*. Volume 1 1901-13, Ed. James T. Boulton, Cambridge: Cambridge UP, 1979, (39-41): 40.

13. Gilles Deleuze, "Nietzsche and Saint Paul, Lawrence and John of Patmos," in *Essays Critical and Clinical,* Trans. Daniel W. Smith and Michael A. Greco, Minneapolis: U of Minnesota P, 1997, 36-52. This essay first appeared in French as the Preface to the French translation of Lawrence's *Apocalypse* in 1978. Deleuze's great admiration for Lawrence is obvious too throughout his (and Félix Guattari's) *Capitalism and Schizophrenia*, Vol. 1 of their *Anti-Oedipus*.

14. D.H.Lawrence, *The Symbolic Meaning: The Uncollected Versions of "Studies in Classic American Literature,"* New York: Viking P, 1964, 17. See in this connection an essay I co-authored with M.Elizabeth Sargent, "D.H.Lawrence and the Dialogical Principle: 'The Strange Reality of Otherness,'" *College English* 63:4, (March 2001): 409-36.

15. D.H.Lawrence, "Study of Thomas Hardy," in *Study of Thomas Hardy and Other Essays,* Ed. Bruce Steele, Cambridge: U of Cambridge P, 1985, (7-128): 18-19; henceforth *STH;* the volume abbreviated as *STHOE*.

16. In the short essay on "The Future of the Novel" (originally published as "Surgery for the Novel—Or a Bomb"), in *STHOE* 151-55, we find Lawrence maintaining that the novel and philosophy "should come together again, in the novel" (*STHOE* 154).

17. D.H.Lawrence, "1024. To Lady Cynthia Asquith, 21 October 1915," in *The Letters of D.H.Lawrence*. Volume 11. 1913-16, Ed. George J. Zytaruk

and James T. Boulton, Cambridge: Cambridge UP, 1981, (414-15): 414. F.R.Leavis used this sentence as the last of three epigraphs to his pioneering book *D.H.Lawrence: Novelist* (1955).

18. Andrew Moss, "Sporting with the Literary Corpis," *Hungry Mind Review*, Summer 1998, 27. At the end of the review we are told that Moss is "a transplanted Briton" working in San Francisco.

19. Richard Locke, "James's Gang," *BookForum*, Apr/May 2007, (26-7, 53): 53.

20. I am drawing in this paragraph on my essay "Rethinking This-Worldly Religion: D.H.Lawrence and French Theory." *Études Lawrenciennes* 21, "D.H.Lawrence: After Strange Gods," 2000, 21-49.

21. Georges Bataille, *The Accursed Share: An Essay on General Economy*, Vols. 2 (*History of Eroticism*) & 3 (*Sovereignty*), Trans. Robert Hurley, New York: Zone, 1995; henceforth *AS 2* and *AS 3*. I am quoting here from Hurley's note on p. 431.

22. Georges Bataille, "The Notion of Expenditure" (1933), in *Visions of Excess: Selected Writings 1927-1939*, Trans. Allan Stoekl, Carl R. Lovitt and Donald M. Leslie, Jr., Minneapolis: U of Minnesota P, 1985, (116-29): 118.

23. Georges Bataille, *The Accursed Share: An Essay on General Economy*, Vol. 1 (*Consumption*), Trans. Robert Hurley, New York: Zone, 1995, 25; henceforth *AS 1*.

24. Georges Bataille, *Theory of Religion*, Trans. Robert Hurley, New York: Zone, 1994, 49.

25. Jacques Derrida, *Given Time: 1. Counterfeit Money* (1991), Trans. Peggy Kamuf, Chicago: U of Chicago P, 1992, 137; henceforth *GT*.

26. Ross Posnock, *The Trial of Curiosity: Henry James, William James, and the Challenge of Modernity*, New York: Oxford UP, 1991, 81.

27. I'm thinking of a number of things here; first of Bataille's observation that the satisfaction promised by Hegel's quest for Absolute Knowledge carries with it the implication that "nothing (at least nothing important) remains to be discovered" (*Inner Experience* [1954], Trans. Leslie Anne Boldt, Albany: State U of New York P, 1988, 108); then of George H. Mead's objection to "absolute idealism," that "there can be nothing novel in the absolute," "that everything is all accomplished in the Absolute. All that is to take place has already taken place in the Absolute. But our life is an adventure" (*Movements of Thought in the Nineteenth-Century*, Chicago: U of Chicago P, 1936.508); then of Gudrun's response to her sister's question ("But do you hope to get anywhere by just marrying?") three pages into *Women in Love*: "It seems to be the inevitable next step" (9). I should say that I owe my second example

to Posnock, who cites Mead's objection as that of William James's "fellow pragmatist" (*Trial* 96).

28. Michael Foucault, "Maurice Blanchot: The Thought From Outside" (1966), Trans.Brian Massumi, in *Foucault/Blanchot*, New York: Zone, 1990, (7-58): 19.

29. See too Michael B. Smith's *Toward the Outside: Concepts and Themes in Emmanuel Levinas*, Pittsbugh: Dusquesne UP, 2005.

30. Jacques Derrida, *Of Grammatology* (1967), Trans. Gayatri Chakravorty Spivak, Baltimore: John Hopkins UP, 1976, 158.

31. D.H.Lawrence, *The Virgin and the Gipsy* (1930), Harmondsworth: Penguin, 2002, 19.

32. D.H.Lawrence, "Pan in America," in *Phoenix: The Posthumous Pap*ers (1936), (22-31): 26.

33. Gilles Deleuze and Félix Guattari, *What is Philosophy?* (1991), Trans. Hugh Tomlinson and Graham Burchell, New York: Columbia UP, 1994, 203. Lawrence's review is clearly a major reference point in the last chapter ("Conclusion: From Chaos to the Brain") of this book.

34. Martin Buber, *I and Thou* (1916), Trans. Walter Kaufmann, New York: Charles Scribner's, 1970, 58.

35. Hent De Vries, *Minimal Theologies: Critiques of Secular Reason in Adorno and Levinas* (1989), Trans. Geofrey Hale, Baltimore and London: John Hopkins UP, 2005: 349; henceforth *MT.*

36. John D. Caputo, *The Prayers and Tears of Jacques Derrida: Religion Without Religion*, Bloomington and Indianapolis: Indiana UP, 1997, 209; henceforth *Prayers.*

37. D.H.Lawrence, Rev. of "Chariot of the Sun, by Harry Crosby," *Phoenix.* 255-62. This review is untitled in *Phoenix* but I think usefully given the title "Chaos in Poetry" in D.H.Lawrence, *Selected Literary Criticism*, Ed. A. Beal, London: Heinemann, 1955.

38. We might be reminded here of the need Bataille and others felt to combat the Hegelian system with its claim to have achieved Absolute Knowledge.

39. D.H.Lawrence, "Life," *Reflections on the Death of a Porcupine.* (13-18): 16.

40. See "Sauf le nom"—in Derrida's *On the Name,* Trans. John P. Leavey Jr., Ed. Thomas Dutoit, Stanford: Stanford UP, 1995, (35-85): 37—where we find Derrida reflecting on the question as to whether this desire "come[s] from God in us, from God for us, [or] from us for God?"

41. Emmanuel Levinas, "Preface" to *Outside the Subject* (1987), Trans. Michael B. Smith, Stanford: Stanford UP, 1993. 3.

42. D.H.Lawrence, *Studies in Classic American Literature* (1924). London: Martin Secker, 1933. (ch. 6 Poe): 72.

43. D.H.Lawrence, "The Crown," in *Reflections on the Death of a Porcupine and other Essays,* (251-306): 280-81.

44. The translator explains that he is translating "*'autrui'* (the personal Other, the you) by 'Other,' and *'autre'* by 'other'" (*TI* 24).

45. D.H.Lawrence, "Morality and the Novel," in *Study of Thomas Hardy and other Essays,* (171-76): 172.

46. Later on, in chapter four of *Study of Thomas Hardy* we find a variation on this wording: "Is not his own soul a fighting line, where what is and what will be separates itself off from what has been?" (35).

47. D.H.Lawrence, "Reflections on the Death of a Porcupine," in *Reflections on the Death of a Porcupine and other Essays,* (347-63): 358.

48. See Richard O. Young's "'Where even the Trees Come and Go': D.H.Lawrence and the Fourth Dimension." *D.H.Lawrence Review.* 13:1 (Spring 1980): 30-44. See too Linda Dalrymple Henderson's *The Fourth Dimension and Non-Euclidean Geometry in Modern Art.* Princeton, NJ: Princeton UP, 1983. For our purposes here it is perhaps worth noting Lawrence's claim that "a perfected relationship" opens up a fourth dimension and that "[i]t is into this perfected relationship that every straight line *curves*, as if to some core, passing out of the time-space dimension" (my italics, "Reflections" *RDP* 361). For his part, Levinas explains the fact that "the Other is placed higher than me" with reference to what he calls a "curvature of space" that he suggests "is, perhaps, the very presence of God" (*TI* 291).

49. Emmanuel Levinas, "Ethics as First Philosophy" (1984), in *The Levinas Reader,* (76-87): 86.

50. Levinas quotes this in his *Ethics and Infinity: Conversations with Philippe Nemo* (1982), Trans. Richard A. Cohen, Pittsburgh: Duquesne UP, 1985; henceforth *EI.*

51. Amit Chaudhuri, *D.H.Lawrence and "Difference,"* Oxford: Clarendon P, 2003, 59.

52. It was only after writing this that I came upon Derrida's brief discussion of Lawrence's poem "Snake," which I will comment on in the next chapter.

53. D.H.Lawrence, *The Rainbow* (1915), Ed. Mark Kinkead-Weekes, Cambridge: Cambridge UP, 1995, 409. Penguin edition has same pagination.

54. I'll have something to say about negative theology a bit later but this may be a good place to note two of the questions raised by Hent De Vries in his *Philosophy and the Turn to Religion* (1999): "Why, notwithstanding the expectations raised by so many of his titles (e.g., 'How to Avoid Speaking'

and *Sauf le nom*), is Derrida's inquiry into the argumentative and rhetorical protocols of negative theology and mysticism centered, not so much on the problem of the sayable and the unsayable but rather on the question of *le lieu*, the locus, the place, the situation, in which or from which or through which words may be spoken or sent? How, moreover, are we to relate these notions to concepts and tropes such as dimension, horizon, the desert, the island, the gorge, Mount Moriah, and Jerusalem, but also the utopian (*le non-lieu*), not to mention the 'space' that has in our day become prefixed by that most transgressive of all apophatic terms, the adverb *hyper*?" (*PTR* 108)

55. I'm only aware of one reference to Lawrence in Levinas's work and it occurs in an essay on Jean Wahl (to whom *Totality and Infinity* is dedicated):

> The interchangeability of the *beyond* and the *hither side* [of the body]—of the *very high* and the *very low*—is a permanent temptation to which Wahl will always yield, and which belongs to the deepest part of his thought ... God is what is said about that *hither side* or that *beyond*—that gap, that break in continuity. No matter whether it be "what D.H.Lawrence called the dark God" or the one James speaks of in his *Varieties of Religious Experience*, evoked by Wahl in the opening pages of his *Expérience métaphysique* ..." (*Outside the Subject* 75)

56. Georges Bataille, *Inner Experience*, 5.

57. We might also think here of Lawrence's critique of "kodack vision" in his "Art and Morality" essay (see *STHOE* 168).

58. "There is," Derrida adds, "no coming or event that is not, that does not imply[,] the coming of the heterogeneous, the coming of the other" ("Politics and Friendship: An Interview with Jacques Derrida, *The Althusserian Legacy*, Ed. E. Ann Kaplan and Michael Sprinkler, London & New York: Verso, 1993, [183-231]: 216).

59. This distinction seems similar, incidentally, to the one Eric Santner tells us Franz Rosenzweig drew between "the *metaethical self*" and "the concept of the 'personality,'" with the latter signifying "what is *generic* about a person, that is, everything about a person that can be subordinated to some sort of universal or genus" ("Miracles," *The Neighbor* 96). And in a similar vein, later on in the same piece, Santner tells us that "[Saint] Paul's great achievement, in [Alan] Badiou's eyes, was to have articulated the procedures for and virtues appropriate to the composition of a subjectivity correlative to 'that uncountable infinity constituted by a singular human life,' a subjectivity thereby in excess of the predicative particularity of any sort of cultural identity" (117;

Santner is quoting in this sentence from Badiou's *Saint Paul: The Foundation of Universalism,* 10). The fact that Badiou is (elsewhere) openly hostile to Levinas (and that Santner is not thinking of the latter here) makes these momentary convergences all the more interesting. Badiou's references to "a subject without identity" (*St Paul* 5), and his critique of "identitarian logic" (8, 9, 11) and of the "predicative traits" (10, 57, 63, 76) he associates with it are also worth noting in this connection.

60. D.H.Lawrence, "The Horse-Dealer's Daughter," in Lawrence's *England, My England and Other Stories* (1922), Ed. Bruce Steele, Introduction Michael Bell, London: Penguin, 1995, 145.

61. Thus, in his fine "Introduction" to the collection in which the story appears, Michael Bell writes this:

> As the girl-friend of his youth, Jesse Chambers, said, he always saw the numinous (the magical or the divine) in the everyday. This is suggested in his ability to change the original title "The Miracle" to the more down-to-earth "The Horse-Dealer's Daughter," for the story contains both aspects. Lawrence's constant sense of something out of reach, something that always escapes the fixture of language, is not therefore to be understood as striving to get beyond the tangible and visible world. It is rather an attempt to respond to that world fully...(xxvi)

62. "A new relation, a new relatedness hurts somewhat in the attaining: and will always hurt" ("Morality in and the Novel" 174).

63. Maurice Blanchot, "Literature and the Right to Death" (1949), in *The Gaze of Orpheus and Other Literary Essays,* Trans. Lydia Davis, Barrytown, New York: Station Hill P, 1981, (21-62): 42.

64. Gerald L. Bruns, *On the Anarchy of Poetry and Philosophy: A Guide for the Unruly,* New York: Fordham UP, 2006, 164.

65. In "'The Fact, and the Crucial Significance, of Desire': Lawrence's *The Virgin and the Gipsy, English* 34 (Summer 1985): 131-56, I emphasized the ways in which the Gipsy's glamour is shown by the text to be generated by mimetic desire. Though I still think the workings of the latter vitally important, I would read the novella somewhat differently today.

66. Kevin Hart, *The Dark Gaze: Maurice Blanchot and the Sacred,* Chicago: U of Chicago P, 2004, 10.

67. Levinas is explaining that he reached this conclusion at the end of his early *Existence and Existents* but that it "is the kernel of all [he] would say later" (*Righteous* 46).

68. In her book on Levinas, Jill Robbins notes that, "like Blanchot and Levinas, Bataille also develops independently the thought of the *il y a*, in texts such as *Inner Experience*. As [Joseph] Libertson puts it: in each of their writings from the 1940s, the *il y a* is 'a common denominator'...Libertson points out that the writings which present the *il y a* are 'thematically disparate'...For Levinas it is associated with horror and suffocation; for Bataille with ecstasy, joy, and celebration, and for Blanchot...it has, at the very least, a *literary* specificity" (*Altered Reading* 97).

69. Simon Critchley explains that "[a]lthough Levinas is not afraid to use the word 'God'...he employs the term 'Illeity' in order to avoid the inevitable onto-theo-logical thematization (i.e. God is a being) that the word 'God' entails. Illeity describes my non-thematizable relation with the Infinite, the direction of transcendence; it does not buttress any positive theology (*AE* 188/*OB* 147)" (*The Ethics of Deconstruction: Derrida and Levinas,* West Lafayette, Indiana: Purdue UP, 1999 [2nd ed.], 114). "Illeity," Levinas tells us, "lies outside the 'thou' and the thematization of objects. A neologism formed with *il* (he) or *ille*, it indicates a way of concerning me without entering into conjunction with me" (*Otherwise than Being Or Beyond Essence* (1974), Trans. Alphonso Lingis, Pittsburgh: Duquesne UP, 1998, 212).

70. De Vries is referring here to Derrida's texts.

71. Jacques Derrida, "From Restricted to General Economy: A Hegelianism Without Reserve (1967)," in *Writing and Difference*, Trans. Alan Bass, Chicago: U of Chicago P, 1978, (251-76): 265. "*Erinnerung* is the Heggelian, speculative concept of interiorizing memory" (336).

72. It might be said that something like a negative theology seems to be at work in the second passage. I'm thinking here of two passages from Derrida's "How to Avoid Speaking: Denials" that De Vries quotes:

> Suppose, by a provisional hypothesis, that negative theology consists of considering that every predicative language is inadequate to the essence, in truth to the hyperessentiality (the being beyond Being) of God; consequently only a negative ("apophatic") attribution can claim to approach God, and to prepare us for a silent intuition of God. By *a more or less tenable analogy*, one would thus recognize some traits, the *family resemblance* of negative theology, in every discourse that seems to return in a regular and insistent manner to this rhetoric of negative determinatioon, endlessly multiplying the defenses and the apophatic warnings...(qtd. in *PTR* 97)

...

From the moment a proposition takes a negative form, the negativity that manifests itself need only to be pushed to the limit, and it at least resembles an apophatic theology. Every time I say: X is neither this nor that, neither the simple neutralization of this nor of that with which it *has nothing in common*, being absolutely heterogeneous to or incommensurable with them, I would start to speak of God, under this name or another. God's name would then be the hyperbolic effect of that negativity or of all negativity that is consistent in its discourse. (qtd. in *PTR* 98)

Look, in the light of this, at the ways in which the second description of Ursula employs the negative: "the immanence of her beauty, that was not form or weight or colour," the failure of language, the words that sound untrue, like lies. The stripping down process that we noted earlier (getting rid of jobs, clothes etc.) now reaches the "I," which also gets erased.

But at the same time as his old self has perished, thanks to his marriage with Ursula, Birkin has been resurrected. In other words, it isn't just a matter of a negative theology at work here. At one point in his *Minimal Theologies*, De Vries speaks of "the *via negativa* and the *via eminentiae*—ascesis and excess, saying less (or the least) and saying more (the most or too much), negative and positive theologies—touch[ing] upon each other, solicit[ing] each other, collaps[ing] or dialectically revert[ing] into each other, and thus becom[ing] virtually indistinguishable from each other" (*MT* 607-8). De Vries has Adorno in mind here but his words can help us see what is going on in these two descriptions of Ursula. If the second highlights more of a negative theology, the first shows us more of a positive one ("so new, so tender, so made perfect," Birkin's feeling that he can't "bear to look on her," "so wonder-clear, so undimmed"), a clear case, surely, of "saying more (the most or too much)." But here too it is a matter of both these modes becoming intermingled.

See also the "Pseudo-Dionysius's *hyper*" section of the "Hypertheology" chapter of De Vries's *Philosophy and the Turn to Religion*. And the paragraphs in which Derrida calls himself an "incorrigible hyperbolite" and claims that "[e]verything that proceeds under the name of 'deconstruction' arises from [hyperbolism]" (*Monolingualism of the Other; or, The Prosthesis of Origin* [1996], Trans. Patrick Mensah, Stanford: Stanford UP, 1998, 48, 49).

73. Jill Robbins quotes this from Levinas's "Un Dieu homme?" in *Exercises de la patience* 1 (1980), 72. See *Altered Reading* 37.

74. I'm thinking here of Derrida's parenthetical suggestion that it "is far from being clear" that "in what they say in general Heidegger and Levinas are not Christian" (*GD* 48).

75. Also worth pondering in this connection: "The religious truth is the same now as it ever has been: that preceding all our knowledge or will or effort is the central creative mystery, out of which issues the strange and for ever unaccountable emanation of creation: that the universe is a bush which burns for ever with the Presence, consuming itself and yet never consumed" (D.H.Lawrence, *The Symbolic Meaning*, 38). Charles Burack cites this passage and notes that in "Kabbalah, the burning bush is associated with the Crown because at the bush Moses heard the divine name 'I will be what I will be'" (*D.H.Lawrence's Language of Sacred Experience: The Transfiguration of the Reader*, New York: Palgrave, 2005, 174, n.21).

76. Emmanuel Levinas, "Jacques Derrida: Wholly Otherwise," in Levinas's *Proper Names*, Stanford: Stanford UP, 1996, (55-62): 55, 56.

Notes to Chapter Five

1. i. Or as Levinas puts it here:

> Beyond the other there is the third party. He is also an other, also a neighbor ... Who then is the first one to whom I must respond, the first to be loved?...It is the hour of justice...The unique incomparables must be compared. We must, out of respect for the categorical imperative or the other's right as expressed by his face, de-face humans, sternly reducing each one's uniqueness to his individuality in the unity of the genus, and let universality rule. Thus we need laws and, yes, courts of law; institutions and the State, to render justice. (*Righteous?* 246)

2. Though Critchley's sentence has it the other way around, I take his point to be that each side needs to be supplemented by the other side.
3. For Bruns anarchy is "not chaos, but that which is older than the distinction between chaos and order" (*Maurice Blanchot* 32).
4. Hent De Vries, "Violence and Testimony," *Violence, Identity, and Self-Determination*, (14-43): 19.
5. Richard Rorty, "Remarks on Deconstruction and Pragmatism," in *Deconstruction and Pragmatism*, Ed. Chantal Mouffe, London & New York: Routledge, 1996, (13-18): 17.
6. "Remarks on Deconstruction and Pragmatism," in *Deconstruction and Pragmatism*, (77-88): 87.
7. Jacques Derrida, "Force of Law" (1989), in *Acts of Religion*, (230-98): 247.
8. "On Forgiveness: A Roundtable Discussion with Jacques Derrida," in *Questioning God*, (52-72): 67.

9. For Levinas on Abraham, see "A Propos of 'Kierkegaard vivant'" in *Proper Names,* (75-9):77.
10. Slavoj Žižek, *On Belief,* London: Routledge, 2001. 150-51.
11. The next paragraph begins as follows:

> Let us not look for examples, there would be too many of them, at every step we took. By preferring my work, simply by giving it my time and attention, by preferring my activity as a citizen or as a pro-fessorial and professional philosopher, writing and speaking here in a public language, French in my case, I am perhaps fulfilling my duty. But I am sacrificing and betraying at every moment all other obligations...(*GD* 69)

12. See too Derrida's admission in his "Remarks on Deconstruction and Pragmatism" that "what interests [him] in deconstruction [is] a hyper-po-liticization" (85). Also worth considering here is his claim that "it is in the zone of hyperbole, of aporia and paradox that we should often have to stand or move in this reflection on forgiveness" ("To Forgive," in *Questioning God,* [21-51]: 42).
13. Sean Hand, "Introduction," *The Levinas Reader,* (1-8):1.
14. For Christopher Hitchens the idea that "the sins of the fathers will be visited on their children 'even unto the third and fourth generation'...negates the moral and reasonable idea that children are innocent of their parents' offenses"(*God Is Not Great* 99).
15. Orlie explains what she means in terms of her experience of "[r]enting an apartment in a neighborhood undergoing gentrification," in "the then less-than-fashionable south end of Park Slope in Brooklyn." Her point is that "[g]ood and harm are done simultaneously and in ways that perpetuate pow-er relations that precede new activities" (2-3).
16. I'm thinking of passages like the following:

> The "we" to which I refer includes all those who have some mea-sure of power and agency, that is to say, those who are not wholly dominated. I am theorizing situations from the perspective of those who have some measure of agency that implicates them, however unwittingly, in harm to others; those who, like myself, exercise relatively pronounced social effects as a consequence of their race, class, education, and the like. To be sure, even an un(der)employed U.S.citizen who purchases a "Nike" product made by women work-ers in another part of the world under laws that are illegal in the United States, stands in a position of advantage to those women,

or at least is implicated in their harm. Nonetheless, I always have in mind the former, relatively more privileged cases when I invite identification with "we." (200)

I should point out that Orlie takes over the term "trespass" from Hannah Arendt (see 200, 201) and that Arendt and Foucault are major influences on her thinking. She makes no mention of either Derrida or Levinas—nor, for that matter, of Lawrence, though her discussion of the azure bell interestingly links up with and it seems to me productively complicates what he has to say about the umbrella.

17. Jacques Derrida, "Violence and Metaphysics: An Essay on the Thought of Emmanuel Levinas," *Writing and Difference*, Trans. Alan Bass. Chicago: U of Chicago P, 1978, (79-153): 96.

18. Theodore W. Jennings, Jr., *Reading Derrida/Thinking Paul: On Justice*, Stanford: Stanford UP, 2006, 164.

19. Walter Benjamin, "Theses on the Philosophy of History B" (1940), Trans. Harry Cohn, *Illuminations*, ed. Hannah Arendt, London: Collins/Fontana, 1970, (255-66): 266.

20. Alphonso Lingis, the translator here, explains that he translates "*autrui*" [the personal Other, the you) by 'Other,' and '*autre*' by 'other'" (*TI* 24).

21. "The Villanova Roundable: A Conversation with Jacques Derrida," in *Deconstruction In A Nutshell*, (3-28): 17–18.

22. *Specters of Marx*, Trans. Peggy Kamuf, New York & London: Routledge, 1994, 28.

23. Furthermore, at the end of the first chapter of Lawrence's *Study of Thomas Hardy* we find this: "I tremble at the inchoate infinity of life" (13), which it might be interesting to ponder in the light of Jean-Luc Nancy's claim that the "whole series of tremblings" to be found in Hegel involve "the trembling of the finite seized by the infinite: it is," he adds, "the sensibility of the infinite in the finite" (*Hegel: The Restlessness of the Negative*, Trans. Jason Smith and Steven Miller, Minneapolis: U of Minnesota P, 2002, ["Trembling" 4–5] 44).

24. *The Complete Poems of D.H.Lawrence*, Eds. Vivian de Sola Pinto and Warren Roberts, New York: Penguin, 1993, 250.

25. There would be many things to point to here but I will limit myself to the following:

But do, for God's sake, mistrust and beware of these states of exaltation and ecstasy. They send you, anyone, swaying so far beyond the centre of gravity in one direction, there is the inevitable swing back with greater velocity to the other direction, and in the end you exceed the limits of your own soul's elasticity, and go smash...

Besides, there is no real truth in ecstasy. All vital truth contains the memory of all that for which it is not true: Ecstasy achieves itself by virtue of *exclusion*; and in making any passionate exclusion, one has already put one's right hand in the hand of the lie. (Letter 20 dec. 1914; *The Letters of D.H.Lawrence*. Vol. 2, 246–7)

26. One might recall here Lawrence's insistence in "The Crown" that "It is wrong to make the lion lie down with the lamb" (*RDP* 261). As the editors of the Cambridge edition point out, this is presumably an allusion to Isaiah (11:6): "The wolf also shall dwell with the lamb, and the leopard shall lie down with the kid" etc. Giorgio Agamben sees implicit in this "messianic prophecy" (which as he says "so pleased Ivan Karamazov") "the idea that animal nature will...be transfigured in the messianic kingdom" and that man "will be reconciled with his animal nature" (2002, Trans. Kevin Attell, *The Open: Man and Animal*, Stanford: Stanford UP, 2004, 3). But clearly this version of the messianic did not appeal Lawrence, partly, no doubt, because of the ways in which he was already reconciled with *his* animal nature. One might point to a variety of things here but Agamben's reflections (in the "Physiology of the Blessed" section of *The Open*, 18-19) on the concern expressed by such thinkers as William of Auvergne and Thomas Aquinas over the question as to whether or not we should think of there being excrement in Paradise (with Aquinas forcefully excluding the possibility), this might remind us of the moment in Lawrence's great essay "A Propos of '*Lady Chatterley's Lover*'" when he illustrates the mind's "grovelling fear of the body" with Jonathan Swift's "poem to his mistress Celia, which has the maddened refrain, 'But—Celia, Celia, Celia s***s! (the word rhymes with spits).'" ("A Propos of *Lady Chatterley's Lover*," in *Sex, Literature, and Censorship*, Ed. Harry T. Moore, New York: Viking P, 1959, [82-111]: 86.)

27. I am borrowing here from Henry Staten, who refers to an "excluding inclusion or including exclusion" (*Nietzsche's Voice*, 22). And it's worth noting that, in Nietzsche's case too, this results in passages every bit as ugly as the Lawrentian one I cite here.

28. Jacques Derrida, *Rogues: Two Essays on Reason*, Trans. Pascale-Anne Brault and Michael Naas, Stanford: Stanford UP, 2005, 5.

29. "Mary, Maternity, and Abrahamic Hospitality in Derrida's Reading of Massignon," chapter 5 of *Derrida and Religion*, (73-94): 74, 75.

30. *The Living Principle: "English" as a Discipline of Thought*, London: Chatto & Windus, 1975, 236; henceforth abbreviated as LP..

31. Jacques Derrida and Bernard Stiegler, *Echographies of Television* (1996), Trans. Jennifer Bajorek, Cambridge: Polity P, 2002, 24.

32. Jacques Derrida, "Hospitality, Justice and Responsibility: A dialogue with Jacques Derrida," in *Questioning Ethics: Contemporary Debates in Philosophy*, 74.

33. F.R.Leavis, *The Great Tradition* (1954), New York: New York UP, 1967, 1, my italics; henceforth GT.

34. F.R.Leavis, *Nor Shall My Sword,* London: Chatto & Windus, 1972, 64; henceforth NS.

35. Andrew Gibson, *Postmodernity, Ethics and the Novel: From Leavis to Levinas,* London and New York: Routledge, 1999, 1; henceforth PEN.

36. Slavoj Žižek, *Did Somebody Say Totalitarianism?,* London and New York: Verso, 2001, 1; henceforth DSS. I commented on Frank Lentricchia's thoughtful (Foucault-indebted) reflections on this phenomenon in Chapter Three.

37. Alain Badiou, *Ethics: An Essay on the Understanding of Evil* (1998), Trans. Peter Hallward, London: Verso, 2001, 41-2; henceforth E.

38. Badiou says this about Paul, the "poet-thinker of the event" (*Saint Paul* 2). As Peter Hallward points out in his Introduction to *Ethics*, for Badiou there are "four and only four fields of truth...love, art, science, and politics" (xi). The figure of the militant belongs to the latter.

39. Thomas Keenan, *Fables of Responsibility: Aberrations and Predicaments in Ethics and Politics,* Stanford: Stanford UP, 1997, 193

40. It first appeared in his journal *Scrutiny* in 1951–52 and then in *D.H.Lawrence:Novelist* in 1955.

41. D.H.Lawrence, *Studies in Classic American Literature* (1924), New York: Martin Secker, 1933, (ch. 2), 16–17, 22.

42. Luce Irigaray, *I Love To You: Sketch of a Possible Felicity in History*, trans. Alison Martin. New York and London: Routledge, 1996, 62.

43. Giorgio Agamben, *The Coming Community* (1990), Trans. Michael Hardt, Minneapolis: U of Minnesota P, 1998, 68; henceforth *CC*.

44. D.H.Lawrence, *The Rainbow* (1915), (Harmondsworth: Penguin, 1995), 9; henceforth R.

45. To reiterate a point I made much earlier, the fact that Badiou is usually assumed to be writing *against* an ethics of otherness (see, for example, section 4 ("Abandoning the Ethics of Otherness" of Hallward's Introduction to Badiou's *Ethics*) makes his relevance here all the more striking.

46. In *Women in Love* Birkin charges Gerald Crich with "ignoring the demands of the soul" and I have written about this in an essay entitled "The

Lawrentian/Birkinian Version of the Care of the Self: Attending to the Demands of the Soul," in Jean-Paul Pichardie and Philippe Romanski (eds.) *Like a Black and White Kaleidoscope: Essays on D.H.Lawrence's "Women in Love,"* Rouen: Université de Rouen, 2001, 175-199.

47. F.R.Leavis, *D.H.Lawrence: Novelist* (1955), New York: Clarion (Simon & Schuster),1969, 104; henceforth DHL:N.

48. Thus, in *Rogues*, Derrida writes that '[i]f an event worthy of this name is to arrive or happen, it must, beyond all mastery, affect a passivity"; it must involve "something like a passive decision" (152).

49. Claiming that "[e]vents are what happens," John Caputo praises Heidegger for speaking of "the anonymous, impersonal, improper 'it gives' (*Es gibt*), although," he thinks, "'it happens' (*es geschieht*) would have been still better" (*Against Ethics,*Bloomington: Indiana UP, 1993, 97, 98; henceforth AE).

50. In his *Of Spirit: Heidegger and the Question*, Trans. Geoffrey Bennington and Rachel Bowlby, Chicago: Chicago UP, 1989, Derrida points out that "resolution...plays a decisive role, in fact the role of decision itself, in [Heidegger's] *Sein und Zeit*" (44).

51. Luce Irigaray, *An Ethics of Sexual Difference* (1984), Trans. Carolyn Burke and Gillian C. Gill, Ithaca: Cornell UP, 1993, 81.

52. F.R.Leavis and Q.D.Leavis, *Dickens the Novelist* (1970), Harmondsworth: Penguin, 1972, 296.

53. As Leavis put it elsewhere, "Blake was speaking out of the 'identity' when he said: "Tho' I call them Mine, I know that they are not Mine'" (*LP* 44). Leavis is quoting from Blake's letter to Dr. Trusler on August 16, 1799. This is clearly *not* the "instrumental identity" we saw Lawrence referring to ("Crown" *RDP* 272) in the previous chapter.

54. F.R.Leavis, *Thought, Words and Creativity: Art and Thought in Lawrence,* London: Chatto & Windus, 1976, 26; henceforth TWC.

55. Considering the large element of self-sacrifice in all three examples, it seems appropriate to note a footnote to her "Introduction" (1966) to Charlotte Bronte's *Jane Eyre* (Harmondsworth: Penguin, 1985, 7-29) in which Q.D.Leavis quotes George Eliot saying that "All self-sacrifice is good" and adds this: "We note that the enlightened George Eliot acquiesces in a Victorian assumption—'All self-sacrifice is good'—which Charlotte Brontë would never have done, since it is exactly such unrealities, dangerous and damaging, that it is Emily and Charlotte's distinction to be always alert to expose in the concrete human actualities" (21).

56. Georgio Agamben, "The Messiah and the Sovereign: The Problem of Law in Walter Benjamin" (1992), in *Potentialities* (160-74), 162-3; henceforth "Messiah."

57. Albert J. Guerard, "Introduction"to Joseph Conrad, *Heart of Darkness and The Secret Sharer,* New York: Signet, 1950, 22.

58. Giorgio Agamben, "Walter Benjamin and the Demonic: Happiness and Historical Redemption" (1982), in *Potentialities,* (138-59): 146, 147.

59. Frank Kermode, *The Genesis of Secrecy: On the Interpretation of Narrative,* Cambridge, MA.: Harvard UP, 1979, 40.

60. Joseph Conrad, *The Secret Sharer,* in *Heart of Darkness and The Secret Sharer,* Signet ed.; henceforth *TSS.* 20, 21.

61. Richard Kearney, "Desire of God," in *God, the Gift and Postmodernism,* 126. Kearney is quoting from "Hospitality, Justice and Responsibility," his dialogue with Derrida in *Questioning Ethics,* 70-1.

62. Jacques Derrida, "Discussion with Richard Kearney," in *God, the Gift and Postmodernism,* 133; henceforth DRK.

63. Jacques Derrida, *Adieu to Emmanuel Levinas,* Trans. Pascale-Anne Brault and Michael Naas, Stanford: Stanford UP, 1999, 111.

64. Emmanuel Levinas, "Cities of Refuge," in *Beyond the Verse: Talmudic Readings and Lectures* (1982), Trans. Gary D. Mole, Bloomington: Indiana UP, 1994, (34-52): 39.

65. Georgio Agamben, *Homo Sacer: Sovereign Power and Bare Life* (1995), Trans. Daniel Heller-Roazen, Stanford: Stanford UP, 1998, 51; henceforth *HS.*

66. F.R.Leavis, "The Secret Sharer" (1966), in *"Anna Karenina" and Other Essays.* London: Chatto & Windus, 1967, 111; henceforthy SS.

67. Indeed, in his *Modernity at Sea: Melville, Marx, Conrad in Crisis,* Minneapolis: U of Minnesota P, 2002, Cesare Casarino argues that *"The Secret Sharer* brings back from *The Nigger of the "Narcissus"* both Donkin and James Wait so as to incorporate them into one single, negated body of labor and racial difference: it is," Casarino maintains, "the murder of such a body that enables the coming-into-being of what is nonetheless a liberating narrative of same-sex desire" (244).

68. Drucilla Cornell, *The Philosophy of the Limit,* 66.

69. Caputo is drawing here on Derrida's first essay on Levinas ("Violence and Metaphysics" 127, 138), in which we do indeed find Derrida maintaining that "[t]he other...would not be what he is (my fellow man as foreigner) if he were not alter ego"; and, even more paradoxically, that "the other is absolutely other only if he is...the same as I" (127).

70. "Developing a suggestion of Jean-Luc Nancy, we shall," Agamben tells us in his next sentence, "give the name *ban* (from the old Germanic term indicating both exclusion from the community and the power of the sovereign)

to this original legal structure, through which law preserves itself even in its own suspension, applying to what it has excluded and *abandoned*, that is, banned" ("Messiah" 162).

71. Georgio Agamben, "In This Exile (Italian Diary, 1992-94)," *Means Without End: Notes on Politics*, Trans. Vincenzo Binetti and Cesare Casarino, Minneapolis: U of Minnesota P, 2000, (121-42): 135.

72. In a somewhat similar vein, we find Agamben elsewhere referring to "the refugee that [today's citizen] he or she is" and claiming that "the refugee is perhaps the only thinkable figure for the people of our time and the only category in which one may see today...the forms and limits of a coming political community" (*Means Without End,* 26, 16).

73. At one point in *Homo Sacer* Agamben approvingly refers to Jean-Luc Nancy's "attempts to conceive not only our time but the entire history of the West as the 'time of abandonment.'" "To *abandon*," he quotes Nancy as saying, "is to remit, entrust, or turn over to...a sovereign power, and to remit, entrust, or turn over to its *ban*, that is, to its proclaiming, to its convening, and to its sentencing" (*HS* 58). I'm suggesting that, however much we might prefer to deny it, most of us (readers) are likely to be closer to "sovereign power" than to its victims (even if, for some of the time, we are also in the position of its victims).

74. Jacques Derrida, *Of Hospitality* (1997), Trans. Rachel Bowlby, Stanford: Stanford UP, 2000, 125; henceforth OH.

75. Jacques Derrida, "Eating Well," in *Points...: Interviews, 1974-1994,* Trans. Peter Connor and Avital Ronell, ed. Elizabeth Weber, Stanford: Stanford UP, 1995, 279.

76. Søren Kiekegaard, *Fear and Trembling* (1843), Trans. Alastair Hannay, Harmondsworth: Penguin, 2003. 81.

77. Terry Eagleton, "Subjects and Truths," *New Left Review,* 9, May-June 2001, (155-160): 156. This is a review of Alain Badiou's *Ethics: An Essay on the Understanding of Evil.* Eagleton presumably has the following passage from Hallward's Introduction to this book in mind here:

> Like Badiou, Derrida is careful to distinguish the realm of decision from the realm of knowledge. To reduce my decision to respond to the calculus of reasons and the assessment of possibilities is to eliminate its radical character as a *decision.* The decision must always concern what I cannot *know.* Ethics is a matter of "responsibility in the experience of absolute decisions made outside of knowledge or given norms." But Derrida does not stop there. The responsible decision must concern not only the not-known, it must evade

conceptualization altogether. "In order for [absolute responsibility] to be what it must be it must remain inconceivable, indeed unthinkable." (xxv)

78. De Vries is quoting here from Derrida's "Force of Law: The 'Mystical Foundation of Authority,'" (*Acts of Religion* 251-2).
79. Alasdair MacIntyre, *After Virtue: A Study in Moral Theory*, Notre Dame, Indiana: U of Notre Dame P, 1981, 144 (my italics).
80. For more of Leavis's reflections on the "religious," see *LP* 234-36.
81. Of course, Levinas, on the other hand, gives priority to the ethical, loving it, as Caputo says, "like a rabbi," but what Levinas calls "ethics, which is philosophy, is everything that philosophy resists, excludes, expels in the hope of preserving its good name." Caputo goes on to wonder if Levinas hasn't "carried out, in the name of Abraham and his descendants, the greatest deconstruction of ethics since Johannes de Silentio decided to break his silence about the father of faith" (*AE* 14).
82. In effect, though he himself doesn't have either Derrida or any suspension of the ethical in mind, Ian Robinson's criticism of Leavis in *The English Prophets: A Critical Defense of English Criticism,* Pockthorpe Cottage, Denton: Edgeways Books, 2001, is that he wants what Derrida wants: the messianic without messianism (in its Christian form). Whereas I think Leavis is right to want this. Robinson agrees with Ian Watt that *The Secret Sharer* is "a dramatization, not a manifesto; it is a fictional narrative, not [as presumably Leavis would have it] a testament" (qtd. by Robinson, 196). Though Robinson reaches a very different conclusion to my own, his discussion of what he calls Leavis's "theology" (*The English Prophets*, 199) is closely argued and deserves to be read.

One of the ways in which I think we can see Leavis embracing the messianic and rejecting any messianism is to be found in his explanation that when he chose the Blakean title *Nor Shall My Sword* for one of his works, he was definitely *not* committing himself "to anything in the nature of building Jerusalem" (*NS* 27) and he was quite consciously rejecting "the kind of preoccupation with *telos* [Leavis uses Greek letters here], or final cause, that belongs to the period side of [Blake]" (*NS* 19). On the other hand, unlike Derrida, who gives the impression he rejects teleological thinking *tout court*, Leavis elsewhere uses Majorie Greene's notion of the "telic" positively, when the telos in question is "an implicit denial of finality" (see "'Believing in' the University," in *The Critic as Anti-Philosopher*, Ed. G. Singh, London: Chatto & Windus, 1982, [171-85]: 181). See too in this connection what he does with Majorie Greene's phrase the "pull from the future" (qtd. by Leavis, *LP* 66).

What seems to me crucial here is the effort made by both Leavis and Derrida to keep open the possibility of a future.

83. See also Slavoj Žižek and Glyn Daly, *Conversations with Žižek,* Oxford: Polity Press, 2004, 162-63.

84. Sarah Kay, *Žižek: A Critical Introduction,* Oxford: Polity Press, 2003, 103.

85. Slavoj Žižek, *The Fragile Absolute—-or, Why is the Christian legacy worth fighting for,?* London: Verso, 2000, 150.

86. Or as Žižek puts it in *The Ticklish Subject: The Absent Centre of Political Ontology,* London and New York: Verso, 1999, "there is...something inherently 'terroristic' in every authentic act" (377).

Notes to Chapter Six

1. "Introduction." *Twilight of the Idols and The Anti-Christ* (1889, 1895), Trans. R.J.Hollingdale, Harmondsworth: Penguin, 1990, (7-24): 9.

2. Kenneth Burke, *Attitudes Toward History* (1937), Boston: Beacon P, 1961, 218.

3. D.H.Lawrence, "Books," *Phoenix* (731-34): 734.

4. Alain Badiou, *Polemics,* Trans. Steve Corcoran, London & New York: Verso, 2006, 9.

5. *Middlemarch: A Study of Provincial Life* (1871-2), London: Oxford UP (World's Classics), 1961, (ch.15) 151-52.

6. I'm reminded here of Sam Harris's to-my-mind ludicrous footnote to the sentence "Thousands of years have passed since any Western philosopher imagined that a person should be made happy, peaceful, or even wise, in the ordinary sense, by his search for truth" (*The End of Faith* 215). The footnote starts off as follows:

> Thus, a man like Heidegger, who was an abject admirer of Hitler, can nevertheless be commended to our attention, with scarcely a hint of shame, as one of the giants of European thought. (281 n.9)

However much one might wish that one of the giants of European thought had not been complicit with fascism nothing whatsoever is gained by denying his stature as a major thinker. The rest of the footnote seems to be suggesting that because Schopenhauer "hurled a seamstress down a flight of stairs" and because "Wittgenstein was a manifestly tortured soul" (281) they can't be major thinkers either.

7. When Hent De Vries tells us (approvingly) that for Derrida "[a]ll genuine responsibility must respond to a 'restless excess' that disrupts all 'good

conscience'" (*PTR* 410), he conveys the clear impression that he and Derrida think precisely *all* forms of "good conscience" are necessarily hypocritical and self-deceiving. In a similar vein, Simon Critchley approvingly summarizes Levinas's intention to disrupt "all claims to good conscience" (*Ethics* 4) and Derrida insists that (again in Critchley's words) "an experience of undecidability is at the very antipodes of complacency ..." (261). In both cases, the assumption seems to be that anyone who believes his or her conscience is clear must be incredibly complacent at best. But it seems to me just as possible for someone to be complacent about having a *bad* conscience.

8. *Beyond Good and Evil: Prelude to a Philosophy of the Future* (1886), Trans. R.J.Hollingdale, Harmondsworth: Penguin, 1990, 39.

9. "Introduction [to *Beyond Good and Evil*]," (7-26):17.

10. Staten is quoting here from the opening of the "On the Gift-Giving Virtue" section of Part One of Nietzsche's *Thus Spoke Zarathustra* (1885), in *The Portable Nietzsche,* 186-87.

11. Matthew Arnold, *Culture and Anarchy: An Essay in Political and Social Criticism* (1869), Ed. Ian Gregor, Indianapolis & New York: Bobbs-Merrill, 1971, (ch.4) 107-8; henceforth *CA*.

12. Or as Richard Dawkins puts it, "the Christian focus is overwhelmingly on sin sin sin sin sin sin sin. What a nasty little preoccupation to have dominating your life" (*God Delusion* 252).

13. Stephen Mulhall, *Philosophical Myths of the Fall*, Princeton & Oxford: Princeton UP, 2005, 6. As Mulhall says, such a doctrine "is fundamentally offensive to any conception of morality that places human autonomy at its heart; for it entails that our very ability to orient ourselves toward the good is dependent upon transcendental spiritual sources ..." "For the Christian," he then adds, "our only hope of regaining any contact with goodness is by dying to ourselves" (7). For D.H.Lawrence too, of course; just as he too had his own myth of the Fall.

14. "Structure, Sign, and Play" (1966), *Writing and Difference,* (278-93): 292.

15. I will admit that I find Christopher Hitchens's inability to refrain from a kind of slave-bashing both revealing and (in its own way) rather amusing. Here are some examples: (i) "The holy book in the longest continuous use— the Talmud—commands the observant one to thank his maker every day that he was not born a woman. (This raises again the insistent question: who but a slave thanks his master for what his master has decided to do without bothering to consult him?)" (54); (ii) "The three great monotheisms teach people to think abjectly of themselves, as miserable and guilty sinners prostrate before

an angry and jealous god who, according to discrepant accounts, fashioned them either out of dust and clay or a clot of blood. The positions for prayer are usually emulations of the suppliant serf before an ill-tempered monarch" (73); (iii) "I shall always remember his [Hitchens' schoolfriend's] upright posture while [during compulsory school prayers] others hypocritically knelt or inclined themselves, and also the day I decided to join him. All postures of submission and surrender should be part of our prehistory" (285). As Hitchens sees it, one of the "four irreducible objections to religious faith" is that "it manages to combine the maximum of servility with the maximum of solipsism" (4).

16. I argue for the relevance of this passsage in the fourth chapter ("The Feminist Leigh: Two Women 'on the other side of silence,'"my discussion of *Bleak Moments* and *Hard Labour*) of my book on *The Cinema of Mike Leigh: A Sense of the Real* (2004).

17. Julian Young's recent book (*Nietzsche's Philosophy of Religion*, Cambridge: Cambridge UP, 2006) is worth consulting in this connection. Young argues that Nietzsche was "a pantheist" but that (or, and therefore) he struggled frequently with "the problem of death *and pain*" (199).

18. Friedrich Nietzsche, *The Birth of Tragedy* (1871), Trans. Walter Kaufmann, in *Basic Writings of Nietzsche*, ed. Walter Kaufmann, New York: Random House, 1968, (sec. 21) 127. Shaun Whiteside's translation of this passage can be found on p. 101 of the most recent Penguin edition of *The Birth of Tragedy*.

19. Friedrich Nietzsche, *The Gay Science* (1882, 1887), Trans. Walter Kaufmann, New York: Vintage, 1974, (Book 4, sec. 337) 268.

20. This passage comes on p. 39 of the Penguin edition.

21. While the "question of pity...is never long out of sight in Nietzsche's texts, and Zarathustra calls pity his 'deepest abyss,'" Staten tells us that "this question plays no significant role in any of the commentaries on Nietzsche" that he knows of (1). Staten's book was first published in 1990. I was drawn to read it by Michael Tanner's praise of it both in his *Nietzsche*, in the Past Masters Series, Oxford: Oxford UP, 1994, and also in the "Further Reading" section that follows his Introduction to the Penguin edition of *The Birth of Tragedy*. The latter singles out the pages in the Appendix to *Nietzsche's Voice* that I am drawing on here. Finally, I recommend in this context Tanner's own comments on Nietzsche's attitude to pain and pity in his Introduction to *The Birth of Tragedy*, Harmondsworth: Penguin, 1993, xxii–xxiii.

22. And also, incidentally, if he isn't making Nietzsche sound (in claims I've deliberately ignored even though they are interspersed throughout the

section I'm quoting from) too nostalgic and Rousseauistic. I feel this needn't concern us here.

23. If Derrida and Leavis ask us to imagine ourselves in the positions of (respectively) Abraham and Conrad's young Captain, John Millbank puts us into the position of Gauguin. "Was," he asks, "the painter Gauguin right to leave wife and children to go to Tahiti?" Millbank is arguing against Bernard Williams, who he tells us has "suggested that only the success of Gauguin's wager on being a good painter can retrospectively justify this decision." Millbank summarizes Williams's view as follows:

> He [Gauguin] comes to enjoy the moral luck of finding he has a talent (a "gift"), or that his talent was able to come to fruition. But it might have been otherwise. Williams's analysis assumes that this instance is an anomaly, and that *normally* an intention to do something is not at all like Gauguin's intention to be a painter. Hence one can usually know that one can realize one's intention, and exactly what that intention is (whereas Gauguin does not really know what *kind* of painter he will turn out to be). ("The Midwinter Sacrifice," in *The Blackwell Companion to Postmodern Theology*, Ed. Graham Ward, Oxford: Blackwell, 2002, 115)

Over and against this, Millbank argues that "all of us are always in the situation of Gauguin." This is so partly because one cannot usually know either "that one can realize one's intention" or "exactly what that intention is" but mainly because, "as Derrida suggests, the giving of ourselves to one person or purpose frequently involves sacrificing other goods or people, and often without reason." Or rather, as Millbank implicitly goes on to admit, it doesn't just to do this "frequently" or "often," it *always* does it:

> Our sense of responsibility *must*, in order to fulfil itself, be always exceptional and particular because attentive to a specific unique demand, yet to be responsible it must also by definition be answerable to a public forum. But how can these two demands ever be reconciled? And what explanation could ever be given to the neglected ones? There are *never*, it seems, any *adequate*, that is to say, publicly stateable reasons for lavishing devotion on one person rather than another—to the public gaze this will always appear excessively aesthetic or erotic. Yet to the private impulse it may appear to fulfil the logic of the ethical itself. (116)

In the light of this significant area of agreement, we might expect Millbank to draw Derrida's twofold conclusion: (i) we are all guilty; and (ii) our responsibility is infinite. But this doesn't exactly happen, mainly because, with reference to Shakespeare's *The Winter's Tale*, he moves into the conditional tense:

[S]hould *our* polity be restored by grace, would not anxiety about our necessary preference for some not others, and our apparent [?] sacrifice of some for others, be eased in the knowledge that we are to love our *neighbours*, because we know that others are loving theirs? In other words we would rediscover that even the condition of *agape* can only be fulfilled within a polis where each of us exercises a particular—albeit unique and non-identically repeated—role. (121)

24. Matthew Arnold, "The Function of Criticism at the Present Time" (1864), in *Four Essays On Life And Letters*, ed. E.K.Brown, New York: Appleton-Century-Crofts, Inc., 1947, 13.
25. Søren Kierkegaard, *The Present Age* (1846-7), Trans. Alexander Dru, London: Collins (Fontana), 1969, 55.
26. Matthew Arnold, "The Study of Poetry," in *Four Essays on Life and Letters,* 64.
27. Slavoj Žižek, "Neighbors and Other Monsters," in *The Neighbor: Three Inquiries into Political Theology* (134-90): 186.
28. He seems to mainly have in mind "the latest version of the critique of ethical violence...proposed by Judith Butler" (137). See chapter two ("Against Ethical Violence") of Butler's *Giving an Account of Oneself,* New York: Fordham UP, 2005.
29. I am reminded here of something Geoffrey Galt Harpham says in a recent exchange with Žižek: "Such heroic terms as *breakthrough, action,* and *ruthless radicality* are indiscriminate and ethically indifferent; they leave all the important judgments and decisions—the ones that would distinguish mere terror from the forms of force that are sometimes necessary to secure the dignity and well-being of peoples in a peaceable environment—yet to be made" ("Critical Response 11: Response to Slavoj Žižek," *Critical Inquiry* 29 (Spring 2003) (504-7): 506. This comes in Harpham's response to Žižek's response to Harpham's "Doing the Impossible: Slavoj Žižek and the End of Knowledge" in the same issue of *Critical Inquiry*: 543-85. I should perhaps add that Harpham finds much to admire in Žižek, as I do too, not least (in my case) Žižek's interest in heroism.
30. Even though he has in mind a different set of opposites, it may nevertheless be useful to think here of the way in which Martin Jay praises Adorno in the penultimate paragraph of his book on him:

Adorno stubbornly resisted choosing between flawed alternatives or positing a harmonious meditation between them. Negative ontology or historicism, transcendent or immanent critique, autonomous art or art in the service of the revolution, speculative theory or empirical investigation—these and other antinomies Adorno held on to without forcing their reconcilation. (*Adorno*, London: Fontana, 1984, 163)

31. Friedrich Nietzsche, "On the Uses and Disadvantages of History for Life" (1874), Trans. R.J.Hollingdale, in *Untimely Meditations*, Cambridge: Cambridge UP, 1989, (57-123): 76.

Notes to Chapter Seven: Conclusion

1. Annie Dillard, *Holy the Firm* (1977), New York: Harper & Row, 1984, 36.
2. I will be drawing throughout much of the rest of this Conclusion on my essay, "Rethinking This-Worldly Religion: D.H.Lawrence and French Theory," *Études Lawrenciennes*, No. 21, 2000, 21-49. The essays in this issue are collected under the heading "After Strange Gods."
3. Derrida also claims that "in taking God as witness, even when he is not named in the most 'secular' <*laïque*> pledge of commitment, the oath cannot *not* produce, invoke or convoke him as already there." For Derrida, God is "the witness as 'nameable-unnameable,' present-absent witness of every oath or of every possible pledge" (*FK* 27). Derrida's *The Politics of Friendship* is also worth consulting in this connection, especially chapter six, "Oath, Conjuration, Fraternization or the 'Armed' Question."
4. Hannah Arendt, *The Human Condition*, Chicago: U of Chicago P, 1958, 126-7.
5. André Gorz, *Critique of Economic Reason* (1988), Trans. Gillian Handyside and Chris Turner, London: Verso, 1989, 13.
6. Gorz explains that he is drawing here on a study by Christian Topalov's "L'invention du chômage," *Les Temps Modernes*, Nov.-Dec. 1987.
7. Gorz gets this from Topalov but the original source seems to be the Royal Commission on the Poor Law and Relief of Distress in 1910.
8. For a quick reminder of how economic prospects have changed for the worse over just the last couple of decades consider the significance of Gorz's observation that at a 1988 conference of communist workers in Italy "Antonio Bassolino, speaking in the name of the PCI leadership, declared the thirty-five-hour week an objective for the century 'in a European perspective.'

He presented a reduction in working hours as the 'link between the struggle for liberation *in* work and the struggle for liberation *from* work: the point [Bassolino maintained] is to liberate ourselves from the domination of the economy over our lives'" (Gorz 213).

Also worth noting here is the more recent *Post-Work* essay collection (ed. Stanley Aronowitz and Jonathan Culler, New York & London: Routledge, 1998), especially its long "Post-Work Manifesto." In the latter we learn that, while "few American workers have as much as even three weeks vacation and average U.S. working hours have been steadily climbing," "French, German and many other European workers are engaged in a determined struggle for shorter hours—in many French workplaces, this has succeeded in cutting the workweek to thirty-seven hours, in German workplaces to thirty-five, while it is common in both countries to find five-and six-week paid vacations." The four writers of this Manifesto argue that:

> At a fundamental level, the first thing required is a change in ideas... Unless we begin to think differently about work itself...collective anxieties are likely to steadily worsen. Unless we rethink our basic vision there will be little hope for people in the middle and working classes—or for those who are poor—in generations to come. (38)

Amongst other goals, the Manifesto maintains that the "struggle for a thirty-hour week, and a six-hour day with no overtime and no decrease in income is primary for providing decent living standards but also for reviving the great dream of a grassroots democracy" (73-4).

9. Hence, as I see it, the wisdom of André Gorz's insistence that, in the present circumstances (which in this respect are unlikely to change in the forseeable future), we need to affirm *both* the right to a guaranteed minimum income *and* the right to (significant) work (even if only for a few hours a day). Gorz reasons as follows:

> If I am relieved of any social obligation and more precisely of the obligation to "earn my living" by working, be it only for a few hours, I cease to exist as an "interchangeable social individual as capable as any other": my only remaining existence is private and micro-social. And I cease to experience this private existence as my personal sovereignty because it is no longer the obverse of compelling social obligations. The customary balance of living in a macro-socially organised society is upset...My existence collapses into the private sphere...
>
> This is the condition of those who are involuntarily unemployed; and the guarantee of a social minimum will do nothing to

change that (nor indeed will giving him or her an *unreal* job, a job which is not needed by society...It is for all these reasons that the right to an income and the right to macro-social work must not be dissasociated...(206-7)

Measures like these are necessary to provide at least a minimum level of security and safety, something that, in the opening pages of his "Study of Thomas Hardy," Lawrence too readily seems to assume can be taken for granted. As, for example, in the following:

[I]nstead of producing our flower, instead of continuing our activity, satisfying our true desire, climbing and clambering till, like the poppy, we lean on the sill of all the unknown, and run our flag out there in the colour and shine of being, having surpassed that which has been before, we hang back, we dare not even peep forth, but, safely shut up in bud, safely and darkly and snugly enclosed, like the regulation cabbage, we remain secure till our hearts go rotten, saying all the while how safe we are.

No wonder there is a war [World War 1]. No wonder there is a great waste and squandering of life. Anything, anything to prove that we are not altogether sealed in our own self-preservation as dying chrysalides. Better the light be blown out, wilfully, recklessly, in the wildest wind, than remain secure under the bushel, saved from every draught. (*STH* 15–16)

On the other hand, here is an extract from one of Lawrence's letters to Bertrand Russell in 1915:

There must be a revolution in the state. It shall begin by the nationalising of all [...] industries and means of communication, and of the land—in one fell blow. Then a man shall have his wages whether he is sick or well or old—if anything prevents his working, he shall have his wages just the same. So we shall not live in fear of the wolf—no man amongst us, and no woman, shall have any fear of the wolf at the door.... Something like this must be done. It is no use saying a man's soul should be free, if his boots hurt him so much he can't walk... (*The Letters of D.H.Lawrence*, Volume 11 1913–16, 282–83).

10. See my article on "The Lawrentian/Birkinian Version of the Care of the Self: Attending to the Demands of the Soul."

11. At the same time, Birkin is well aware of the existence of "married people" who "shut their doors...and shut themselves in to their own exclusive alliance with each other," "mistrustful couples insulated in private houses or private rooms...and no further life" ("Man to Man" 199).

12. On the other hand, one of the ways in which we can side-track the demands of the soul is by the following way of understanding and trying to fulfill the command to "love my neighbour as myself":

> I am as anxious about his pecuniary welfare as I am about my own. I am so sorry for him, the poor X. He is a man like me. So I lie to myself and to him. For I do not care about him and his poverty: I care about my own unsatisfied soul. But I side-track to him, my poor neighbour, to [vent] on him my self-pity. (*STH* 18)

13. Arendt strikes an even clearer Lawrentian note when, a few sentences later, she suggests that "Perhaps nothing in our history has been so short-lived as trust in power, nothing more lasting than the Platonic and Christian distrust of the splendor attending its space of appearance" (204).

14. In *Fantasia of the Unconscious* (1921) we find this: "Primarily and supremely man is always the pioneer of life, adventuring onward into the unknown, alone with his own temerarious, dauntless soul. Woman for him exists only in the twilight, by the camp fire" (with *Psychoanalysis and the Unconscious*, ed. Philip Rieff, New York: Viking P, 1968, ch. 9, 143–4).

15. At the same time, while it is surely true to say that maternity can never mean the *complete* relinquishment of the adventure to the unknown, there is a difference it seems important to note between becoming, as Anna does, "a door and a threshold" for others to go through (*R* 182) and being the one who adventures out oneself.

16. "What is it that really matters?...for Dido...that she become herself" (*STH* 12).

17. Friedrich Nietzsche, *Ecce Homo* (1888), Trans. R.J.Hollingdale, Harmondsworth: Penguin, 1980.

18. James Miller, *The Passion of Michel Foucault*, New York: Simon & Schuster, 1993, 5.

19. I am quoting here from Catherine Madsen's fine novel, *A Portable Egypt* (Orders@Xlibris.com, 2002, 49), since this is where I first encountered it but see also Martin Buber, *Hasidim and Modern Man*, Trans. Maurice Friedman, New York: Horizon, 1958, 140.

20. Especially interesting, some might feel, in the light of what we noted in the last chapter about Stephen Mulhall's book *Philosophical Myths of the Fall*.

21. Walter Benjamin, "Theses on the Philosophy of History," 256 (second italics mine).

22. Theodor Adorno, *Minima Moralia: Reflections from Damaged Life* (1951), Trans. E.F.N.Jephcott, London: Verso, 1984, 247.

23. On the other hand, considering the use I have made of Giorgio Agamben earlier, I should note that he is not so impressed; indeed, he sees the passage as evidence that, "[d]espite appearances, negative dialectics is an absolutely non-messianic form of thought, closer to the emotional tonality of Jean Améry than that of Benjamin." See Agamben's *The Time That Remains: A Commentary On The Letter To The Romans* (2000), trans. Patricia Dailey, Stanford: Stanford UP, 2005, (35-8):38.

24. I'm afraid, however, that I have no answer to the question as to where this "demand thus placed on thought" comes from. The best I can do for now is point to some of the terms provided by Eric Santner in his section of *The Neighbor*, entitled "Miracles Happen: Benjamin, Rosenzweig, Freud, and the Matter of the Neighbor." Santner argues that each of his three German-Jewish thinkers "arrived, by radically different pathways, at the same conclusion, namely, that to even conceive of radical shifts of direction in life—of a genuine exodus from deep individual and social patterns of servitude—human beings, both individually and collectively, require the notion of an interpellation beyond (ideological) interpellation" (132). And with reference to Rosenzweig in particular, Santner says this:

> Rosenzweig...concluded that the very fact that we arrive at such an impossible notion—an interpellation beyond interpellation—in the first place, testifies to the ongoing necessity of theological thinking ...What makes this thinking new is that it works at showing how this necessity emerges out of the immanent impasses of secular thought. (132–33)

NAME INDEX

SUBJECT INDEX

17340660R00158

Printed in Great Britain
by Amazon